TREATING
CHILD SEX
OFFENDERS
AND VICTIMS

This manual is dedicated to the pioneers of
sex offender treatment in Vermont:

William Young
William Pithers
Philip White

who trained the rest of us

Finkelhor ch5
Salter ch 12 pp 182-205

TREATING CHILD SEX OFFENDERS AND VICTIMS

A Practical Guide

by
Anna C. Salter

SAGE PUBLICATIONS
The International Professional Publishers
Newbury Park   London   New Delhi

For information address:

SAGE Publications, Inc.
2455 Teller Road
Newbury Park, California 91320

SAGE Publications Ltd.
6 Bonhill Street
London EC2A 4PU
United Kingdom

SAGE Publications India Pvt. Ltd.
M-32 Market
Greater Kailash I
New Delhi 110 048 India

Printed in the United States of America

Library of Congress Cataloging-in-Publication Data

Salter, Anna C.
  Treating child sex offenders and victims.

  Bibliography: p.
  Includes index.
  1. Child molesting—Treatment. 2. Child
molesters—Family relationships. 3. Sexually
abused children—Mental health. 4. Psychotherapy.
I. Title.
RC560.C46S35   1988   616.85′83   87-28691
ISBN 0-8039-3181-6
ISBN 0-8039-3182-4 (pbk.)

95 96 97 98 99 20 19 18 17 16 15 14 13

CONTENTS

ACKNOWLEDGMENTS

I am indebted to Fay Honey Knopp, a pioneer of sex offender treatment in this country, whose competence, personal graciousness and rock-solid integrity stand as a model for researchers in this field. Honey has been generous with her time and her expertise.

I would like to thank Gregory Teague, Ph.D., for his articulate and thoughtful critique of this book. The ideas within are better developed and more gracefully written for his contribution.

My appreciation goes to Steve Kairys, M.D., Director of the Children at Risk Program at Dartmouth Hitchcock Medical Center, mentor, colleague and friend, for introducing me to this field and providing the support through the Children at Risk program that has made my work possible.

Andrew Garrod, Ed.D., Assistant Professor of Education at Dartmouth College, was kind enough to edit this book, and introduce a measure of correctness to the syntax that it did not universally have before his editing. His grasp of the written word has been much appreciated.

I have been fortunate to have two talented research assistants: Lorraine Shea and Marie McAndrew Taylor. Lorraine has contributed in innumerable ways to the preparation of this book. Without her energy and competence it is unlikely that this book could have been completed. Marie McAndrew Taylor tracked and obtained research articles with the zeal of a bloodhound. No article was too obscure or too difficult to find.

My secretary, Robin Berry, brought an unusual amount of professionalism and skill to the final manuscript preparation.

Finally, this manual was initially supported by a grant from the Department of Social and Rehabilitation Services of the State of Vermont, to which I am grateful.

INTRODUCTION

There was a time when learning one particular school of therapy was deemed sufficient empowerment to treat all manner of clients—or at least sufficient to make one feel obligated to treat all manner of clients. If psychoanalytically trained, one applied psychoanalytic theory with impunity to depression, schizophrenia, sociopathy, and to sexual abuse. Nor did other schools of therapy separate out any more carefully the problems treatable by their approach from those that were not.

With time, specific treatments began to be developed for particular problems. Alcoholism became widely recognized as a problem that necessitated a particular type of therapy. Phobias were found to respond best to behavioral treatment. Chemotherapy became a necessary component of the rehabilitation of adult psychosis. The family practitioner model of mental health began to give way to the notion that some problems yielded to very particular and specialized forms of treatment. Treatment began to be problem specific rather than school oriented.

For mental health clinicians, the pressure of feeling obligated to treat any problem that walked through the door (no matter how far from one's experience base) has begun to be replaced by a new pressure: the necessity of keeping up in a field where, seemingly, every new day sees a new type of therapy for a new type of problem.

The treatment of sexual abuse offenders and victims has only recently evolved into a specialized field. Although for many years there have been a few specialized treatment programs available in a few states, it is only recently that the need to set up many specialized treatment programs in every state has been recognized. This recognition has been spurred on by two factors: the increasingly widespread acknowledgement of the extent of the problem (see Chapter 1) and the increasing acceptance of the fact that traditional forms of therapy are not effective with this population (Crawford, 1981). Happily, specialized treatment does appear to have an impact (Knopp, 1984, p. 100).

The intent of this manual is to put together in one place information regarding the treatment of sex offenders, their families, and victims such that a mental health clinician, experienced in treating clients in general, might use this manual as an entry to the process of developing specialized skills in child sexual abuse treatment. It is not intended to be primarily a theoretical book, although issues of treatment cannot be totally separated from the theory informing them, but primarily a "nuts and bolts" manual. I write with no illusion that a manual alone can replace clinical experience and adequate supervision. I do believe, however, that a manual can provide a foundation of information on which clinical experience and supervision may build.

The more experienced reader may be surprised to discover that I treat intrafamilial and extrafamilial abuse similarly unless otherwise noted. In fact, although the clinical literature routinely distinguishes between the two types of offenders, the research literature is equivocal on differences (Murphy, Haynes, Stalgaitis, & Flanagan, 1986). In addition, many successful treatment programs for offenders that have excellent results do not distinguish in their assessment and treatment between the two types of offenders. The argument put forth by such programs as Northwest Treatment Associates is that the patterns of deviancy are similar for both types of offenders and that the patterns, therefore, necessitate similar treatments. Even where there are differences, programs such as Northwest's advocate putting the offenders in the same groups, as there is less danger of offenders colluding with each other when their dynamics are somewhat different.

Certainly, the dynamics differ for victims, although it is unclear at present whether one type of abuse produces more long-term harm than another (Browne & Finkelhor, 1986). Victims of either type of offense have some treatment needs in common, for example, the need not to be blamed, the need for adequate information, and the need to be reassured and supported.

At present there is insufficient evidence to separate totally the discussion of extrafamilial and intrafamilial abuse. Comments regarding child sexual abuse in this book may be fairly taken to indicate either type unless otherwise specified.

The term sexual abuse in this book will be defined as sexual activity between a child or adolescent with an adult or another child five years or more older than the child. Sexual activity will include exhibitionism, voyeurism, fondling, oral genital sex, attempted intercourse, "dry" intercourse (rubbing the penis between the thighs or buttocks of a child), intercourse (penetration), photographing or otherwise exhibiting children sexually, exposing children to pornographic literature, and forcing or manipulating children to engage in sexual acts with each other or with animals. Sexual experiences with relatives and violent or coerced experiences will be automatically considered sexual abuse regardless of the age differential. Consenting sexual experiences with nonrelated peers within five years of the child's age will not be considered sexual abuse. There are exceptions to the age-differential criterion when common sense will indicate that a particular situation is abusive, for example, manipulated consent of a retarded child by a nonretarded child of a similar age. In this case the chronological age is the same, but the mental age sufficiently different.

Even with careful definitions of child sexual abuse the prevalence studies cited in Chapter 1 may surprise many readers. My own experience of treating victims and offenders has been supplemented by lectures to public groups. It is the latter experience that has afforded me the most striking evidence of the accuracy of the research. At almost every lecture in the last several years, someone has reported to me a personal story of sexual abuse. In a small town in New Hampshire, a woman spoke to me afterwards. "Let me tell you," she said, "a way that offenders have of keeping victims silent that you didn't mention. My physician father told me he'd kill the mother I dearly loved if I told, and so, for a long time, I didn't."

During a lecture at a university, an undergraduate interrupted the lecture by banging her fist on the desk and saying loudly, "You can't say that offender doesn't love that child." I had not commented either way, but the student repeated insistently, "You can't say that offender doesn't love that child." After the lecture she approached me to say that her mother had sexually abused her throughout her childhood.

After a lecture to a medical school class, I received a letter in the mail from a young woman who told me she had been raped 15 years previously and had an out-of-body experience that still frightened her. Did I have any references, she asked, on out-of-body experiences?

Following a three-hour workshop with a group of public health nurses, a woman came to see me who said she spent the entire three hours trying not to cry. She had not previously revealed to anyone her long-term abuse by her grandfather.

On a trip to Seattle, Washington, I was the only passenger on the airport bus. The driver asked the reason for my visit to Seattle, and when I told him I was there to visit a sexual abuse treatment program, he replied, "Sexual abuse! Don't talk to me about sexual abuse. My father abused my sister and made me watch, and I can't talk about sexual abuse without going into a rage."

In working with an excellent prosecuting attorney in New England on a child molestation case, I said to him, "You do an excellent job."

"I give these cases the same priority I give murder cases," he said, "and actually, the recidivism is higher."

"Why do you do that?" I replied. "No one else does that."

"Because," he said, "I was sexually abused as a child."

Almost everywhere I speak now I ask the audience to fill in a questionnaire listing anonymously how many people they know personally, not professionally, who have been sexually abused. The questionnaire is divided into "less" serious forms of abuse—exhibitionism, obscene phone calls, voyeurism, frottage—and more serious forms—incest, child molestation, rape, and attempted rape. The figures are impressive each time. A medical school class of 71 students knew 185 people personally (2.6 per person) who had been the victims of more serious sexual offenses, and 464 people (6.5 per person) who had been the victims of less serious offenses. A group of 120 public health nurses knew 510 people personally (4.25 per person) who had been the victims of more serious offenses and 604 (5 per person) who were the victims of less serious offenses. Many people have commented they thought of more victims later—thus the initial response by any group is probably a serious underestimation.

While the prevalence of child sexual abuse can no longer be disputed, neither can there be any doubt of its harmfulness. My own clinical experience with victims tells me that. The voluminous research literature confirms it (Alter-Reid, Gibbs, Lachenmeyer, Sigal, & Massoth, 1986; Anderson, Bach, & Griffith, 1981; Badgley, 1984; Bagley, 1985; Bagley & McDonald, 1984; Becker, Skinner, Abel, & Cichon, 1986; Briere, 1984; Browne & Finkelhor, 1986; Donaldson, 1983; Goodwin, McCarty, & DiVasto, 1982; Harrison & Lumry, 1984; Herman & Hirschman, 1981; Meiselman, 1978. No less an observer than Anna Freud (1981, p. 34) has commented on the harmfulness of incest:

Far from existing only as a fantasy, incest is thus also a fact.... Where the chances of harming a child's normal developmental growth are concerned, it ranks higher than abandonment, neglect, physical maltreatment or any other form of abuse. It would be a fatal mistake to underrate either the importance or the frequency of its actual occurrence.

This book is one effort among many to further the process of providing adequate assessment and treatment to child sex offenders and their victims. Only by focusing on child sexual abuse specifically and implementing specialized techniques can we begin to rehabilitate the offenders and to contribute to the healing of the victims.

PART I

OCCURRENCE OF CHILD SEXUAL ABUSE
Prevalence and Responsibility

1

PREVALENCE

Sexually abused children live with secrecy and isolation. Only a small minority ever reveal the abuse during childhood (Donaldson, 1983; Finkelhor, 1979, 1984; Silbert, 1984). Because of the secrecy, a sexually abused child typically feels different from her[1] peers and frequently believes her abuse is an isolated and unique event. Would that it were so. In fact, the widespread sexual abuse of children is, in Florence Rush's words, "the best kept secret" (Rush, 1980).

While studies of sexual abuse in clinical populations find extremely high rates of sexual abuse (Benward & Densen-Gerber, 1975; Briere, 1984; Goodwin, McCarthy, & Divasto, 1981, 1982; Meiselman, 1978; Silbert, 1984; Summit & Kryso, 1978), they are not considered here, as they represent skewed samples and illustrate better the harmfulness of sexual abuse than its prevalence. The focus of this chapter is on child sexual abuse found in research studies that utilize nonclinical populations. As can be seen in Table 1.1, studies of nonclincial populations have found rates ranging from 7.7% to 38%. The Fritz, Stoll, & Wagner study (1981), which found the lowest rates of abuse, excluded adolescents, both as offenders and as victims. Adolescents, however, both commit a sizable proportion of offenses and are victimized in considerable numbers (Knopp, 1982; Russell, 1984, p. 79). By contrast, one of the more comprehensive and rigorous studies, that by Russell, found the highest rates.

Other studies find rates in the middle. Within this group a number of studies utilized college populations (Briere & Runtz, 1985; Finkelhor, 1979; Fritz et al., 1981; Fromuth, 1983; Sedney & Brooks, 1984; Seidner, Calhoun, & Kilpatrick, 1985; Sorrenti-Little, Bagley & Robertson, 1984). These "college" studies have the disadvantage of underrepresenting the lower socioeconomic levels, thereby possibly underestimating the incidence of child sexual abuse. This weakness is demonstrated by Finkelhor's finding that lower-income females in his 1979 study were 60% more likely to experience child sexual abuse (both extrafamilial and intrafamilial) than the middle-income females. Most of these college studies utilized an age differential as the criterion by which a sexual experience was judged abusive, with the exception of Sedney and Brooks (1984). Most commonly the studies required a five-year differential (Briere & Runtz, 1985; Finkelhor, 1979; Seidner et al., 1985), although at least one utilized a three-year differential (Sorrenti-Little et al., 1984). Studies differed as to how precisely sexual abuse was defined, ranging from general definitions such as that of Sedney, who considered sexual abuse to be "sexual experiences involving other people while they were growing up" (Sedney & Brooks, 1984, p. 215), to Finkelhor's more precise categories, which included intercourse, fondling, and exhibitionism, and to Sorrenti-Little's strict categories, which included only fondling or intercourse with the child's unclothed genitalia. These differences may partially explain the differences in findings, which ranged from 11% to 22% for females if we remove the Fritz study, which excluded adolescent victims and offenders. The average rate of abuse for females from all studies, including the Fritz study, was 15.3%; without the Fritz study it was 16.9%. Results of the surveys of males show greater agreement with a range of from 5% to 9%.

Many studies utilized noncollege populations (Badgley, 1984; Finkelhor, 1984; Kercher, 1980; Kilpatrick, 1986; Russell, 1984). These typically were more representative of the general population, with several (Badgley, 1984; Kercher, 1980; Russell, 1984) utilizing random samples. These studies generally defined their categories of sexual activity precisely, although not all defined an age differential. It is not possible, therefore, in those studies that did not

TABLE 1.1
Recent Prevalence Studies of Sexual Abuse

Study	N	% Females	% Males	Age Abuse Began	Population
Badgley, 1984	1006	15		< 16	Canadian national
		22		< 18	random survey
	1002		6	< 16	
			9	< 18	
Briere & Runtz, 1985	278	15		< 15 with offender 5 years older	college students
Finkelhor, 1979	530	19		victim < 13 with offender 5 years older or victim 13-16 with offender 10 years older	college students
	266		9		
Finkelhor, 1984	334	15		< 16 with offender 5 years older	Boston parents
	187		6		
Fritz, Stroll & Wagner, 1981	540	8		< puberty with postadolescent	college students
	412		5		
Fromuth, 1983	482	22		victim < 13 with offender 5 years older or 13-16 with offender 10 years older	college students
Kercher, 1980[3]	593	11		< 17	Texas driver's
	461		3	< 17	license holders
Kilpatrick, 1986	501	24		< 15	women aged 18-61
Russell, 1984	930	28		< 14	door-to-door
		38		< 18	random sample
Sedney & Brooks, 1984	301	16			college students
Seidner et al., 1985	595	11		< 18 with offender 5 years older	college students
	490		5		
Sorrenti-Little et al., 1984; also Bagley, 1985	404	19		< 16 with offender 3 years older or use of force by peer	college students
	164		11		

to distinguish between consenting sex play between peers and sexual abuse (Kercher, 1980; Kilpatrick, 1986). The Kilpatrick study included all sexual activity under the age of 15 and found that 55% of the 501 respondents had one or more sexual experiences prior to that age. Because the study did not distinguish between exploratory sex play between peers and sexual abuse, that figure was not reported in Table 1.1. Rather, the 24% of women who had had sexual experiences with relatives was reported, as those experiences were more clearly abusive.

Of particular note were the Russell study and the Badgley study. The former was marked by the care and precision of Russell's methodology. She defined her categories exactly, trained her interviewers extensively, and took a door-to-door random sample. Following strict definitional guidelines, she excluded hands-off offenses such as exhibitionism at all ages. Her definition of extrafamilial abuse included the unwanted fondling of children under 14 as sexual abuse, along with rape and attempted rape. For children ages 14 through 17, she only defined attempted or completed forcible rape as sexual abuse. Incestuous relationships were more broadly defined: Any sexual activity with a relative was included. Despite the narrowness of her definitions, she obtained the highest rates.

Among the contributions made by Russell's study was her analysis of data by age of the respondents. With this form of analysis, she determined that younger women reported more intrafamilial abuse than did older women. The rates of extrafamilial abuse did not differ, however, thus ruling out faulty memory or reluctance on the part of older women to discuss sexual abuse as possible contributors. On the basis of her data, Russell stated unequivocally that "What is clear now is that despite fluctuations, incestuous abuse increased over the years from 1916 to 1961, while extrafamilial child sexual abuse merely fluctuated without significantly decreasing or increasing during this period" (Russell, 1984, p. 214).

The Badgley study, titled the National Population Survey, was a Canadian national random survey to which 94.1% of those queried responded. Like the Russell study, the Badgley study did not restrict the definition of sexual abuse to an age differential between offender and victim, but inquired about unwanted sexual touching or assault, defined primarily as penetration or attempted penetration of the anus or vagina.[2] Of the female respondents, 15.2% had been molested under the age of 15, and the figure rose to 21.9% under the age of 18. Of the males, 5.9% had been molested under the age of 15 and 9.4% under the age of 18 (Badgley, 1984; Bagley, 1985). By combining results from three other surveys that the Badgley Commission made—one of police forces, one of hospitals, and one of child protection agencies—Badgley concluded that 60% of the victims under 16 had been either physically forced or threatened by the offender. The National Population Survey found that 9% of the males and 19.9% of the females reported physical injuries during the assault.

The Badgley study and the Russell study were noteworthy not only for their sampling, but for their definitions of sexual abuse, which included any unwanted sexual activity. The majority of studies thus far cited utilized only an age differential as the criterion for sexual abuse, thus eliminating coercive and even violent sexual interactions with peers as well as incestuous experiences with relatives of a similar age. This is particularly unfortunate given that studies of rape victims indicate that adolescents are particularly at risk to be raped (Amir, 1971; Katz & Mazur, 1979; Mulvihill, Tumin, & Curtis, 1969; Russell, 1984). A number of studies have found that 14 is the modal age for victimization by rape (Hayman, Stewart, Lewis, & Grant, 1968; Hursch, 1977; Schiff, 1969); Peters's study found 15 to be the the the modal age, with an average age of 20 (Krasner, Meyer, & Carroll, 1976). Amir (1971) found that 27.8% of rape victims were under 15, whereas 52.7% were less than 20. Svalastoga (1962) found that approximately half of the victims were from 15 to 19. The modal age for victim's rape in Russell's study was 16 (Russell, 1984), whereas the average age was 21. Women aged 16 to 20 made up 36% of rape victims (Russell, p. 81). The National Commission on the Cause and Prevention of Violence (Mulvihill et al., 1969) found in a 17-city study that 47.4% of the victims were under 18 (p. 212). Katz and Mazur (1979) in a summary of 11 empirical studies found that adolescents represented the largest single age group of victims reported to police.

Male rapists, like their victims, are found disproportionately in the adolescent and young-adult age groups (Amir, 1971; Eisen-hower, 1969; MacDonald, 1971; Svalastoga, 1962; Wright, 1980). Amir, for example, found that 43.9% of his sample of rapists were under 20. The National Commission found that 20.9% of rapists were under 18, whereas 48% were between 18 and 25 years old (Mulvihill et al., 1969, p. 212). Wright (1980) found that 27.3% of their 202 offenders were under 21. Thus studies that excluded unwanted sexual activity between peers and only rely on an age differential as the sole criterion for sexual abuse will underestimate the extent of the problem by excluding significant numbers of victims who have been forcibly raped by peers.

The rates reported in all the studies summarized are uniformly high. The most complete studies (Badgley, 1984; Russell, 1984) found rates of from 22% of females to 38%, whereas the Badgley study found almost 10% of males under 18 had been sexually abused. Of all the puzzling aspects of the field of sexual abuse, one of the most puzzling is how so much sexual abuse could have gone on for so long with so little attention, either from the public or from the professionals. A preliminary answer would be that the information was not available. Sex offenders did not reveal their offenses, children were too afraid to tell, and often their parents didn't believe them when they did. Proponents of this argument would argue that the studies cited above are all recent studies and represent new data. Although plausible, this answer will not do. A summary of incidence studies of sexual abuse available in the professional literature for many decades is presented in Table 1.2. While few of the old studies addressed male victimization, the same cannot be said for female. Rates of sexual abuse of female children ranged in these studies from 24% to 37%.

As older studies, they lack the sophisticated methodology and the careful definitions of more recent research. The Hamilton study (1929, p. 334) reported the percentage of those who stated that before puberty they had been "frightened or disgusted by the sexual aggressions of [persons of the opposite sex]." Unquestionably, this may have included some experiences with nonrelated peers that might more appropriately be classified as sex play. However, of the examples of experiences given by men in the study, 24 of 30 could certainly be classified as sexual abuse. Of those by women, 37 of 55. Since some respondents may have given more than one example, the actual percentages cannot be known.

The actual question in the Terman 1938 study was "Before the age of fifteen, did you encounter any incident connected with sex, which shocked or greatly disgusted you at the time?" (Terman, p. 250). Sexual abuse was defined in the Landis study (Landis, 1940, p. 278) as "sex aggression" by an older boy, adult, or family member. Landis distinguished the number of individuals molested by someone outside the family from those molested by a family member. Since the degree of overlap is unknown, the exact total cannot be computed; only the minimum and maximum molested can be estimated. Terman's 1951 study inquired about "sex shock" (p. 136). Kinsey's 1953 study included sexual approaches in which no contact

TABLE 1.2
Older Prevalence Studies of Child Sexual Abuse

Study	N	% Females Abused	% Males Abused	Age Abuse Began	Population
Hamilton, 1929	120	37		< 16	
	110		27		
Terman, 1938	752	32		< 15	married women
Landis, 1940	153	27-39		prepuberty	"normal women"
	142	20-33			"abnormal women"
Terman, 1951	556	25		< 16	gifted, married
Landis, 1956	1800	35	30	< 20	college students
Kinsey, 1953	4441	24		preadolescent	middle class
Gagnon, 1965	1200	28		< 13	

was made (9%) along with exhibitionism, fondling, oral genital sex, and intercourse (Kinsey, Pomeroy, Martin, & Gebhard, 1953). The Gagnon study was based on a subset of Kinsey's sample (approximately one-fourth) who were queried more extensively regarding the nature and extent of the sexual incidents.

Granted, the methodology of these earlier studies was generally less sophisticated than current ones, their definitions were imprecise, and the sexual milieu at the time was such that "sexual aggressions" that "frightened" or "disgusted" a young female were not all what would be classified today as sexual abuse. Some of the incidents would no doubt be classified as sex play among agemates, although both Kinsey et al. (1953) and Landis (1956) eliminated those by requiring significant age differences between offender and victim. Moreover, an examination of examples cited in these studies reveals numerous incidents that today would be definitely classified as sexual abuse. While these studies are generally methodologically crude (with the exception of Kinsey's), and the actual rate of sexual abuse in the early part of this century is unknown, it is striking that the rates reported were extremely high and represented what was thought to be sexual abuse at the time.

Why then was this information attended to so little? Clinicians trained as late as the 70s were instructed that sexual abuse was extremely rare and cited figures for incest as low as one in a million (Weinberg, 1955; Weiner, 1962). Yet studies dating from 1929 documented extraordinarily high rates of sexual abuse at a time when the culture was considerably less sexually permissive than today. Sins of omission are more difficult to track in the literature than sins of commission, as they leave fewer trails. However, Kinsey's reasons for not publicizing child sexual abuse can be derived from his writings. First, although his own research documented a 24% rate of sexual abuse of females (including both intrafamilial and extrafamilial), he nonetheless maintained that heterosexual incest was to be found more in the imagination of therapists than in the lives of their patients (Kinsey, Pomeroy, Martin, & Gebhard, 1948, p. 558). Second, despite the fact that 80% of the victims in his study reported being upset or frightened by the experience, he felt there was no logical reason that children should be disturbed by sexual abuse. Since his views on this topic accurately describe the zeitgeist of the times, they are worth quoting fully.

> It is difficult to understand why a child, except for its cultural conditioning, should be disturbed at having its genitalia touched, or disturbed at seeing the genitalia of other persons, or disturbed at even more specific sexual contacts. When children are constantly warned by parents and teachers against contacts with adults, and when they receive no explanation of the exact nature of the forbidden contacts, they are ready to become hysterical as soon as any older person approaches, or stops and speaks to them in the street, or fondles them, or proposes to do something for them, even though the adult may have had no sexual objective in mind. Some of the more experienced students of juvenile problems have come to believe that the emotional reactions of the parents, police officers, and other adults who discover that the child has had such a contact, may disturb the child more seriously than the sexual contacts themselves. (Kinsey et al., 1953, p. 121)

Such hysterical warnings, Kinsey felt, could result in false accusations.

> A problem that deserves noting is that of the old men who are apprehended and sentenced to penal institutions as sex offenders. These men are usually charged with contributing to delinquency by fondling minor girls or boys; often they are charged with attempted rape. Among the older sex offenders who have given histories for the present study, a considerable number insist that they are impotent, and many of them give a history of long-standing impotence. A few of these man may have falsified the record, and many courts incline to the belief that all of them perjure themselves. We find, however, definite evidence in the histories that many of these men are in actuality incapable of erection. The usual professional interpretation describes these offenders as sexually thwarted, incapable of winning

attention from older females, and reduced to vain attempts with children who are unable to defend themselves. An interpretation that would more nearly fit our understanding of old age would recognize the decline in erotic reaction, the loss of capacity to perform, and the reduction of the emotional life of the individual to such affectionate fondling as parents and especially grandparents are wont to bestow upon their own (and other) children. Many small girls reflect the public hysteria over the prospect of 'being touched' by a strange person; and many a child, who has no idea at all of the mechanics of intercourse, interprets affection and simple caressing, from anyone except her own parents, as attempts at rape. In consequence, not a few older men serve time in penal institutions for attempting to engage in a sexual act that at their age would not interest most of them, and of which many of them are undoubtedly incapable. (Kinsey et al., 1948, pp. 237-238)

Finally, Kinsey felt the punishment for offenders was disproportionate to the crime. "In many instances the law, in the course of punishing the offender, does more damage to more persons than was ever done by the individual in his illicit sexual activity" (Kinsey et al., 1953, p. 20).

Excellent discussions by both Russell (1984) and Herman (1981) point out that Kinsey's associates continued to promulgate the thesis that the sexual abuse of children was not intrinsically harmful to them throughout the 70s, when their comments appeared in such journals as *Forum* and *Penthouse* (Herman, 1981, pp. 23-25).

Although intriguing, the larger problem of decades of cultural denial is beyond the scope of this book. Related aspects—blaming the victim and her family with concurrent minimization of offender responsibility—will be discussed as they relate directly to treatment.

NOTES

1. Female pronouns will be used throughout this manual to describe sexually abused children and male pronouns to describe offenders. This is not to imply that only female children are abused, since surely they are not, nor that only males are offenders. However, all existing studies find more female children abused than male and more offenders to be male than female. For this reason those pronouns will be used that reflect the majority of cases.

2. The study did include exhibitionism, but tabulated those results separately.

3. Of the total sample of 1,054 Texas residents, 71 evidently did not answer this question, as the combined "yes" and "no" responses equalled 983. However, Kercher did not indicate the sex of the nonrespondents; thus they cannot be subtracted from the figures.

2

THE CASE AGAINST THE VICTIM AND NONOFFENDING FAMILY MEMBERS

The literature on child sexual abuse in this century has often held victims and their mothers responsible for the sexual abuse, particularly in cases of incest, frequently with little mention of the role of the offender. Attributing responsibility to the child was more prevalent in the early part of the century, although there is literature in the 80s that continues this tradition. Holding the mother and nonoffending family members responsible has been more frequent in the past 30 years, and is currently the dominant position in the field in incest cases.

THE CASE AGAINST THE VICTIM

In 1907 Karl Abraham published a paper entitled "The Experiencing of Sexual Traumas as a Form of Sexual Activity" (Abraham, 1927). His thesis was that "in a great number of cases the trauma was desired by the child unconsciously, and that we have to recognize it as a form of infantile sexual activity" (p. 48). While he blamed the victim for the abuse, his stance was nonetheless an improvement over Freud's position that reports of child sexual abuse by adult women represented Oedipal fantasies. The fallacy inherent in that position has by now been well documented and will not be examined here (Herman, 1981; Masson, 1984; Rush, 1980).

What will be examined is the position of the psychoanalytic movement in those cases in which the reality of the assault was admitted. Abraham, for example, believed that children not only unconsciously desired sexual assault but were responsible for its occurrence, since (referring to previously published cases of his) "in all of them the trauma could have been prevented. The children could have called for help, run away, or offered resistance instead of yielding to the seduction" (p. 50).

Children who did resist fared no better. Abraham himself cited the case of a 9-year-old girl who was enticed into the woods by a neighbor, who "then attempted to rape her" (p. 51). The little girl physically resisted and managed to free herself. She then ran home without telling her parents what had happened. Abraham wrote that the girl "had allowed herself to be seduced. She had followed the neighbour into the woods and allowed him to go a long way in carrying out his purpose before she freed herself from him and ran off. It is not to be wondered at that this child kept the occurrence secret" (pp. 52-53).

If Abraham did not admit the existence of physical coercion, could we expect him to recognize psychological coercion? Those children who are psychologically manipulated or coerced into sexual relations were dismissed entirely as having an "abnormal desire for obtaining sexual pleasure, and in consequence of this undergo sexual traumas" (p. 54). Hysterics were, for example:

> those interesting people to whom something is always happening. Female hysterics in particular are constantly meeting with adventures. They are molested in the public street, outrageous sexual assaults are made on them, etc. It is part of their nature that they must expose themselves to external traumatic influences. There is in them a need to appear to be constantly subjected to external violence. In this we recognize a general psychological characteristic of women in an exaggerated form. (p. 57)

Abraham's opinions were not eccentric commentary outside the mainstream of psychiatric and psychological opinion. By 1937

Bender and Blau would specifically cite Abraham's work in their indictment of victims:

> This study seems to indicate that these children undoubtedly do not deserve completely the cloak of innocence with which they have been endowed by moralists, social reformers and legislators. The history of the relationship in our cases usually suggested at least some cooperation of the child in the activity, and in some cases the child assumed an active role in initiating the relationship. This is in agreement with Abraham's views. It is true that the child often rationalized with excuses of fear of physical harm or the enticement of gifts, but these were obviously secondary reasons. Even in the cases in which physical force may have been applied by the adult, this did not wholly account for the frequent repetition of the practice. . . . Furthermore, the emotional placidity of most of the children would seem to indicate that they derived some fundamental satisfaction from the relationship. . . . Finally, a most striking feature was that these children were distinguished as unusually charming and attractive in their outward personalities. Thus, it is not remarkable that frequently we considered the possibility that the child might have been the actual seducer rather than the one innocently seduced. (p. 514)

Weiss, Rogers, Darwin, and Dutton (1955) agreed. In a study of 73 girls sexually molested as children they looked for factors within the child's personality that would explain the sexual abuse. Of their 73 victims the authors concluded that 21 could be termed "accidental" and 44 "participating" (with 8 undetermined). The division "was made on the basis of the writers' overall evaluation of the child's personality, but it could have been made on the basis of a single factor, that is, the frequency of the child's sexual experiences (more than one sexual experience with one, or more than one, adult" (p. 2). Basically, accidental victims were those children molested once by a stranger, without "remuneration" (bribes), who told their parents immediately afterwards. Victims of repeated abuse at the hands of relatives or acquaintances were termed "participating." The "participating" victims had "typical" personalities, and were described as being

> often very attractive and appealing. She establishes a superficial relationship with the psychiatrist almost immediately. She does not hesitate to enter the playroom, and, once there, she is more interested in the psychiatrist than in the playroom toys. She may behave with the male psychiatrist as if he is an exalted authority. She

may be submissive or sexually seductive with him, or she may attempt to win him masochistically by humiliating herself in order to gain pity.

Certain tendencies are frequently revealed in the playroom fantasies of the typical participant victim. Her fantasies may contain masochistic elements. For instance, she may enact a scene in which a girl doll is misunderstood and unfairly punished by a parent doll; or she herself may lie on the floor, pretending to be completely paralyzed by poliomyelitis, and ask to be fed. Her play reveals, too, her unresolved conflicts about looking and being looked at (scopophilia and exhibitionism). She may fantasize a situation in which a child peeks at her parents in bed, or she may slyly remove the trousers from one of the dolls and giggle. Another of her playroom preoccupations is with family conspiracies, and in her doll play she may have a girl doll and a father doll keep a secret from the mother doll, or she may have the daughter and the mother keep a secret from the father. (pp. 4-5)

While the study went on to examine certain family dynamics that the authors felt contributed to the sexual acting out, the authors concluded that the family dynamics were not sufficient to explain the sexual abuse, since "An understanding of the child's acting out must be in terms of the structure of the child's own personality" (p. 26).

The distinction between "accidental" and "participating" victims was to endure (Gagnon, 1965; Krieger, Rosenfeld, Gordon & Bennett, 1980; MacVicar, 1979). Gagnon (1965) divided his sample into accidental and nonaccidental victims, both further divided into single and multiple "events." The criterion for single accidental was "a single event with a single offender without any buildup of social interaction apparent in the record" (p. 180). Multiple accidental victims were separated out for discrete analysis, since they "might have in fact been more provocative in the offense than the bare bones of the description might allow" (p. 180).

All other events were defined as nonaccidental, and divided into collaborative and coerced. Of the 31 nonaccidental cases, Gagnon classified 5 as coerced. All others were defined as collaborative, and it was thought that the children "sustained the offense out of their own interest" (p. 184). These did include 12% who had sexual contact with total strangers. It is striking, however, that Gagnon felt that there were far fewer collaborative victims than previously thought, and found that only 7.8% of his sample of 333 fell into that category (p. 181).

Moreover, he did not assign full responsibility to the child, and at least alluded to the role of the offender:

There are those males who have histories of extensive contact with prepubertal children, a minority of all those who have sexual contact with children to be sure, who have learned techniques of dealing with children in sexual situations such that the child derives fundamental satisfactions from the act or is not sufficiently disturbed to report the event to his or her parents. The social and sexual skills of the offender, as well as some aspects of physical situation, are external to the character of the child and operate as strains toward cooperation or resistance. The most eager child will be put off by pain, and the most recalcitrant interested by charm and adult affection. (p. 185)

Other researchers, however, have been less convinced that the offender has a role. Revitch and Weiss (1962) stated flatly that "The majority of pedophiles are harmless individuals and their victims are usually known to be aggressive and seductive children" (p. 78). Their position is clear: "the child victim is aggressive and seductive and often induces the adult offender to commit the offense" (p. 74). While admitting that they "rarely" interviewed the victims and relied almost entirely on the word of the offenders, nonetheless they concluded:

The precocious and aggressive children quickly sense the infantile characteristics of the pedophile and very soon lose the awe of adult authority and treat him as if he were one of them. The pedophile will complain that the children annoyed him, that they followed him into the bathroom when he had to urinate, and *that they exploited him through accepting his gifts and money* which he allegedly distributed just because of friendly feelings or in order to help a deprived child. (p. 75, italics added)

Likewise Mohr, Turner, and Jerry (1964) described the child as "a willing participant if not the instigator of a sexual act with an adult" (p. 34). Regarding incest, Henderson (1975) felt, "The daughters collude in the incestuous liaison and play an active and even initiating role in establishing the pattern" (p. 1536). Sarles (1975) agreed. "Although public and professional sentiment is generally empathetic toward the daughter and negative toward the father, there are indications that the daughters may play an active and initiating role in the incestuous relationship" (p. 637).

Other writers have echoed similar themes. Lukianowicz (1972) noted that many incest victims accepted their father's behavior as "normal" and that in those who later became promiscuous, they almost always chose adult males rather than peers. He concluded, therefore, that "this behaviour might further suggest that at least some of the girls might have played an active part in the initiation of the incestuous relations and that not all of them were only 'innocent victims'" (p. 307).

Weiner (1962) stated that "the length and frequency of these incestuous contacts and the absence of any complaints on the part of the daughters indicate that these girls were not merely helpless victims of their fathers' needs but were gratified by the relationship, if not . . . active initiators of it" (p. 628). Weiner explained the fact that many victims behaved as though they did not enjoy the activity by describing an adult survivor who allegedly stated that she had felt intense pleasure but hid it from her father in order to make him feel more responsible for the incest and her less guilty. Weiner concluded, "It is quite likely that many incestuous daughters avoid guilt feelings by denying their enjoyment of the sexual experience and behaving in an outwardly passive manner during sex contacts" (p. 614).

Various theories have been developed to explain "the child's acting out." Gordon (1955) felt it represented revenge directed at the mother for pre-Oedipal frustrations. Weiner (1962) felt it reflected penis envy and revenge against the mother deemed responsible for the lack of a penis. Friedlander (1947) thought the child's Oedipal wishes were responsible. Kaufman, Peck, and Tagiuri (1954) wrote that the incest was the child's response to abandonment by the mother, whereas Rascovsky and Rascovsky (1950) felt it involved "Overcompensation of the primary maternal frustration through the father's penis" (p. 46). In their case study of an adult involved in an incestuous relationship with her father, the father was "placed in the position of compensating the oral frustrations inflicted by the mother" (p. 44). The authors traced extensively the psychopathology of the daughter prior to the initiation of incest but did not comment on the father's. It was unclear in any case the degree of harm Rascovsky and Rascovsky attributed to this activity, since they wrote that "the actual consummation of the incestuous relation . . . diminishes the subject's chance of psychosis and allows better adjustment to the external world" (p. 45).

Whatever the theory, the assumption was the same. The child, not the offender, was responsible for the sexual aggression directed toward her. This view may be less popular currently, but it is by no means absent.

Virkkunen (1981) cited Fattah's division of victims of crimes into five categories (Fattah, 1967) as the most suitable categorization for looking at pedophilia. The categories consist of nonparticipating victims, latent or predisposed victims, provocative victims, participating victims, and false victims. Nonparticipating victims are those who do not contribute in any way to the commission of the crime. Latent or predisposed victims are those who, because of "peculiar predispositions or traits of character, are more liable than others to be victims of certain types of offenses" (Fattah, 1967, p. 165). Provocative victims either incite the criminal to commit the crime or create a situation in which a crime is likely to occur, whereas participating victims contribute to the crime while it is happening. False victims are not the victims of crimes committed by others, although they may either believe and/or say they are.

Virkkunen found a pedophilic act was primarily incited by a "provocative" or "participating" victim on an offender who was a "timid person, usually without adult contacts, childish and immature" (1975, p. 123). Such individuals were "in a pronounced manner gentle, fond of children and benevolent" (p. 179). His 1975 study found a lower incidence of intelligence in the offenders than controls, and he felt that their limited capacities made them less able to resist victim precipitated molestation: "in victim-precipitated cases opportunity makes the thief" (pp. 178-179). In his study of 64 victims of extrafamilial abuse, he found that the child had initiated the sexual activity in 31 of the 64 cases (Virkkunen, 1975). Virkkunen concluded his 1981 review by stating that "Without doubt, the child victim's own behaviour often plays a considerable part in initiating and maintaining a pedophiliac crime" (pp. 130-131).

As further proof of his thesis, Virkkunen cited studies indicating both that acquaintance between victim and offender is common prior to the abuse and that many children are molested repeatedly. "Repeated visits to the offender in spite of continuous criminal behaviour is of course proof of the cooperation of the victim" (Virkkunen, 1981, p. 128). In addition, he referred to a study in 1965 by Gebhard, Gagnon, Pomeroy and Christenson in which 48% of offenders who had committed crimes against female children stated that the child had encouraged the sexual activity (as opposed to 16% in the official records). In this study 37% of the offenders indicated that the child had not resisted (as opposed to 8% in the records), and only 15% of the offenders reported that the child had actively refused (as opposed to 75% in the records). Virkkunen clearly implied that the offenders should be believed over the official records. Gebhard himself was more ambivalent and raised at least the possibility that "the more reprehensible the offense, the more the offender endeavors to bend the account in his favor" (p. 797).

Nor are Virkkunen's views an isolated phenomenon. Mohr (1981) objected to the view current in some quarters that offenders are responsible for sexual assaults against children. "There is a cultural assumption, if not a conspiracy, to look at and present the phenomenon of pedophilia in a way that excludes its treatment as an interaction phenomenon" (p. 41). Of perhaps more concern, however, is his objection to the fact that the sexual interactions between adults and children are "seen as highly problematic and characterized as deviant and criminal" (p. 51). Were we to look at most of these interactions "it is difficult to understand why this should be, although there can be no doubt about the level of anxiety such incidents arouse in adults. This anxiety and the demonology to which it gives rise is not accounted for by pedophilic incidents themselves" (p. 51). Evidently, Mohr felt the current tendency to view the sexual abuse of children as criminal may cause anxiety in the offenders.

West (1981) wrote that "controversy arises over the criminalization of consensual acts as "sexual assaults" (p. 266), and he explored alternatives to the current policy of protecting children categorically by age. The law should take into account that at least some instances of incest involved "completely mutual relationships" (p. 262). Thus he argued that "Libertarian principles suggest the abolition of the legal fiction of an age of consent and the introduction of a requirement to have a complaining victim before a criminal charge can be brought" (p. 266). While admitting there were "substantial" problems with this approach, particularly in the case of very young children and children under the physical or psychological control of the offender, he nonetheless felt the arguments against it were "not completely convincing" (p. 266). He noted that pregnancy was the chief social evil likely to occur from pedophilic activity, and as an alternative to the current policy, suggested that "it might be more logical to criminalize neglect of contraception than to criminalize sex itself" (p. 267). In any case, many instances of child sexual abuse "could best be dealt with informally by the families concerned, with or without the help of social workers or doctors" (p. 268).

Slovenko (1971) directed a scathing attack at the concept of statutory rape, focused on the concept of lecherous females and innocent males. He quoted a 1923 court with which he evidently agreed:

A lecherous woman is a social menace; she is more dangerous than TNT; more deadly than the "pestilence that walketh in darkness or the destruction that wasteth at noonday." . . .

This wretched girl was young in years but old in sin and shame. A number of callow youths, of otherwise blameless lives so far as this record shows, fell under her seductive influence. . . . She was a mere "cistern for foul toads to know and gender in." Why should the boys, misled by her, be sacrificed? (p. 158)

Slovenko continued, "the male offender in the case of statutory rape has no special pathology; the girl is usually more in need of psychiatric care or other attention. She may be seductive or aggressive, or apathetic about life" (p. 158). That he did not simply oppose the charging of agemates with statutory rape is shown by his objection to the fact that elderly offenders were not allowed to use impotence as a defense.

Conclusions

The tendency to blame the child victims of sexual abuse thus continues into the '80s, although it is no longer the dominant approach in the field. The tendency is puzzling. It would seem obvious, but apparently is not, that one should not confuse the effects of child sexual abuse with the cause. A child whose interactions with adults are sexualized by child sexual abuse may then go on to act seductively toward other adults. Her personal interactions may well be disturbed and her ability to express nonsexual affection may be impaired. It is a stunning leap of illogic to state that these existed prior to the abuse, and in fact, were the cause of the abuse. Even in recent articles the anguish experienced by the incest survivor is still being used as evidence she may have initiated the incest in the first place. Henderson (1983) has written "It is at least a possibility that the all-pervasive anguish to which incestuous behavior is a dysfunctional solution is the same anguish which we later identify in the subsequent adult life of the little girl who was the alleged victim of this interaction—that the intense personal pain preceded the incestuous interaction and was in part motive rather than its consequence" (p. 34).

Likewise, the literature's silence on the issue of psychological coercion is unfortunate. Children generally obey their elders, especially when their elders are in positions of power over them.

Although many children intuit from early ages that something is wrong with the type of touching the offender seeks, it is a rare child who knows what to do about it. Adults use their superior cognition to convince children that they, and not the offenders, will be blamed. Various threats and bribes are employed to ensure the child's silence. Even in Virkkunen's 1975 "victim-precipitation" study he found that 74% of the offenders had used bribes to entice the children. Many children are afraid of their offenders and believe that they or nonparticipating members of their families will be harmed. One client reported that at age 7 she did not tell that a babysitter was molesting her because he told her he would lock her in a dark basement the next time he babysat if she did. At 7 she did not understand he would not be babysitting for her if she told, and she did not. Other children sometimes love an offending parent and believe his statement that he will go to jail if she tells, thus abandoning her. This is extremely effective in securing a child's silence, as the threat of abandonment by a parent can be quite terrifying to children.

A child who engages in sexual activity with an adult through ignorance, confusion, manipulation, fear, or psychological dependency should not be labeled "participating," with the implication that the child sought and willingly continued the sexual relationship. The fact that an offender gained repeated access to the child is evidence not of the child's planning and persistence in the deviant behavior but of the offender's. If that child then generalizes the behavior and approaches other adults as she has been taught, to exchange sex for affection, it would seem unsupportable to label her as "provocative," rather than as injured by her experiences.

Likewise the issue of responsibility has been confused in the literature. Much has been written that seems to imply that the offender has no control over his behavior, and that responsibility for setting appropriate standards of behavior is appropriately delegated to children. Even if a child, sexualized by a previous assault, were to approach an adult sexually, whose responsibility would it be to set limits on inappropriate behavior? The literature cited above implies it would be the child's.

While it is difficult to understand these types of logical errors in a current article, perhaps older studies can be forgiven for confusing correlation with causation, and for eliminating adult responsibility. What, however, explains the *virulence* of the attacks on the children (Bender & Blau, 1937; Revitch & Weiss, 1962; Slovenko, 1971)? There is nowhere in the literature the kind of animosity shown toward offenders that has repeatedly been expressed toward the victims and their mothers.

THE CASE AGAINST THE FAMILY

It is less fashionable currently to hold the victim accountable for her own abuse, although, as we have seen, it continues to occur. In general, however, the focus of the literature in incest has shifted from assigning responsibility to the victim to assigning responsibility to the family in general and the mother in particular. "Despite the overt culpability of the fathers, we were impressed with their psychological passivity in the transactions leading to incest. The mother appeared the cornerstone in the pathological family system" (Lustig, Dresser, Spellman, & Murray, 1966, p. 39). Some authors have specifically limited the culpability of spouses to cases of father-daughter incest.

> It is primarily in father-daughter incest that family dysfunction plays the most significant role. In other forms of incestuous relationships, individual pathology assumes greater importance as a motivating force. For example, in father-son incest, homosexual conflict often underlies the offender's behavior. In sibling incest, individual pathology also dominates the picture. (Mayer, 1983, p. 21)

Thus it is explicitly in cases of male aggression against female children where the mother is thought to hold the major responsibility.

The literature on the subject of the mother's responsibility for father-daughter incest is quite sizable and can be divided according to the authors' views of the nature of the mother's culpability. Authors differ as to whether the mother (1) actively encourages the incest to occur, (2) is indirectly responsible, (3) fails to set appropriate limits to prevent the incest, and/or (4) is aware of the incest but does not allow herself to acknowledge it.

Actively Encourages the Incest

Kaufman et al. (1954) felt mothers unconsciously give their daughters permission for the incest. "The mother did this not only by being absent, but more actively by setting up a situation where this could occur" (p. 276). They cited the example of a mother who placed her daughter in bed with her husband while going herself to another room to escape his snoring.

Lustig et al. (1966) felt that the mothers encouraged incest because of both hostility and homosexual feelings toward the daughters:

> The mother's role in facilitating the incestuous relationship involved both strong unconscious hostility toward the daughter and considerable dependency upon her as a substitute wife-mother. (Hostility toward the child was not a striking feature of the fathers.) . . . Indications of unconscious homosexual strivings in the mothers were abundant, and the fathers may well have acted as vehicles for the mothers' unconscious homosexual impulses toward the daughters. (p. 34)

Lustig et al. also noted that the "vehicle" fathers "do not typically choose the more sociopathic forms of acting out, such as promiscuity outside the family" (p. 33).

Indirectly Responsible

Mothers are frequently held responsible for the abuse by virtue of "denying" sexual relations to their husbands (James & Nasjleti, 1983; Justice & Justice, 1979; Lustig et al., 1966; Maisch, 1972; Weiner, 1962). A number of authors have taken the view that this has a direct and sometimes *intended* connection with the incest. Henderson (1975) felt that such mothers "promote the occurrence of incestuous liaison by frustrating their husbands sexually or symbolically deserting them" (p. 1536). Lustig et al. (1966) wrote that "these women had a history of sexually rejecting and deprecating their husbands" (p. 34). In addition, he observed that, "While rejecting their husbands sexually and generating in them considerable sexual frustration and tension, they played conspicuous roles in directing the husbands' sexual energies toward the daughters" (p. 34). Sarles (1975) agreed. The wives "promoted the incestuous relationship by abandoning or frustrating their husbands sexually, or by actively altering the living arrangements to foster incest" (p. 637).

Numerous authors have commented on role reversal, the assignment of the maternal role to the child by an absentee mother, which is thought to encourage incestuous behavior on the father's part (Forward & Buck, 1978; Heims & Kaufman, 1963; Henderson, 1975; Justice & Justice, 1979; Lustig et al., 1966; Kaufman et al., 1954). For Justice and Justice, the role reversal is likewise *intended* to include sex. "In inviting the daughter to take over her role, she is suggesting that the daughter also become her mate's sex partner" (p. 97). Such a mother "feels relief when the daughter substitutes for her" (p. 97). Henderson (1975) agreed. "These mothers push their daughters prematurely into a mothering role, and that eventually includes sexual partnership with father" (p. 1536).

There are, however, numerous other ways in which a mother's behavior has been considered responsible for sexual abuse. Justice and Justice (1979) commented that the nonparticipant (i.e., "colluding") mother "keeps herself tired and worn out. This is yet another invitation for the daughter to take over" (p. 98). They noted also that the nonparticipant mother may be weak, dependent, indifferent, absent, depressed, or promiscuous. Each of these were listed as ways the mother *contributes* to the incest.

In a case presented in 1971, Bell and Hall reported that a child molester's behavior was determined in part by his "fixation at a stage of psychosexual development due to his mother's intimacy" (p. 93). This hypothesis was forwarded despite the fact that the offender had been sexually abused at the age of 4 by his father, who later left the family. The sexual abuse is only noted in passing; it is not mentioned at all in the summary of the different factors that contributed to the offender's sexual deviancy (p. 93).

Fails to Set Limits

Other authors do not imply the mother initiated the abuse or even that her behavior was indirectly responsible for its occurrence. They do, however, hold her responsible for a failure to stop the abuse. Tormes (1968) has written of some of her sample of child abusers that they had locked a mother in the closet while abusing the child, broken a radio over a mother's head, or burned children with hot irons, but concluded that the cause of the incest was "the failure of the mother to protect her child" (p. 27).

Denies Her Knowledge of It

A number of authors have concluded that mothers of incest victims are aware of the abuse, either unconsciously or consciously.

Forward and Buck (1978) identified the majority of mothers (80% to 90%) as either active partners or silent partners, who know of the incest but neither prevent nor stop it. Justice and Justice (1979) disagreed only with the percentage. They indicated that every mother of an incest victim was either directly involved and participating or "colluding and indirectly involved when her husband carries on sexual activity with their daughter while the mother remains a member of the family. In either case, she cannot escape sharing responsibility for the problem" (pp. 96-97). Thus incest is considered to be the mother's responsibility even when she does not know it is occurring. James and Nasjleti (1983) agree, listing as one of their misconceptions about sexual abuse that "Mothers who are not aware of the child sexual abuse in the family have no responsibility for it" (p. 1).

Justice and Justice held, in any case, that the mothers are at least unconsciously aware of the incest and chose not to acknowledge it: "They simply prefer to keep knowledge of the sex out of their awareness since it serves their emotional needs for the daughter to become the wife as well as the mother" (p. 102).

Much has been written about the extent to which the mother's knowledge combined with a failure to act is etiologically responsible for the incest (Henderson, 1975; Justice & Justice, 1979; Meiselman, 1978). Clark, O'Neil, and Laws (1981), for example, wrote of the "collusion of the 'silent' partner" (p. 19) and went on to specify that "incest usually requires the passive cooperation of the wife" (p. 19). They continued: "Through denial and the use of other defenses, the passive parent allows the incest to continue, apparently unwilling to disturb the tension reducing function that is effected by the abuse" (p. 19).

Mothers and No-Win Situations

It would seem from the literature that almost anything that mothers do can be and has been taken as a sign they approved, encouraged, or at least tolerated incest. Despite the oft-cited notion that mothers do not intervene in incest, Justice and Justice (1979) and Henderson (1975) both reported incidents in which a mother stopped the incest by reporting it. They found, however, other reasons to explain the mother's report, other than an objection to the husband's behavior and a desire to protect the child. Justice and Justice stated that "often this occurs when the wife seeks retaliation against her husband for some other grievance he has caused her" (p. 102). Henderson wrote that the report is, "often precipitated by anger over some other matter and appears as much linked to that as an expression of real objection to what is taking place between father and daughter" (p. 1536). Lustig et al. (1966) felt that such a mother would sometimes report the incest when confronted by it since she could not tolerate the conscious recognition of incest as it threatened her sense of her own competence as a female. Likewise Lukianowicz (1972) conjectured that in two cases in which discovery was followed by divorce, the mothers had surely known of the incest for years and "might even have tacitly encouraged it" (p. 305).

Weiss et al. (1955) cited a case of sexual abuse in which, prior to committing incest with his 6-year-old daughter, the offender had encouraged his daughter to go nude and had gone nude himself in front of her. The mother had objected. Weiss et al. made the point that the parental conflicts about the expression of sexuality were responsible for the "child's" sexual acting out, not the behavior of the father. In reality, the father's behavior was typical "grooming" behavior of a sex offender toward a child. Had the mother agreed with him that he and the child should go nude together, is it to be imagined that she would have been thought less culpable by Weiss?

Even mothers who, far from encouraging their daughters to participate in incestuous relationships, explicitly warn their children against sexual advances by adults, have been held culpable for their warnings. Weiss et al. (1955) described such a case and stated that the mother "in so doing made the child aware of the possibility of sexual relationships with adult men; the mother's warnings were at the same time prohibiting and stimulating to her child" (p. 7). In many cases, the conclusion that the mother's behavior was contributory to the incest seems to have been made independent of the nature of the behavior.

Family Involvement

A number of authors have proposed that incest is a symptom of family dysfunction and therefore, the responsibility of all members (Alexander, 1985; Gutheil & Avery, 1977; James & Nasjleti, 1983; Lutz & Medway, 1984; Mrazek & Bentovim, 1981; Taylor, 1984). Gutheil and Avery noted that incest expressed "the collective psychopathology of all the family members" (p. 105). DeYoung

(1982) agreed, "Incest is a product of family pathology and, except for the rarest occasions, all family members contribute in some way to the pathology that breeds the incest" (p. 9). For Mayer (1983) the culpability of the family is specifically restricted to father-daughter incest, as other forms of incest involve individual offender pathology and therefore individual responsibility. "In father-daughter incest, the entire family is involved and each member is active in perpetrating the abuse" (p. 22).

Nor is the philosophy that families are responsible for child sexual abuse restricted to academics. The Child Sexual Abuse Treatment Program (CSATP) in San Jose, California, one of the oldest, largest and most widely emulated treatment programs in the country, writes in its statement of philosophy that "Incestuous behavior is one of the many symptoms of a dysfunctional family" (Giarretto, 1982, p. 19). An independent evaluation of the program wrote of the mothers that, "By termination, 50% of the evaluation's sample admit that they were 'very much responsible,' compared to none at all claiming responsibility at intake. Giarretto commented that, "This change of attitude comes from learning that a failing marriage is, invariably, one of the precursors to incest" (p. 54). Evidently, in Giarretto's program, it is considered a sign of progress for mothers who did not believe they were responsible for the incest when they entered the program to believe they were responsible by termination.

CONCLUSIONS

Florence Rush (1980) writes of "this relentless tendency to blame women for male sexual transgression" (p. 194). It is indeed striking that the emphasis has evolved in recent years, not toward the offender as responsible for sexual abuse, but toward his nonparticipating spouse and family. The most objectionable part of this literature is not that which implies *some* mothers *actively* collude with incest; some mothers clearly do. Of more concern is the implication that all mothers know, whether or not they, their partners, and their children say they know of the abuse, and the assumption that a lack of knowledge would not render them blameless in any case. Of the myriad ways in which the mothers are alleged responsible for the incest, the most frequently cited is marital sexual dysfunction. Nicholas Groth (1979), however, in his work with incarcerated offenders, did not find that lack of access to sex explained the behavior of the child molesters:

> In fact, the sexual encounters with children coexisted with sexual contacts with adults. For example, in the incest cases, we found that the men were having sexual relations with their daughters or sons in addition to, rather than instead of, sexual relations with their wives. Those offenders who confined their sexual activity to children did so through choice. There was no one for whom no other opportunity for sexual gratification existed. (p. 146)

If asked, however, many sex offenders will blame their sexual deviancy on either their wife's behavior or their victim's. Such "explanations" are all too often accepted uncritically. As noted previously Virkkunen (1981) accepted the account of offenders regarding the behavior of their victims over the official records in his review of Gebhard's 1965 study. Accepting the offender's rationalizations for his behavior is naive and can only lead to error. This author interviewed an offender about whom a previous psychologist had written that he had molested a 9-year-old male neighbor out of sexual frustration, *because* his wife had ceased to have sex with him five years previously. In a more confrontational interview, the man admitted that he had had fantasies of male children for 10 years, and that five years after the fantasies began he was no longer interested in having sex with his wife.

Other types of marital problems may be as likely to occur after the incest as before. The literature, based on characteristics of families at discovery, rather than prior to the beginning of the incest, makes no distinction between correlation and causation.

Becker and Coleman (forthcoming) have written the following:

> Family dysfunction may be a result of incest rather than its cause. Incest may occur because the husband or stepfather is a pedophile who attempts to isolate the family, places the daughter in the role of an adult, and ignores the wife (who is consequently physically or psychologically absent). It is of interest that in cases of incest, the family, to date, has been the target of intervention rather than targeting the perpetrator.

To support their contention they note that in their sample of incest offenders, 44% had also molested unrelated female children, 11% had molested unrelated male children, 18% had raped, 18%

had engaged in exhibitionism, 9% in voyeurism, 5% in frottage, 4% in sadism, and 21% in other paraphilias. Well over half (59%) of their sample of child molesters had experienced the onset of their deviant arousal during adolescence, well before the entry of the "seductive" victim, the "colluding" spouse, and the "involved" family.

A review of the history of the sexual abuse literature suggests that responsibility for child sexual abuse was first assigned to the victims, regardless of their degree of immaturity or the degree of psychological or physical coercion applied against them. Although there are current writings that still reflect this bias, increasingly in the past 20 years the fashion has turned from holding victims accountable for their own abuse to holding their mothers and other nonparticipating family members responsible. As will be demonstrated in Chapter 3, there are findings from the research literature that suggest that some of the family correlates of abuse referred to in the clinical literature do, in some cases exist. The findings do not, however, have the explanatory power assigned to them. An individual who commits a sexual molestation is, ultimately, responsible for it. Summit and Kryso (1978) have written:

> The father is the key to the disturbed dynamics and is responsible for the choice to eroticize the relationship with the daughter. Whatever else is said in sympathy with his motivations, and regardless of the contributions of the wife and daughter, that responsibility must be emphasized and must be identified in any therapeutic encounter. (p. 242-243)

A spouse's knowledge or lack of knowledge of the offender's behavior, her ability or inability to control his behavior, and the quality and quantity of the sexual relationship between them are all peripheral issues, and do not in any way diminish an offender's responsibility for his own behavior. It is troubling that the field of sexual abuse has had such difficulty accepting the offender's responsibility for sexual molestation.

3

THE ROLE OF THE OFFENDER

An array of factors are cited in the literature as either causal or correlates of intrafamilial child sexual abuse:

Factor	Studies
social isolation	Finkelhor, 1979; Justice & Justice, 1979; Riemer, 1940; Weinberg, 1955
unsatisfactory marital sexual relationship	Browning & Boatman, 1977; Cormier, Kennedy & Sangowicz, 1962; Henderson, 1975; James & Nasjleti, 1983; Justice & Justice, 1979; Lustig et al., 1966; Machotka, Pittman & Flomenhaft, 1967; Maisch, 1972; Meiselman, 1978; Molnar & Cameron 1975; Peters, 1976; Riemer, 1940; Sarles, 1975; Weinberg, 1955; Weiner, 1962
marital discord	Browning & Boatman, 1977; Gruber & Jones, 1983; Maisch, 1972; Molnar & Cameron, 1975; Mrazek, Lynch & Bentovim, 1983; Weinberg, 1955; Weiner, 1962
role reversal	Eist & Mandell, 1968; Forward & Buck, 1978; Heims & Kaufman, 1963; Henderson, 1975; Herman, 1981; Herman & Hirschman, 1977,

	1981; Justice & Justice, 1979; Kaufman et al., 1954; Lustig et al., 1966; Machotka et al., 1967; Meiselman, 1978; Riemer, 1940; Sarles, 1975
wife colluding, passive, powerless or dependent	Clark et al., 1981; Cormier et al., 1962; Forward & Buck, 1978; Henderson, 1975; Herman, 1981; James & Nasjleti, 1983; Justice & Justice, 1979; Kaufman et al., 1954; Machotka et al., 1967; Meiselman, 1978; Peters, 1976; Sarles, 1975; Tormes, 1968; Weinberg, 1955; Weiner, 1962
wife mentally ill	Browning & Boatman, 1977; Herman, 1981; Herman & Hirschman, 1977, 1981; Justice & Justice, 1979;
wife physically ill or psychosomatic	Finkelhor, 1984; Herman, 1981; Herman & Hirschman, 1977, 1981; Kubo, 1959; Maisch, 1972; Meiselman, 1978; Swanson, 1968
sex punitive mother	Finkelhor, 1984
absent mother	Browning & Boatman, 1977; Cormier et al., 1962; Finkelhor, 1984; Herman & Hirschman, 1977, 1981; Justice & Justice, 1979; Kubo, 1959; Meiselman, 1978
family dysfunction or involvement	Alexander, 1985; Cormier et al., 1962; DeYoung, 1982; Eist & Mandel, 1968; Giarretto, 1982; Lutz & Medway, 1984; James & Nasjleti, 1983; Machotka et al., 1967; Maisch, 1972; Mrazek & Bentovim, 1981; Mayer, 1983; Sarles, 1975; Sgroi, 1982; Taylor, 1984
alcoholism	Browning & Boatman, 1977; Cormier et al., 1962; Gebhard et al., 1965; Herman, 1981; Herman & Hirschman, 1981; Howells, 1981; Kaufman et al., 1954; Maisch, 1972; Meiselman, 1978; Molnar & Cameron, 1975; Mrazek et al.1983; Peters, 1976; Rada, 1976; Riemer, 1940; Swanson, 1968
seductive child	Abraham, 1927; Bender & Blau, 1937; Henderson, 1975; Justice & Justice, 1979; Lukianowicz, 1972; Mohr et al., 1964; Revitch & Weiss, 1962; Weiss et al., 1955

While some of the studies cited rely on clinical impressions, others (for example, Finkelhor, 1984; Gebhard et al., 1965; Gruber & Jones, 1983; Herman, 1981; Herman & Hirschman, 1977, 1981; Maisch, 1972; Meiselman, 1978) are research studies that find that some of the factors do appear to be present to a greater degree in index cases than controls. These are most frequently factors that define the lack of a restraining influence on the father (wife absent, physically or mentally ill, powerless or dependent), marital, sexual, or emotional dysfunction, and alcoholism. Seductiveness of the child and whole family involvement are more in the eye of the beholder than in the research literature.

However, even for those factors that are sustained by the research literature, how much *explanatory* power do they have, and to what extent do they mitigate the responsibility of the perpetrator of the offense? Of all the responses, for example, to marital problems tried by unhappy husbands—counseling, divorce, drinking, work, depression, even extramarital affairs—why do some men instead turn to incest? Is it likely that the reasons will be found in the details of the unhappy marriage? Is the answer to be found in the wife's emotional or physical health, in her degree of passivity or assertiveness? It seems unlikely. Cormier et al. (1962) noted that "Many husbands are faced with similar problems, and find other solutions" (p. 204).

Child sexual abuse cannot be explained on the basis of the number or type of nonsexual problems with which the offender is faced, even though there is evidence that perpetrators frequently face nonsexual problems. These problems appear quite ordinary, and are not unique to sex offenders. Clinical impressions suggest some of the problems offenders face may, on occasion, be quite subtle: for example, power struggles with a child, boredom when not working, or annoyance that a spouse has gone to work. Secondly, nonsexual problems can be solved (or avoided) nonsexually.

The appropriate analogy is to alcoholism. Unquestionably some alcoholics drink to escape problems at work or at home. The solution, however, lies not in blaming the problems at work or at home, but in teaching the alcoholic that problems are no excuse for drinking. The solution cannot be to eliminate problems, nor should it be to imply, either to the offender or his family, that anyone except the offender is responsible for the drinking behavior. On the contrary, the approach utilized by many alcohol treatment programs is frequently to encourage other family members to stop taking responsibility for the offender's behavior.

Child sexual abuse can be conceptualized similarly and should be managed similarly. To the extent that nonsexual problems are found to correlate with child sexual abuse, it is the propensity of offenders to convert those problems into inappropriate sexual behavior that is the issue, not the existence of nonsexual problems per se.

It is nonetheless true that an adequate treatment program will focus in part on nonsexual problems. This is because many offenders are unable to solve nonsexual problems, or even to tolerate certain feeling states (most often anger or depression), without relying on sexual behavior as an escape. Programs will not be successful that simply try to block the offender's habitual response to stress, i.e., sexual acting out, unless they also teach him how to solve the problems directly. Crawford (1981) has written that

> it has been recognized that to concentrate on deviant arousal alone whilst ignoring other problems is too narrow. The hope that if patients could abstain from their deviant sexual behaviour for a sufficient period of time then other types of nondeviant sexual behaviour would fill the vacuum . . . has proved over-optimistic. Unless other problems are tackled as well, the evidence suggests that deviant behaviour is likely to return. (p. 195)

Even so, it is not clear that all incest offenders are simply converting nonsexual problems into sexual behavior. It has long been known that pedophiles, men who repetitively molest children outside the family, are sexually attracted to children. Described in the literature as a deviant arousal pattern, the attraction is found to be quite stable over time, frequently beginning in adolescence (Abel, Mittelman, & Becker, 1985; Knopp, 1984). Abel reported that 42% of their overall sample of paraphiliacs had a deviant arousal pattern by age 15 and 57% by age 19. Those who molested male children had the earliest onset; 53% reported an arousal to younger males by age 15. Mohr et al. (1964) reported that 18% of their sample of offenders were under 20. Thus sexual deviancy can frequently be noted by adolescence in men who either then or later commit sexual offenses.

While a pedophile may explain his behavior as a response to stress, in fact, the data suggest otherwise. Pedophiles molest children with great regularity, regardless of their life circumstances. In a study by the New York State Psychiatric Institute, 232 child molesters guaranteed confidentiality admitted they had attempted 55,250 acts of child molestation and had completed 38,727 of them (Abel et al, 1985). Freeman-Longo and Wall (1986) reported that 53 offenders had committed an estimated 25,757 sexual crimes. Pedophiles often claim that they "love" a particular child, but if that child becomes unavailable as a victim, other children soon replace him or her. Plummer (1981) quotes a pedophile as saying, "I get so desperately in love with these people. Any of them, you know" (p. 233).

Pedophiles are sometimes attracted to adults and children but more frequently to children alone. Mohr et al. (1964) found that 59% of their female-oriented pedophiles and 37% of their male-oriented pedophiles over the age of 20 were married, whereas an additional 32% and 16% respectively had been married. Only 2 of their 22 heterosexual offenders and 9 of their 19 homosexual offenders over the age of 20 had never been married. Gebhard et al. (1965) found that 56% of their "patterned" (repetitive) offenders against female children were married as opposed to 76% of their "incidental" (not repetitive) offenders. Of those offenders who molested male children, 47% of both the "patterned" and the "incidental" groups were married. Rada (1976) found that 59% of their total group of child molesters were married. This included 43% of those who molested male children, 72% of those who molested female children, and 62% of those who molested both. However, it is unknown how often marriage represents a true indication of the adult's attraction to women. Many pedophiles will admit in treatment that they fantasize sex with children while engaging in sex with adults.

It is not known in what manner some males' sexual arousal becomes attached to children rather than adults. A background of sexual abuse sometimes correlates with a pedophilic orientation, but the correlation is by no means perfect. Incidence rates vary widely. Groth (1979) found that 46% of a sample of fixated pedophiles were molested as children. Seghorn, Boucher, and Cohen (1983) found that 59% of their incarcerated child molesters had been sexually abused as children.

Some studies have found considerably lower rates. Gebhard et al. (1965) found that 9.6% of their incarcerated offenders who had molested female children had been previously abused by an adult female and 24.4% by an adult male. Of those offenders who had molested female minors, 15.8% had been previously molested by an adult female and 14% by an adult male. Of the male-oriented offenders against children, 7.7% had been previously abused by a female and 32.1% had been abused by a male. Of those who molested male minors, 6% had been previously abused by an adult female and 34.6% by a male (Gebhard et al., 1965, p. 466; Russell, 1984, p. 240). Langevin (1983, p. 309) found no differences in rates of previous abuse between incest offenders and normal heterosexual controls.

Knopp (1984) cited studies that found rates of previous sexual abuse ranging from 22% to 82%. Thus there are a number of studies that do not find that the majority of offenders were sexually molested as children, although the rates exceed those found in incidence studies of the general population by wide margins (see Chapter 1). In addition, there are no accurate data on the number of nonabusing males who were sexually molested as children. It may well be that the majority of males molested as children do not become abusers. Therefore, the pedophilic orientation, while well documented, has never been satisfactorily explained etiologically.

The division of offenders into two types, one with a chronic repetitive pattern of abuse related to deviant arousal and the other with a more episodic pattern related to nonsexual problems, has previously met with widespread acceptance in the literature, although the names and descriptions of the two types have differed somewhat. Much of the literature has made the division along the lines of incest versus extrafamilial abuse. Individual authors have developed particular typologies. Gebhard et al. (1965) described "patterned" and "incidental" offenders. Swanson (1968) described "individuals to whom the child represents the sexual object of choice" compared to "those at the other end of the continuum where the choice of an immature sexual object is virtually a matter of convenience or coincidence" (p. 681). Freund discussed offenders who used the child as a surrogate object for an adult female versus offenders who were primarily attracted to children (Freund, McKnight, Langevin, & Cibiri, 1972). Lanyon (1986) described situational versus preference offenders. (For a complete review of the classification of sex offenders see Knight, Rosenberg & Schneider, 1985.) The most frequently cited classification is that by Groth, who divided offenders into regressed versus fixated (Groth, 1982).

According to Groth, fixated offenders (pedophiles) are described as having certain specific characteristics. The sine qua non is a persistent sexual attraction to children regardless of external stress. Pedophilic interests typically begin in adolescence. Crimes are premeditated, and are primarily targeted toward males. Such offenders are usually single, with little sexual contact with agemates. They identify with children and prefer the company of children to adults. They usually do not have a history of alcohol and drug abuse. They are thought to have characterological immaturity and inadequate personalities.

Groth describes regressed offenders as being primarily sexually attracted to agemates. Their sexual involvements with children are thought to be more impulsive and to occur under stress; they are less continual and more episodic than the offenses of fixated offenders. The sexual deviancy more often begins in adulthood, focuses primarily on female children, and concurs with adequate sexual functioning with agemates. The offense is more often alcohol related.

Unfortunately, both ways of categorizing offenders, as intra-familial versus extrafamilial or as fixated versus regressed, rest entirely on the offender's honesty in reporting his sexual and social interests, most frequently the number, sex, and relationship of victims, and his degree of social and sexual comfort and experience with adults. As such they are subject to considerable distortion.

Recently the question has been raised as to what extent different categories of offenders, particularly intrafamilial and extrafamilial, are different from each other (Abel, Becker, Murphy, & Flanagan, 1981; Becker & Coleman, forthcoming; Murphy et al., 1986). Certainly crossovers between categories as they are currently conceptualized are common. Incest offenders are frequently seen who also molest children outside the home, or who molest sequentially every child within the home, and later, when oppor-tunity affords, grandchildren as well. As reported previously, Becker and Coleman found that 44% of their incest offenders who had molested female children in the home had also molested female children outside the home, whereas 11% had molested unrelated male children. "Incest" offenders have been known to marry in succession into different ready-made families, each of which has children of their preferred age and sex whom they then molest. This author saw an offender who molested his own daughter, his daughter's best friend, propositioned the best friend's mother, and sexually harassed subordinates at work. Nor are regressed versus fixated categories any more distinct as they are now defined.

Numerous offenders present with a chronic, repetitive pattern of molesting *female* children outside the home. Abel et al. (1981) found that heterosexual pedophiles had an average of 62.4 victims. Female victims often recite experiences that indicate clearly premed-itation and planning. Male-oriented pedophiles are sometimes discovered who are married and functioning adequately sexually with their wives and well socially with their friends. As cited previously, Mohr et al. (1964) found that 37% of their male-oriented pedophiles were married. This overlap has raised for some the possibility that incest and out-of-home offenders do not represent distinct categories, but instead that incest offenders are simply, in Lynn Sanford's term, "lazy pedophiles." Abel conducted a study of plethysmograph assessment of incest offenders versus extrafamilial offenders and did not find differences in the arousal patterns of the two groups. He concluded, "A classification system relying on recorded sexual arousal patterns would redefine heterosexual incest cases as heterosexual pedophiles" (Abel et al., 1981, p. 126).

Of particular concern is the fact that the categories of fixated versus regressed or incest versus extrafamilial can be manipulated by an offender who is being dishonest about his sexual interests and his social and sexual history. Quinsey (1977) has summarized studies that rely on an offender's report of his interests and history and concluded, "Unfortunately, it is difficult to know what a given child molester's sexual preferences are. . . . It is well known that institutionalized child molesters often report appropriate sexual preferences in order to obtain release from custody" (p. 207). In fact, those programs that are the most confrontive and that use objective measures of sexual attraction such as the penile plethysmograph are often the most pessimistic regarding the existence of "regressed" offenders. Roger Wolfe of Northwest Treatment Associates has said that his program would be happy to treat a first-time incest offender with no previous history of sexual deviancy when they find one (personal communication, January 1986). In a decade of treatment of sex offenders, his group of specialists has failed to find the differences in pedophiles and incest offenders that the literature describes.

Certainly many a clinician working in the area has had the unsettling experience of having an offender who appears to be a classic example of a "regressed" offender turn out to have a far more extensive history of sexual involvement with children than first thought. In fact, given the social desirability of the characteristics of a regressed offender, can we say with any certainty that we have fixated and regressed offenders or that we have offenders who are more or less honest? Is a regressed offender a fixated offender who minimizes? Is "regressed" the way a fixated offender presents at intake?

Undoubtably many fixated offenders try to pass as regressed. An offender trying to get out of a sexual-assault charge with the fewest constraints on his freedom possible has every reason to deny that he is primarily attracted to children. He will frequently assure the clinician that his adolescence was spent with fantasies of adult women. No indeed, he has never done this sort of thing before, which he did impulsively without malice or aforethought ("I have no idea what I was thinking. I guess I just wasn't thinking"), and yes, it was either the lack of sex with his wife or the alcohol that caused it. Of course he feels terrible about this, and he is quite sure it will never happen again.

Unfortunately, a pedophile is addicted to his behavior, as surely and as entirely as an alcoholic. He will say what he must say in order to protect himself and his addiction. If denial fails, minimization is the most reasonable alternative. Being a "regressed" offender may not be as desirable as not being an offender, but it is certainly easier than admitting to a longstanding sexual preference for children and to a history of previous offenses of different types. Abel and colleagues (Abel et al., 1985; Becker & Coleman, forthcoming) have demonstrated the lengths to which researchers must go in assuring confidentiality, in order to obtain accurate measures of the extent of pedophilic activity in child molesters.

Nonetheless, it is this author's opinion that, while many incest offenders are closet pedophiles, incest offenders exist who are not. In my practice I have seen incest offenders who, I believe, had no prior history of sexual assault prior to the incest, although they frequently had strange practices, beliefs, and opinions regarding sexuality. The incest was, in some cases, a conversion of nonsexual problems into sexual behavior rather than the result of a long-standing sexual interest in children.

A crucially important issue from the clinician's standpoint is how to distinguish different types of offenders. No categorization is likely to be effective in the long run that rests on the offender's word exclusively regarding his sexual proclivities. Even if such a categorization were theoretically accurate, it will be impossible to apply. A better categorization would be to divide offenders into those with a deviant arousal pattern and those without. Offenders with a deviant arousal pattern are categorically sexually attracted to children regardless of their personal circumstances or the amount of stress they are under. The penile plethysmograph (discussed in Chapter 12 on assessment) will measure a deviant arousal pattern far more reliably than verbal report and is most useful in confronting offender denial and encouraging honesty (Abel et al., 1985). By relying on an objective measure, the problem of relying on the pattern and history of offenses is circumvented. While the plethysmograph is not invariably reliable in determining sexual preference (see Quinsey, 1977, for a discussion of voluntary suppression of penile response) it is, in Quinsey's words, "far more accurate than verbal descriptions of the subject's preferences, particularly when the persons being assessed are motivated to bias their test data" (1977, p. 211). In addition to its advantages in terms of objectivity and reliability, a categorization based on measured sexual preference would be useful in determining treatment, since there is little disagreement in the literature that behavioral techniques are the treatment of choice for a deviant arousal pattern.

With this division, all offenders with deviant arousal patterns would be conceptualized and treated similarly, regardless of whether they were male-oriented pedophiles with admitted track records of child molestation since adolescence or whether they insisted they were "first-time" female-oriented incest offenders who "just weren't thinking." Those without a deviant arousal pattern would still be treated, but without emphasis on reducing the nonexistent deviant arousal pattern and with considerable emphasis on the other components of sexual molestation.

By developing categories that can be objectively measured—that is, deviant arousal pattern or not—questions could then be empirically answered regarding the extent to which men with deviant arousal patterns molest female children, the extent to which men without deviant arousal patterns also premeditate their offenses, and regarding the percentage of incest offenders who have a deviant arousal pattern. The answers to these questions must be derived from empirical research and not assumed based on categorizations that rely on an offender's self-report, under circumstances in which honesty frequently leads to incarceration.

CONCLUSIONS

Two conditions must be present for a sexual assault to take place: The offender must be willing and have the opportunity. Willingness occurs as described: either the offender is sexually attracted to children and willing to assault them for sexual gratification, or the offender converts a nonsexual problem into sexual behavior. In either case the motivation for the offense comes from the offender.

The family, however, may wittingly or unwittingly provide the opportunity. It is true that many of the items on the list of causal factors do indeed correlate with child sexual abuse, but not because they cause the abuse to happen. They do not provide the motivation or the willingness to offend. Rather, a sick or absent mother, a helpless or depressed one, an alienated child who is unlikely to tell or to be believed if she does, each allows the offender the opportunity to offend. Maternal dysfunction or absence provides the opportunity in the same manner that a family on vacation provides the chance for a burglar to rob them and implies the same degree of culpability. Therapy may imply increased vigilance on the family's part, but in the same manner that one who chooses to live with a thief must take precautions against being robbed.

4

THE ROLE OF THE SPOUSE
AND CHILD

THE SPOUSE

As noted in Chapter 3, traditional views of the spouse's role in intrafamilial child sexual abuse have treated spouses as invariably colluding with the offender. Some theorists have gone further and contended that spouses are more responsible than the offenders (Lustig et al., 1966). In fact, a considerable amount of sexual molestation occurs after divorce when the spouse is not even present. Mian, Wehrspann, Klajner-Diamond, LeBaron, and Winder (1986) found that 67% of the children reporting intrafamilial abuse came from families in which the parents were separated or divorced, compared with 27% of the children reporting extrafamilial abuse. Even in those cases in which the spouse is in the home, the clinical reality appears to be far more diverse than the literature implies. Figure 4.1 lists a spectrum of spousal involvement derived from clinical experience with spouses of intrafamilial sex offenders. This section will discuss the extent of knowledge about the offense and the range of responses to the offense encountered in spouses.

Did Not Know	Did Not Know	Did Not Know	Knew	Knew
Supports Child	Denies	Sides with Spouse	Did Not Stop Abuse	Sets Up or Participates

Figure 4.1   Spectrum of Involvement and Reaction of Spouse

Did Not Know; Supports Child

Numerous spouses who are told of child sexual abuse do believe their children, and take action immediately upon being told. In his study of intrafamilial and extrafamilial abuse, Peters (1976) found that 41% of the cases were reported to the police by the mother. The major concerns of the adults who came to the clinic with the child were concern for the emotional well-being of the child (63%), concern for the child's physical well-being (57%) and concern for protection for the child (32%). Only 17% of the adults were angry at the child, and only 14% concerned about the effect the incident might have on the family. Undoubtably, the figures would have been somewhat different if the study had been entirely of intrafamilial abuse, but this author's experience suggests that sizable numbers of mothers do believe their children and do act to protect them. In one case the offender lived in one state and worked in another. His wife called the police the day her daughter told her. The police arrested the father when he crossed the bridge linking the two states that evening.

Not all such spouses have any further desire to work out the marriage and the incidence of divorce following discovery has been noted in the literature but interpreted in ways that give little credit to the mothers. (See "Mothers and No-Win Situations" in Chapter 2.) There is little need for tortured explanations of why some mothers divorce following the discovery of incest. It is not an uncommon clinical phenomenon for a spouse to be repulsed by her husband's behavior and to feel she can never trust him again.

There are also spouses who believe the daughter and still wish to save the marriage. "I just want my family back together again," one spouse repeated throughout the intake session. She never denied or minimized the abuse and took appropriate steps immediately to protect her child. She did work consistently, however, for the ultimate reunification of the family.

Did Not Know; Denies

"I can't believe he did that. I couldn't live with him if I thought he did that." Unquestionably a considerable number of spouses deny their husband/partner could have committed the offense, and their denial is taken by many clinicians as equivalent to colluding with the offender. But is it? For many spouses the notion that someone they have loved and trusted has sexually abused their daughter is an emotional earthquake. If it is true, the spouse's internal map of the world changes. She must reassess her relationship with the trusted spouse, and must now doubt her judgment. She will feel considerable guilt that her daughter was abused and she was unable to protect her. She must wonder why her daughter did not tell her immediately.

Nor will the damage be confined to those particular relationships. Some spouses find that, since they had no warning that this incest was occurring, they are unable to trust subsequent relationships in which there is no indication of incest. One spouse, divorced from the offender and involved in a new relationship, reported being afraid to leave her new partner alone with her daughter, despite the fact that she had no indication of abuse and he had no history of abusive behavior. When he offered to take her daughter shopping at a department store, she became obsessed with fears he would molest the girl in the store. She could say rationally that this was unlikely, but found that her capacity to trust had been impaired.

Much is at stake in this issue of denial versus belief. For some women it is the capacity to trust, to believe in their own judgment. If they can be that wrong, can they ever trust their judgment again? The single psychological mechanism that will allow them to avoid reconstructing their internal world along less trusting and more painful lines is denial. If the charge is not true, the spouse has not just spent a given number of years trusting a man who was abusing her daughter. If not true, she does not have to worry about the harm done to her daughter. If not true, she does not have to mistrust her spouse continually and decide whether to terminate the marriage. She does not have to be concerned about whether other men are likely to be more trustworthy than this one. If not true, her judgment is not faulty.

The cognitive dissonance to be overcome before an incest report can be believed by a spouse is considerable. It does not seem surprising that some spouses deny, nor do pathological mechanisms need to be evoked to explain it.

Did Not Know; Sides with Spouse

By all accounts—the client Sandra's, her husband's, and her teenage daughter's—Sandra did not know the incest was occurring. However, in the initial session Sandra stated, "If I had it to do all over again, I'd side with him and not this little twerp." Throughout the sessions she shouted at her daughter and accused her of "seducing" her husband. Sandra's anger was particularly provoked by learning of occasions when her husband had sneaked off to have sex with her daughter before having sex with her, as he did, for example, on her birthday. There were also incidents driving across the country in a camper in which her husband asked her to drive because he was tired. He then molested the daughter in the camper while Sandra drove the car. Nevertheless, Sandra was not angry at her husband, but held her 14-year-old daughter accountable.

This type of inappropriate blaming of the daughters occurs frequently in mothers who feel dependent on the spouses and are frightened of potential loss. It is also a sign that the mother does not have appropriate boundaries between the generations, and thus sees her daughter as a potential rival. Mothers who "confide in" daughters about adult matters and otherwise treat them more as friends than children are particularly at risk to carry this lack of a parent/child relationship into the sexual arena.

Knew; Did Not Stop It

"I walked in on them. I've never been able to get that scene out of my mind. I don't know why, but I see it mostly when I'm driving."

"But why," the client's teenage daughter asked, "didn't you do anything? You didn't say a word; you just walked out."

"Don't you see? It was over. Once I knew, he had to stop it. I knew it couldn't go on after that. I didn't have to say anything."

But it did go on after that, and the rift between mother and daughter was never mended. There are mothers who know and take no action. This is often considered simply collusion. While there are surely cases where this is so, to claim that knowledge invariably amounts to collusion is to ignore the very real issues of power and powerlessness in marriages (Herman, 1981). There are marriages in which a woman's primary experience is of dependency, powerlessness, and sometimes fear. Spouse abuse binds many women to silence. Psychological abuse binds others. For many, a deep passivity and fear of being alone causes women to hold their tongues. This is fair grist for the therapeutic mill, and in fact these are vital issues to be addressed, but are they the same thing as collusion? There is a difference in wanting a child to be abused and feeling profoundly helpless to stop it.

Sets Up or Participates in the Abuse

Grace was a mildly retarded, illiterate woman who had never held a job and could not drive. On the few occasions when her husband was not living with her (as when he was in the service and stationed away from her), she had "nervous breakdowns" and was hospitalized. Her husband had abused at least one daughter (and probably more) for over 10 years. The girl had reported the abuse in several of the states the family lived in, but each time the family moved in time to escape legal action. The abuse only ended when the daughter reported it again, and this time, at 18, moved out of the house.

The daughter stated that not only had her father been abusing her in front of her mother, but that her mother had sex with her while her father watched. When the mother was asked why she did this, she said simply, "Because he asked me to." The mother completely refused to have any contact with the daughter after she reported the abuse, and blamed her for the father's subsequent incarceration.

Mothers have also at times participated by helping to set up the abuse. Mary entered an institution for the mentally retarded at 11 months, diagnosed as retarded, blind, and having cerebral palsy. In fact, she was only blind in one eye. She did not have cerebral palsy, and after spending her entire childhood in the institution, her verbal IQ score at age 25 was found to be 114. In retrospect, Mary's inability to sit up and her development delays at 11 months were unquestionably the result of neglect and subsequent failure to thrive.

Despite the fact that she was not mentally retarded, Mary spent

14 years in the institution for the retarded. She was released at age 14 as the "star pupil" of the institution, to a foster home that had several other children. Beginning with the day she arrived, the foster mother in the home asked her daily if she had started menstruating. The day she did and answered her foster mother affirmatively, the mother took all of the other children grocery shopping. Mary asked to go but was refused. While the other children and the mother were away, the foster father raped her. During all of the eight years Mary lived there, the foster mother continued to take the other children away on a weekly basis and force Mary to stay home with the foster father, who then molested her sexually and abused her physically.

A Spectrum, Not a Single Position

The spouse's knowledge of and response to incest runs the entire spectrum from lack of knowledge and subsequent outrage to active involvement and overt collusion. In between lie degrees of helplessness and the tragic hopefulness of denial. Nothing is more infuriating for a spouse who did not know and is devastated by the discovery than a child-protection worker or a therapist who says, "You didn't know?" and smiles knowingly. For those who indeed did not know, such smug implications can lead either to anger and a failure to cooperate with social services, or to pathological doubt.

"Well, I don't think I knew. Her grades dropped this year. She seemed depressed. Maybe I should have known. How could I not have known?" Such pathological doubt only serves to further devastate the one person who is the child's best hope for healing. Uniform assumptions that all spouses know and all spouses collude can be as harmful as minimization of the involvement of spouses who did know and did not stop the abuse. Even in the latter case the universal assumption that the spouse desired the abuse to occur is not justified, for the underlying mechanism may be powerlessness in the face of an undesired molestation rather than collusion with a desired one.

The clinical material in this area is complex. It is better for clinicians to consider the entire range of options and evaluate each case individually, rather than assume specific ones on the spouse's part on the basis of assumptions in the literature that have neither an empirical nor a solid clinical foundation.

ROLE OF THE CHILD

While most mental health clinicians have ceased blaming children for child sexual abuse, the same cannot be said for offenders. Hamilton in 1929 wrote that "a psychiatrist who becomes a sufficiently ardent advocate of any explanatory formulation whatsoever and a patient who is both loyal and suggestible to a marked degree can between them obtain subjective data almost to order" (p. 328).

If so, any author who would like to prove that child sexual abuse is caused by children can enlist the aid of quite a number of offenders. What rationalizations do offenders use?

"I know she is only 5, Doc, but she looked 6." This is a joke in the field, but it captures almost verbatim what many offenders say. When an offender reports how old his victim looked, it is always wise to ask how old his victim actually was.

"I thought it was my wife." This was said by a large man with a large wife about his 4-year-old daughter. The daughter was sleeping in bed with her parents and her father, "half asleep," reached over to have sex with his wife. Quite "by accident," he had sex with the child instead. He was evidently unable to note the difference in body size between an adult female and a 4-year-old girl. This was, he felt, the daughter's fault, because she "insisted" on sleeping in bed with them.

"I woke up and she had her hand in my pants." From the point of view of offenders, children initiate a considerable amount of sexual activity, although evidently, only in the presence of sex offenders. Even were this so, it would be irrelevant. Children who have not been molested do not initiate sexual activity with adults. Children who have learned to trade sex for affection and attention are exhibiting an acquired behavior. Nicholas Groth's classic response to such a claim is, "And what would you have done if you had woken up and she had her hand on your wallet?"

"She used to wear a little pink nightie around the house." "She sat in my lap." "She ran out of the bathroom nude and ran all around the house." Behaviors are often interpreted as sexual by offenders that are normal behaviors of young children.

Attempts on the part of offenders to externalize responsibility for the sexual abuse onto victims and others is by no means new. Riemer (1940) quoted offenders who justified their behavior by stating that sexual relations with a daughter was less objectionable than "frivolous relations with outsiders" (p. 574), that a daughter at that age would soon have been pregnant anyway, and that the father was simply trying to fight his own venereal disease. (Swedish folklore held that intercourse with a virgin had a therapeutic impact on male venereal disease.) Riemer commented that such attempts to rationalize the behavior constituted "an absurd mixture of surviving values of family solidarity and lack of responsibility" (p. 574). Swanson (1968) noted that sex offenders against children would grasp "at any concept (e.g., alcohol, they were seduced, memory loss) which would serve as an explanation for their behavior, and thus allow them to avoid responsibility for their action and permit continuing passivity regarding their destiny" (p. 678). While the desire to find an acceptable explanation for the behavior is understandable, nonetheless the explanations should not be accepted and condoned. This author once found herself in court with a psychologist who testified that a particular rapist of over 100 women "did not understand that putting a knife at a woman's throat constituted force." Empathy for how difficult it is to accept individual responsibility can be therapeutic; acceptance of an evasion of responsibility is not.

What can we say about the actual role of children in child sexual abuse? The one denominator this author has seen is that offenders often choose the one child in the family who is unlikely to tell.

Tanya and her younger sister Norma were adopted at ages 3 years and 18 months, respectively, following severe neglect in their natural home. Tanya weighed 18 pounds. Norma was younger, less impaired, and she bounced back more quickly physically and emotionally than did Tanya. While Norma became a robust, affectionate child, Tanya remained moody and threw temper tantrums that frightened her mother. Her mother vividly remembered an incident in which an angry Tanya threw herself out of a moving swing. The mother became afraid to cross Tanya, and progressively withdrew from her. In any case, Tanya refused to be cuddled unlike her more affectionate sister.

As Tanya entered school, she began to tell "tall tales." Her mother remembered being called by the school in the second grade and asked about Tanya's impending foot operation. "What foot operation?" her mother asked. Tanya had been limping for weeks, she was told, and had said to everyone she was going to have a foot operation.

When Tanya was 9 years old, her father began to sexually molest her.

Tanya's father was aware that this child, already alienated from her mother and the rest of the family, would not be able to tell of the abuse. If she did tell, it would be unlikely that she would be believed. At age 14 Tanya did tell a school guidance counselor. Her father, who had been depressed and at times suicidal, admitted it immediately. The mother had no choice but to believe her daughter and eventually repaired the relationship between them. She maintained, however, that had her husband not admitted it, she would not have believed it.

Annie had a sister the family felt was "perfect." Two years older than she, her sister was adopted as a response to the mother's inability to get pregnant. Annie was subsequently a surprise, although not an unwelcome one, as the family desired other children. However, unlike her mellow and compliant sister, Annie was feisty and moody, with a far more intense personality. She became embroiled in power struggles within the family. The unexpected child became the unwanted child. A younger brother came several years later who, unlike Annie, became an accepted member of the family. Annie's position in the family continued to deteriorate. While her older sister was disdainful of her, and her mother distant, her father became caught up in almost constant power struggles. When she was 8 years old he began to sexually abuse her when her mother was working.

It seems fair to assume that it was no coincidence her father chose the one child in the family least likely to tell. However, in this case there were other factors, too. The abuse appeared to be a way to win a power struggle her father did not always win otherwise. There was no power struggle with the older daughter.

While the role of the child as defined by offenders echoes the statements made in the literature that child victims are seductive and actively initiate their own victimization, the reality is that children in incest cases are often distinguished by their powerlessness and alienation from other family members, particularly their mothers. The antivictim bias of the literature may reflect the unintended results of individual therapy with offenders. Without the kind of information release commonly required by treatment programs today, many therapists were unable to contact victims, family members, or even to obtain police records. They were therefore solely dependent on offenders as the source of information regarding the offenses. Individual therapy often created a therapeutic alliance that—in the absence of contrary information—resulted in identification between offender and therapist. Too often this further resulted in the therapist accepting the offender's version of events as objective reality, rather than the offender obtaining much-needed feedback from the therapist regarding cognitive distortions. (See Chapter 7 for a discussion of the differences between treating sex offenders and other clients.)

Therapists are therefore cautioned against accepting verbatim an offender's explanation for his behavior. Likewise, an account of sexual abuse from a child with a history of emotional difficulties, of telling "tall tales," and of estrangement from the family should not be automatically discounted. The child may have been chosen because her alienation and her emotional difficulties would make it less likely that she would be believed.

PART II

PHILOSOPHY AND STRUCTURE

5

PHILOSOPHY OF
TREATMENT PROGRAMS

Treatment programs are frequently not clear about their philosophy. Yet often clinicians with diverse backgrounds and beliefs regarding child sexual abuse staff such programs. Without a common philosophy there is a risk that the treatments offered by different providers may have little in common. For a program to be truly coordinated and effective, staff members must be working from common premises toward common goals. One of the better ways to begin this process is to develop or borrow a program philosophy. The philosophy recommended by this manual is as follows:

(1) Child molestation is either the result of:
   (a) a deviant arousal pattern and/or
   (b) the inappropriate conversion of nonsexual problems into sexual behavior.
(2) Goals of therapy for offenders are as follows:
   (a) A primary goal is for offenders to learn to control their deviant arousal patterns.

(b) A second goal is to place obstacles in the path of converting nonsexual problems into sexual behavior. These may include removing the father from the home, developing a better mother-child relationship, and improving the ability of the victim to be assertive and to report any attempts at remolestation. A key to minimizing the risk of reoccurence is to strengthen the positive qualities of the mother-child relationship.

(c) A third goal of therapy is for offenders and their families to learn to solve nonsexual problems in nonsexual ways. For example, the offenders need to deal with marital problems, depression, and other life problems directly, without the use of inappropriate sexual acting out.

(3) Offenders must take responsibility for child sexual abuse without minimizing, externalizing, or projecting blame onto others. Manipulation and denial are major behavioral overlays of the offense and the response to discovery.

(4) Each parent must take responsibility for his or her own behavior and not the other's. Spouses are responsible for abuse only if they are involved in sexual abuse. They are responsible for denying and minimizing if they do so.

(5) Child sexual abuse is a treatable problem. Treatable is defined as helping the offender learn ways of minimizing the risk of reoffense. It does not imply cure.

(6) Any dysfunctional family patterns resulting from or providing the opportunity for sexual abuse need to be addressed and changed. These may include but are not restricted to isolation, poor communication, lack of boundaries, and patriarchal entitlement.

(7) Victims are not responsible for child sexual abuse under any circumstances.

(8) Child sexual abuse is harmful to children.

(9) An important goal of a child sexual abuse program is to provide support to other professionals and to network effectively.

Developing or adopting a treatment philosophy is an opportunity for treatment providers to discover similarities and differences in their ways of treating clients. Without explicit discussion, individual assumptions underlying treating may not surface directly, but result in differences in treatment. The result may be a less well-coordinated treatment program and, ultimately, poorer care.

6

STRUCTURING A RESPONSE TO CHILD SEXUAL ABUSE

William M. Young

Any systematic response to child sexual abuse must be structured within the context of a highly cooperative effort involving organizations that are usually independent of each other. Local prosecutors, correctional, probation and parole personnel, police, child protection agencies, and mental health professionals may cooperate around specific cases, but typically do not have methods of doing so that are highly developed and systematic. In responding to child sexual abuse such cooperation is not only desirable, but essential, for without it attempts to provide quality services and protect children will certainly fail.

Cooperation forms the umbrella under which reporting, investigation, prosecution, juvenile proceedings, and treatment are able to function effectively. A competent prosecutor, for example, may be very knowledgeable about dealing with children and child sexual abuse, but without the cooperation of the child-protection service agency and the police, she[1] will find that fewer cases are referred to her office, and that the ones that are, often lack the information that a joint investigation produces. Unless the Department of Corrections cooperates with other agencies, presentence investigations will be denied the essential information about the dynamics of the offense, the offender's risk to the community, and potential for change. Such investigations may result in inappropriate recommendations to the court, with a resulting injustice to the offender, his victim/potential victim, or both.

The desire to avoid, whenever possible, placing children in state custody is widely recognized. Such a desire is understandable given a child's needs to be with her family and the current status of most of the country's substitute care systems. Yet lack of cooperation between protective services, police and prosecutors frequently results in failure to make a sound criminal case against a perpetrator; this leaves the child protective service agency with no alternative but to remove children from their homes in order to protect them. In short, intensive cooperation is a key ingredient to the success of any response to child sexual abuse.

OVERVIEW OF COMPREHENSIVE SERVICES

A thorough response to child sexual abuse should include prevention as well as comprehensive treatment services. Treatment services provide for in- and out-patient therapy for offenders, treatment for victims, and also for other family members. Such services should function under a formal written protocol that specifies how all of the agencies will cooperate with each other. The quality of treatment will be enhanced by the inclusion of casework services provided by the correctional and child protection agencies.

There are two primary goals to such a system:

(1) to prevent child sexual abuse
(2) to provide timely, effective intervention and treatment for victims and their families

All of the work done by such a program, including treatment services for offenders, is aimed at these two goals. While assisting offenders to lead law-abiding, healthier lives is a worthy goal in itself, the most compelling reasons for committing resources to offender treatment are that: (a) they represent a high risk group, most of whom will be released to the community at some point; (b) appropriate treatment significantly reduces the likelihood of recidivism, with some offenders responding to treatment without costly incarceration; and (c) the dynamics of many incest cases demand an approach that includes the perpetrator in order to most effectively help his victim.

The following briefly describes the component parts of a comprehensive system:

Prevention

The need for prevention services is often overlooked amid the immediacy of current workloads. Prevention breaks the offender's pattern by furnishing children, parents, and community members with a most powerful tool—the knowledge necessary to recognize an inappropriate approach, to understand that it is the offender who is responsible for deviant behavior, and to help children and those who care for them learn how to respond when such behavior occurs. All too often in the past secrecy and silence on the part of victims, often over long periods of time, has allowed offenders access to a child without detection.

Prevention may consist of such activities as "personal safety" curricula in the schools, either free-standing or as part of a broader, "family life" program. Ironically, school administrators will find that it is often easier to implement a child sexual abuse prevention program in their schools than it is to convince parents of the need for a sex education program. The earlier that such efforts are begun, the better, since many children are victimized at an early age. A 1981 Vermont Department of Corrections study showed that 47% of the child victims of adult offenders were under 12 years old (Young & Waite, 1982), while a subsequent study by the Vermont Health Department revealed the median age of the victims of juvenile offenders to be 7, with over two-thirds of the victims under age 9 (Wasserman & Kappel, 1985).

While it is important to notify parents that a personal safety program is being implemented in the school, it is wise not to require written parental consent before implementing one. Incestuous parents may not sign release forms for children to view personal safety programs. However, if they receive a written notification of that program, along with other school offerings, they may not wish to draw attention to themselves by demanding that their child be excluded.

Other prevention efforts may involve workshops aimed at teachers, day-care providers and other professionals who work with children, as well as workshops for parents designed to assist them in learning how to help their child avoid being victimized and what to do if she is. Dispelling common misconceptions, such as "kids lie about sexual abuse" or "sex offenders are dirty old men," is an important prelude to discussion of how to avoid victimization and how to respond to it. Response to victimization should be covered in detail, since an inappropriate response may inflict more damage on the child or fail to protect a child from continued victimization. Too many children report that long before their cases came to the attention of the child protection authorities, they told someone only to be answered in a severe voice: "Your father wouldn't do THAT to you, would he?" Such a child may later recall that "When I asked her about it she said nothing was happening." Only by educating people to the reality and prevalence of child sexual abuse can we help them respond appropriately to revelations of abuse by children.

Treatment Services

These must be seen as more than the sum of the parts outlined below. "Treatment" must be recognized as a coordinated effort that includes not only the clinical components traditionally viewed as "treatment," but also the supervision and casework services provided by social workers, probation and parole officers, institutional staff and others, working within the context of written protocols and court-ordered structure. Court structure should always be utilized with offenders, and is desirable with families, although more difficult to obtain in those states that lack a family court system to handle juvenile cases. (See Chapter 7 for a discussion of the necessity for court-mandated therapy.)

(1) Offender Treatment. Treatment for offenders should include clinical services for both adult and juvenile offenders, both incarcerated and out-patient. The need for juvenile services is frequently overlooked, perhaps because sexual aggression in juveniles is often excused as "normal childhood exploration," making it harder to identify youthful offenders and to bring the court process to bear in

their cases. Nevertheless, it is important to provide services for this population, given the large numbers of adult offenders who report that their first offenses occurred in adolescence (with obvious implications for prevention), and the greater prospects for success if intervention can occur before years of behavior establish an entrenched pattern.

In some states, programs for incarcerated adults are housed under the authority of the correctional agency; in others, treatment is provided by transfer or "furlough" from a correctional facility to a closed mental health agency program. A high level of coordination must be present between programs for incarcerated offenders and outpatient services; without it offenders will have trouble with the transition and be likely to fail, often with disastrous results for their victims and loss of public support for treatment efforts. Ideally, treatment modalities should be the same. An offender receiving behavioral modification and group therapy while incarcerated should have those therapies available as part of his after-care. Planning for out-patient treatment should begin and be in place in very specific detail well before release occurs. Each offender should know which therapy group he will be attending, who his therapist will be, who his probation and parole officer will be, and the consequences of not cooperating with outpatient treatment before he is released to the community.

While victim and offender treatment may take place separately, as in the case of a child's victimization by a nonfamily member, it is vital that those working with the offender have a clear understanding of issues relevant to victim treatment; likewise, those who treat victims will be well served by understanding offender issues and treatment. This is not only essential for the mental health professionals involved, but also for corrections, child protection service agency staff, and others. Treatment providers working only with offenders run a very real risk of losing touch with the trauma caused by the offender's act, thereby increasing the risk of buying into a common offender manipulation—minimizing the offense and its impact on the victim.

(2) Victim Treatment. This covers a wide variety of services for children that must be geared to the child's age and developmental level. Some combination of group and individual work must be available to differing age groups, with group work more feasible with adolescents (and more cost effective) and individual work more often necessary with younger victims. Although it is not necessary that services for adult survivors of child sexual abuse be a

formal part of the child sexual abuse treatment program, as they are in the Child Sexual Abuse Treatment Program in San Jose, California (Giarretto, 1982) the need for such services should be supported and coordinated with any program, if not fully integrated. Nor should the importance of victim's advocacy organizations be overlooked. Such groups provide a useful, direct service to victims and are an important source of support for both victim and offender treatment programs.

(3) Family Services. Any treatment program must also recognize the need, in various stages of treatment, for clinical work with different configurations within the family: couples, nonoffending spouse/child, family group, and so on. Such work must be coordinated with other clinical efforts, as well as with the child protective services and correctional agency staff involved with the family.

(4) Protocols. Child sexual abuse is a tremendously complex issue, cutting across law enforcement, corrections, child protection, mental health and judicial systems. An effective response demands a high degree of cooperation that is found only in occasional cases. One of the key first steps in development of a cooperative program is to formalize the manner in which all of those involved will work. The most effective way to do so is to reduce working arrangements to a written agreement, or protocol, that delineates each agency's responsibilities and operating procedures, both internal and external, for responding to child sexual abuse cases. (See Appendix A for a sample protocol.)

At a minimum the protocol should include the following:

- provision for joint investigation of all child sexual abuse reports by the child-protection agency and the police. This involves the social worker and the police officer (preferably both well trained) going out together on every investigation, with close ties to the local prosecutor's office. There should be no compromise with this, since there is no way to know which reports will be confirmed and which will not, and no way to meet the goal of reducing the number of interviews a child is subjected to if the two do not go out together on each report.
- a firm recognition that the strength of the courts must be brought to bear as soon as possible in order to protect the child and other potential victims from further victimization, by placing immediate structure on offender behavior. This necessitates strong support from the area prosecutor in bringing cases to court immediately and seeking appropriate intervention from the judge. Such structure comes in the form of special conditions of release following arraign-

ment, and special conditions of probation after sentencing, or parole following release for incarceration. (See Appendix B for an example of such conditions.) Every effort should be made to enlist the support of the judiciary in providing appropriate conditions and sentencing, and in gaining the training necessary to good judicial involvement in the process.

- provision for referral of the offender, victim, and nonoffending spouse to the treatment program. It is very important that such a referral take place immediately, both because there is an obvious crisis for all concerned upon discovery, and because the chance of gaining the cooperation of a family is often greatest at this point. To assist in such a referral being successful it may be helpful to send a brief program description to area attorneys and mental health professionals who may come into contact with victims and offenders, informing them of the program and soliciting their recognition of the need it meets.

- incorporate a philosophy that the offender should be the one to leave the home and not the child. This may be done by immediate arrest, arraignment, and release on conditions that specify that the offender must move out. In some states police may give the offender the option of leaving the home voluntarily and being "cited" into court, or refusing to leave and being arrested. Whenever possible, it is better to arrest the offender and have his removal from the home one of the conditions of his release pending trial rather than to rely on his voluntary compliance. Removing the offender should be done wherever consistent with the best interests of the child. Unfortunately, there are sometimes cases where the nonoffending spouse is emotionally abusive to the child, blaming her for the abuse and breakup of the family, and/or is unable to protect the child from the offender, allowing him unsupervised visits. In such cases there is no option but to seek removal from the home.

- involve as parties in the protocol at least the following: the local prosecutor, the police (often several different agencies), the mandated child-protection agency, corrections (including probation and parole), and mental health. The protocol should be formally signed by all of the agencies involved. Even after the program is functioning it is important to send the protocol around each year to have any changes in each agency's way of handling such cases updated, and to have each agency again sign the protocol. Otherwise the protocol will, over time, simply be forgotten as personnel change and new people come in. Signing the protocol also carries with it a formal commitment that helps to ensure it will be followed, particularly in difficult cases. It also assists in resolving questions when the protocol is not followed: "Chief, I understand that the night shift didn't send an officer out with our social worker on the child sexual abuse case last night. I know you

and I agreed to do that with the protocol, and wondered if there's a problem here with either your people or mine that we should talk about."
• provide for the sharing of information among participants in the treatment program. Secrecy is one of the major weapons that an offender uses to conceal his behavior. Offenders must know that information will be shared as necessary to protect victims, forestall further victimization and assist in treatment goals. (See Appendix C for a sample Agreement of Nonconfidentiality.)

Treatment-Team Organization

An effective child sexual abuse treatment program will involve simultaneously the treatment of offenders, victims, spouses, and siblings. Extrafamilial offenders can and must be treated without the involvement of their victims, as can victims of intrafamilial abuse in cases where the offender is not reuniting with the family or is refusing to participate. However, in cases in which the offender and the victim are likely to reside eventually under the same roof, the involvement of the offender, the spouse, and the victim in treatment is essential and the involvement of the siblings desirable. Treatment must involve community supervision of the offender, or plans for community release, as well as casework services provided to the family.

These treatment requirements necessitate a coordinated treatment program, as it is neither practical nor desirable for a single-treatment provider to attempt to provide all types of therapy to all family members. Few child therapists have much experience in or inclination toward working with adult offenders; those experienced with adult offenders are rarely comfortable providing play therapy to preschoolers. Nor can a mental health professional provide the community supervision and casework services offered by corrections, probation and parole, and child protective services social workers. A secondary benefit of working with a team is that doing so minimizes the risk of being manipulated by the offender. It is much more difficult to manipulate several individuals at once than one.

Finally, teamwork maximizes the sources of information. Offenders are frequently not honest regarding the type, extent, and duration of their sexual activities. A lone clinician is often totally dependent on the offender's self-report. Even in cases of a cooperative offender, few offenders have the insight to notice slight movement toward their previous pattern of offending that alert spouses and victims may well note.

For these reasons working alone as a clinician with sex offenders is not recommended regardless of the skill level of the clinician. It is of course feasible to work alone with victims of extrafamilial abuse, although the stress of work with large numbers of victims may be alleviated by association with other clinicians engaged in similar activity.

Team members should include as an integral part of the team (and not as occasional guests), probation and parole officers from the department of corrections and social workers from the child protection agency as well as mental health clinicians. Cases of child sexual abuse are typically reported to the child protection agency, either directly or through the police. Social workers typically monitor the safety of the child thereafter, until the case is closed. Corrections becomes involved either through an order from the court for a pre-sentence investigation or after the offender has been sentenced either to probation in the community or incarceration. Mental health becomes involved after a referral to treatment. The typical treatment team, therefore, might regularly consist of the mental health professionals working with offenders, victims and nonoffending spouses, probation and parole officer(s), and social worker(s) assigned to the cases under discussion. Responsibility for scheduling the work of the team may be assigned to a single agency or individual, or may be rotated, although sometimes a single agency may well be the best choice in terms of resources and time to fulfill this need. The team should have a system in place for tracking each person and each family's progress in the program, including current status of any legal proceedings.

Treatment teams are often restricted by financial and time constraints, with agency staff typically coping with overloads and mental health professionals reluctant to devote much time to what they see as indirect service hours. Nonetheless, whether time for the team to meet is funded or voluntary, it must be set aside. Team members must be able to meet to review new referrals, coordinate treatment, share information with probation and parole and child protective services, and review major decision points regarding the families involved, such as offender-victim contact, reunification activities, and reports of offender lapses. The ideal situation would probably be a weekly team meeting, but time and fiscal issues may make a meeting twice a month more realistic. This is feasible if there is the opportunity for communication as needed among the team members in between formal meetings.

WHERE TO BEGIN

One of the questions frequently raised about how to respond to child sexual abuse is which portion of a program should be started first. The only clear answer is that if one waits until all aspects of a program are in place before beginning, nothing will ever happen. In fact, experience around the country reveals a quite varied history of program development, with no set pattern standing out as the "right" way to begin. Victims' services were begun first in Seattle, Washington, and victims' advocates were supportive of the need for offender treatment. In Vermont the first formal effort was begun with a secure treatment program for incarcerated offenders and expanded to out-patient services for victims and offenders. In earlier programs such as Henry Giarretto's Child Sexual Abuse Treatment Program in San Jose, California, protocols were developed as the program grew. Later treatment programs built on that experience and put protocols in place before a program was begun.

The most practical advice is to begin where there is the most support and the greatest likelihood of success: start small and build on success, rather than try to put all program components on line at once and risk failure. It is often unprofitable to obsess about the order in which components should be begun when factors beyond anyone's control—political pressure, community demand, or advocacy by outside groups—may determine what the first steps will be. If at all possible, however, it is not advisable to begin a major prevention campaign until services are available for child victims and a cooperative arrangement has been worked out with the law enforcement system. Most efforts to prevent child sexual abuse by work with the public and particularly with children result in an immediate increase in reports. It is not at all uncommon, for example, for an elementary school class on "Good Touch, Bad Touch" to be followed by one or more students approaching their teacher to say that they are currently being victimized. It would be unconscionable to encourage children to report and then have nothing in place to provide assistance but the old system, which often inflicts as much trauma as the crime.

PREPARATION

Advocates for an appropriate response to child sexual abuse often make the mistake of trying to begin a program by immediately approaching policymakers. They do this with a very specific proposal that seeks support for components of the treatment program. Barring an unusually well-informed administrator or political figure, this is often a mistake and fails because of insufficient groundwork to prepare the decision maker for such a request. Most people are not uncaring; in fact many will personally know someone who has been sexually abused, but they may regard it as an isolated incident rather than the pervasive problem that it really is. A small amount of preparation will go a long way toward resolving such misconceptions and gaining support. The following are very basic suggestions that should not be overlooked in beginning a program. In many areas, however, at least some of the preparation may have been already accomplished by other advocates and media coverage.

(1) Information. Policymakers expect that advocates will have available to them reliable information about the size of the problem. They may need to be convinced themselves that it warrants a significant emphasis that will be supported by the public. Information regarding number of reported and "founded" cases of child sexual abuse—geographical area, age and sex of victims, nature of victimization, relationship of offender to victim, number of children in state custody as a result and at what cost—are usually readily available from the state child protection agency. The state corrections agency, local prosecutors and the judicial system are likewise good sources regarding the number of convicted adult and juvenile offenders, by age and sex, type of conviction and sentence, nature of offense, and other offender characteristics such as marital status, employment history, and history of substance abuse. In addition to data pertinent to a given state or locality, it is also a good idea to have available information regarding the extent of the problem nationally (see Chapter 1), thereby putting local issues in the context of similar problems being faced elsewhere in the nation.

Questions will often be asked about causal factors. While much remains to be learned about cause, it is helpful to be able to present basic material regarding dynamics of offenders, victims, their families, and other relevant data, and to have more extensive references ready if they are requested.

(2) Identifying allies. Attempting to start a program alone can be a frustrating and lengthy process. It is wise at the outset to try to enlist the support of at least several other individuals who are knowledgeable and willing to collaborate in beginning a program. Help may be very useful coming from a local prosecutor, police, child protection agency, corrections, mental health, education professional, or member of a local victims' organization. Obviously when members of agencies essential to a successful program become participants in the original process, it is easier to begin.

It is also helpful to identify and try to enlist support from key decision makers in the appropriate political and organizational structure as soon as possible, always providing them with basic information about incidence as an introduction to the discussion. Such an approach should not be made, however, until there is a clear consensus as to exactly what you want to do. Energy and good will is lost if an "instant sale" is made with a decision maker, but you are unable, when asked, to make a specific proposal.

(3) Public information and support. Use of the media to raise public awareness of the problem and generate support, if not demand, for remediation is always helpful. Media coverage may be gained simply by release of incidence data and recommendations for change. Greater attention to the problem may be gained, however, if the coverage comes as a "media event." Such an event, such as a conference with a nationally recognized expert, accomplishes several purposes, while providing the media with a more interesting story to cover. Media coverage is often prompted by particularly outrageous crimes. It is a sad commentary on how public policy gets made that occasionally it takes a tragic case to generate public interest and support. If anything positive is to come of such tragedies, it may be that they present an opportunity to enlist public support for change at a time when decision makers may be most receptive to it. Arrangements for individual interviews with reporters that center on local statistics and interest stories may also be helpful in bringing a public focus to bear on efforts to begin a program.

(4) Gaining support for a protocol. The importance of agreement on a written protocol, signed by all parties, was stressed earlier. When beginning to develop support for a protocol it is helpful to reach agreement among the core group of organizers as to the basic structure of the protocol, and then to approach all of the future

parties to the protocol with a request for ideas and suggestions. When dealing with many independent organizations and individuals it is usually a good idea to use a "soft sell" rather than a "hard" one. Few people will respond negatively to a request that begins: "I know we've always tried to work cooperatively, and share the same concerns about child sexual abuse. But I think we can do even better, and wonder if you'd be willing to meet with me to discuss it?" If one person or more is hesitant, as well may occur if the area covered includes several communities, approach your strongest supporters first to obtain their signatures on the final copy of the protocol. Ideally by the time you get to your most recalcitrant party, he will be faced with a protocol that has been signed by all of the major agencies in the area that deal with this problem, and all of their counterparts in the other communities in the area. Nor should an absolute commitment be insisted on at the outset. It is better to enlist cautious support and demonstrate by actions that a cooperative effort works better than prior arrangements, if indeed there were any.

(5) Building a treatment team. All the structure and sound organization possible is wasted if not carried out by competent people who share a commitment to the same goals. In selecting a treatment team the objective is to find mental health professionals, probation and parole officers and social workers who are both trained and experienced in working with child sexual abuse in the context of a treatment program. This is often difficult at present since there is a scarcity of trained personnel. In deciding on appropriate members of a treatment team the following questions should be asked:

- What are the proposed individuals levels of experience and training as regards child sexual abuse? Have they worked in any capacity with offenders, victims, and families? Are they familiar with the work of nationally recognized experts like Nicholas Groth, Lynn Sanford, Fay Honey Knopp, Gene Abel, and Henry Giarretto? It is most important to ensure that prospective team members do not adhere to commonly held misconceptions regarding child sexual abuse like "many children desire sexual contact with adults and ask for it." These questions are easily explored and should be easily answered.
- A high level of commitment is necessary to program success, especially at startup. Is an individual willing to commit herself to the time necessary to attend team meetings and coordinate with team members at other times? What have they done on their own to improve their abilities in this field, or that gives an indication of genuine interest?

- Is there agreement as to the goals of the protocol, and the approach of the treatment program in such areas as therapeutic modality, use of the criminal justice system, nonconfidentiality and so forth? While there is no agreement in the country as to the efficacy of a single therapeutic intervention above all others, certainly there must be agreement within the team as to a common approach! Frequently professionals who are experienced in working with substance abusers and their families are more attuned to commonly recommended approaches to work with this population than others.

Team meetings themselves, when they begin, should be as well organized as possible, with an agenda and structured plan for dealing with (a) administrative details, (b) new cases, (c) on-going cases, and (d) case coordination. Since the mental health clinicians may not be members of the same agency, they may not have regular contact outside the team meetings. When they do not, they may wish to set up separate meetings to discuss clinical matters in more detail than the main team meeting can allow.

(6) Funding. There is no one way to fund treatment programs, and there are many options to choose from, the "choice" usually being determined by necessity rather than an abundance of funding mechanisms. The participation of government employees such as probation officers is clearly part of their job and should pose no problem. The same is usually not true of mental health professionals, whose time is an issue either personally or to their organizations. Funding for such services may be completely private, collected by the provider directly from their clients (or through third party payments), or may be partially or totally subsidized by a state or local agency, or some combination of the above. In some areas the courts often demand that an offender who remains in the community pay his victim's treatment costs as a condition of probation. In any event, the costs of out-patient offender treatment should be borne almost totally by the offender. Their participation in and financing of their own treatment should be a condition of probation and parole, and enforced fully by the probation or parole officer, working closely with the treatment provider. Failure to pay should be seen as an indication of a lack of commitment to full participation in the program and dealt with immediately. Often the biggest obstacle to this is that agency staff do not like to see themselves as "bill collectors." Staff should see this aspect of the program as important as all other expectations placed on offenders.

Treatment services for children and nonoffending spouses, usually mothers, may be more of a problem, particularly if the offender is already paying his own way. State child protective service agencies may be able to cover these costs, and certainly should do so for children who have been placed in state custody. In these instances it may be possible to work out a guaranteed fee to the provider, with the agency covering any costs not paid by clients or third-party payments below the guaranteed level. Some programs subsist on grants from various public and private sources. This reliance on grants may be unavoidable, but it should be noted that when subsequent grants are not forthcoming, it leads to considerable program disruption and staff loss.

CONCLUSIONS

Administrators must recognize that a successful program demands long-term effort and commitment. It is not enough to put funding mechanisms and organizational structure in place. With the many different components of the program, there will also, over time, be significant turnover in staff. This requires a continual effort to ensure that staff are appropriately trained and that all of those involved are adhering to desired procedures. For example, every time a local prosecutor is newly elected it will be necessary to start over again with the protocol, providing assistance, encouragement, and whatever persuasion is necessary to ensure continued cooperation. Such continual effort is essential, nonetheless, since the commitment of the treatment provider must be shared by those whose support is vital to its continuation.

Child sexual abuse is gradually being recognized as the major social problem that it is, a problem that taxes the resources of all agencies who must respond. The benefits of active participation in a comprehensive program far outweigh whatever loss of autonomy an agency or individual might experience in order to cooperate. By far the greatest of these benefits is the prospect of higher success in preventing victimization and effective intervention where cases are identified. But it is also true that a cooperative effort makes for more efficient use of scarce resources, renders the individual task of each agency easier, and often achieves an enhanced reputation with the public and with key policymakers.

NOTE

1. In this chapter indefinite pronouns will be alternately designated male and female to avoid the awkwardness of the he/she construction.

PART III

OFFENDER ASSESSMENT AND TREATMENT

7

DIFFERENCES IN TREATING
CHILD SEX OFFENDERS AND
OTHER CLIENTS

The treatment of child sex offenders with individual, insight-oriented psychotherapy has yielded disappointing results (Crawford, 1981; Field & Williams, 1970; Golla & Hodge, 1949; Sturup, 1972). Crawford accurately summed up the opinions of many mental health professionals when he wrote the following:

> Sex offenders are generally regarded as a population unlikely to be responsive to psychotherapy for reasons such as their denial of guilt, lack of motivation to change and failure to cooperate with voluntary treatment. (Crawford, 1981, p. 189)

The failure of psychotherapy in the past to effectively treat child sexual abuse can be attributed partially to the naive belief that the nature of therapy was the same regardless of the issue. The same therapeutic principles were thought to apply whether the problem was depression, marital discord, or child sexual abuse, and the nature of the client/therapist relationship was construed to be the same as well. This position has proved to be unrealistic, for a number of conditions are necessary in order to work effectively with sex offenders. In addition to the necessity of working within a different structure—a team sharing information rather than a lone clinician withholding it—clinicians must hold to different therapeutic principles and tolerate a different type of clinician/client relationship, one marked by less trust and more controls, in order to work effectively with child sex offenders.

My clinical experience has led me to believe that the following differences must be accepted and assimilated by mental health clinicians in order to effectively treat child sex offenders.

MANDATED VERSUS VOLUNTARY TREATMENT

The mental health community has frequently opposed court-ordered treatment in the past. Most clinicians were trained in insight-oriented therapies that required motivation on the part of the client. To require a client to undergo therapy against his will seemed almost to guarantee a therapeutic failure. How could one "make" someone obtain insight into his behavior if he or she did not wish to? Most therapists treating sex offenders were not working as part of a team, were not using specialized treatment techniques, and were instead using the same techniques that worked with voluntary, motivated clients. They were understandably not impressed with the results of forcing sex offenders onto their case loads. They found very quickly that most sex offenders did not believe they had a problem, that they either denied they committed the offense (and any previous offenses) or they admitted the offense but either minimized or defended it.

They also discovered the "two-week cure." "Thank you, doc. That was great. I learned a lot. No, I don't think I need therapy any more. Well, I'll never do that again. So long."

This was particularly vexing given that offenders had often not been reported to the authorities by family, neighbors, and even therapists, but had been allowed to go into voluntary treatment instead. "All I want is for him to get some help for his problem," was the refrain that led many well-meaning people to allow sex offenders to opt for voluntary therapy rather than expose the offender's secret by reporting him to the authorities. What was one to do, then, when the offender left as soon as some time had elapsed and the possibility of legal action was more remote? It was difficult to go back and report a case weeks and months after it occurred. Often those who could have reported even after that period of time did not have access to the information that the offender had prematurely terminated therapy. No release was ever signed, so patient confidentiality protected the offender from his neighbor's finding out that he had stopped seeing a therapist. A long delay before legal action, especially with a very young child, meant that her memory would not be as fresh and the evidence thus less compelling, if she would talk about it at all. Many child victims would resist talking about the molestation after a period of time.

It was particularly embarrassing and distressing when a sex offender who had left therapy with much bravado (after a therapeutic encounter consisting largely of denial and minimization), reoffended. Sex offenders became everyone's least-favorite clients.

However, more effective treatments have now been developed, based not on principles derived from the insight-oriented therapies, but on those derived from the addictive therapies. Drug and alcohol counselors assumed little motivation and cooperation on the part of their clients. They understood that denial and minimization were symptoms of the disorder and not to be taken as a factual account of what happened. They were aware that insight alone is of little consequence in attempting to control an addiction, and that behavioral techniques are appropriate for behavioral disorders.

The major difference in addictive disorders and child sexual abuse is that child sexual abuse is an assaultive behavior that harms children, and thus justifies legal intervention and mandated therapy. Ultimately it is considered an individual's right to drink himself to death, but not to continue to molest children. Court-ordered therapy is an essential tool in treating child sexual abuse, but one typically unavailable to alcohol and drug counselors unless a crime has been committed relating to substance abuse.

Many of the problems therapists previously faced with sex offenders have been alleviated by the use of court-mandated treatment. Contrary to expectations, motivation has been increased by the use of jail as an alternative. The "two-week cure" is seen as the attempt to evade therapy that it is, rather than as an effective course of treatment. The legal authorities are already appraised of the situation, so there is no sense of colluding with the offender to escape detection and community sanction.

Very few specialized sexual abuse programs today refuse to take mandated clients, although many refuse to take voluntary ones. Several of the Vermont outpatient programs, for example, will not take voluntary offenders, refusing to expend the resources of the program in what are considered impossible circumstances for treatment. Those programs that do take voluntary clients are sometimes quick to admit the shortcomings of doing so. Timothy Smith of Northwest Treatment Associates in Seattle, Washington has stated, "Not one in ten will stick with the program" (personal communication, January 1986).

There is no other way to guarantee the safety of the community while treating sex offenders other than to have some legal control over them. Otherwise, one is counting on the offender's ability and willingness to control his behavior, which he has already explicitly demonstrated he is unable to do.

SETTING TREATMENT GOALS

In traditional mental health, it is the client's job and not the therapist's to set the goals of therapy. The client may be morbidly overweight, have a singularly destructive marriage, a conflicted relationship with his children and bouts of debilitating depression but seek therapy for a long-standing problem with his boss. No responsible therapist would fail to raise the other issues and ask whether the client would wish to address them. Therapists may go further and explain the extent to which the presenting problem is interwoven with the others and cannot be resolved without dealing with those also, as in a case where marital conflicts are effecting his mood and behavior at work. Nonetheless, it is ultimately the client's right to refuse to address other issues if he wishes, and to decide what his priorities are. It is by no means uncommon for client and therapist to disagree regarding those priorities, but the therapist must acquiesce in the client's wishes for change or elect to part company. Such election is rare. Few therapists would part company over a client's refusal to address a weight problem, or his desire to keep smoking, but might well withdraw if the client refused alcohol treatment when the therapist believed the sought-after marriage counseling could not be effective so long as the person continued to drink.

The rules must be different with child sexual abuse. It is to be expected that the client will have goals the therapist does not share and the therapist is expected to override the client's wishes. For many clients child molestation is an addiction. They are more frightened of being without the addiction than of continuing it.

Thus the client's goal in the short run may not be to cease molesting children. Instead it may be to seduce the therapist into colluding with the denial or at least agreeing the molestation was not as extensive and certainly not as traumatic as the victim claimed. It may be to convince the therapist to share the view that the spouse, victim, problems at work, or the drinking were the cause of the abuse. It is often to persuade the therapist that the client really does not remember molesting the child, due, for example, to an alcohol blackout at the time. In many cases, it is to get the therapist to agree that either the client does not have to leave his home "Where would I go?" or at least to allow him to return almost immediately "I have already admitted doing it." Whatever else, the goal will probably include asking the therapist to buy the "two-week cure," and to support the client's desire to terminate therapy within a short period of time.

It is the therapist who must set the goals of therapy outlined in Chapter 5 on the philosophy of treatment. It is also the therapist who repeatedly must resist colluding with inappropriate goals, which are all the more insidious for being unspoken and unacknowledged.

EXPLICIT VALUE STANCE

The heart of the therapeutic relationship has traditionally been its nonjudgmental nature. Therapists may help clients to explore the effects that certain things that they do will have on other aspects of their lives, but it is not the therapist's job, for example, to tell the client he should not have an affair because the therapist believes it is wrong. Implicit in the client's right to choose the goals of therapy is his right to hold the values he believes in and act accordingly. This ability of therapists to side with clients, to see the world from their point of view, and to help them determine what they want in their lives is one of the important differences between therapy and advice.

Nonetheless, in child sexual abuse the therapist must set the goals for the client. In doing so the therapist is making de facto a value statement, and it is easier for the client to understand if the therapist is honest and explicit. The client should hear that the therapist does not believe that child sexual abuse is acceptable, that she has no intention of colluding with it in any way, that she believes that children are indeed reliable reporters of child sexual abuse whereas offenders are not reliable reporters of child sexual abuse, and that child sexual abuse is harmful to children. The offender should be further assured that the therapist considers it her job to prevent the reoccurrence of child sexual abuse in any form.

In this the treatment of child sexual abuse does not differ from the treatment of alcoholism and drug addiction. There is little room in such therapies for colluding with the addict's claims that alcohol or drugs are not harmful to him or her. Rather the therapist must be clear from the start that they are, and communicate that explicitly to the client.

SETTING LIMITS

Therapists are not police officers, and often dislike intensely being asked to help control a client's behavior. Nonetheless, working with sex offenders must involve a constant setting of limits. The therapist's presence and her explicit value stand is limit setting. Likewise, the therapist's willingness to disclose information regarding future molestations to the authorities is also limit setting.

In addition to the absolute ban on child molestation, there are frequently other limits that the offender tests and that must be maintained. For example, the therapist of the offender may be asked by the child's therapist to make it clear that the offender is not to come in her room while she is there and "hang around." Word may come back from the spouse's group that the mother feels uncomfortable that the father has "tickling" sessions when he comes to visit the child. It is entirely appropriate that the therapist deal with these issues with the offender. As uncomfortable as it is for many therapists to set limits on the behavior of their clients and enforce them, nonetheless, the therapist's willingness and ability to do so is an important factor in helping offenders to learn to live within the limits of the law. In this the therapist serves less as a model for an observing ego, as she does in other forms of therapy, and more as a model of a superego.

LIMITED CONFIDENTIALITY

Limited confidentiality is a necessity if a child sexual abuse treatment team is to function effectively. In this, sexual abuse differs from all other therapeutic programs known to the author. Confidentiality is guaranteed in the treatment of alcohol and drug addictions by federal law. Even when the client is a minor, therapists are not allowed to reveal information regarding drugs or alcohol to their parents. This is so even if the adolescent drops out of therapy and leaves, as happened in one case, to pursue her addiction to heroin.

There are exceptions to traditional therapeutic confidentiality, but they involve violence to self or others and are specific to emergencies rather than programmatic. A therapist is required to report a homicide threat to the intended victim; sexual or physical abuse must be reported to the appropriate mandated agency; suicidal behavior requires notification of the family. Each of these involve emergencies, however, and not the routine exchange of information in nonemergency situations.

Sexual abuse programs differ from the traditional stance on confidentiality in that individuals are asked to surrender their right to have total confidentiality upon entry to the program and may be denied entry if they do not agree. This involves a radical shift in perspective for a therapist. Therapists have described much initial distress at discussing clinical material in meetings with probation and parole officers and child protection workers. With time (and therapeutic successes) therapists often become accustomed to working within this framework. Initially, however, this is an extremely difficult adjustment for many therapists to make.

TRUST AND SEX OFFENDERS

"I tell my clients that I do not operate on a trust basis. Trust is what is abusable. I communicate to them that I have no intention of feeling confident in them. Feeling confident about them can be dangerous" (Dreiblatt, in Knopp, 1984, p. 70).

In other forms of therapy the client is ultimately the best source of information and the best authority on his own experience. Even where the client's perceptions are not accurate, it is generally considered that it is those perceptions that motivate the client's behavior, and they are taken as the basic data from which the therapist works. Except in rare instances, for example, when the client has psychopathic tendencies, the therapist does not routinely expect that the client is lying to her. Lying is even more unlikely if there is a good therapist-client bond and the client understands that the therapist accepts him even when not at his best. Trust is possible—some might argue necessary—for therapy to be effective.

In child sexual abuse many and perhaps most therapeutic encounters begin with what may be called the fundamental lie: "I didn't do it." Offenders may continue to assert their innocence despite overwhelming evidence and despite good rapport with their therapists. Offenders can be quite convincing when asserting their innocence, and it is a rare therapist who has not wondered whether a particular offender was not telling the truth, despite considerable evidence to the contrary. In this author's experience the offender who was the most persuasive was ultimately ordered out of his home specifically because of his refusal to own responsibility for the offense. He then immediately reversed his story and admitted in detail the charges his daughter had made against him. He was equally persuasive in his reversal.

THE APPEAL TO NARCISSISM

Doc, I've been in Dr. Smith's treatment group over in Riverland and I'm just not getting anything out of it. He just doesn't understand the special problems of alcoholics. I mean, I don't remember a thing about it, and he keeps riding me all the time to say I remember something I just don't remember, and the parole officer said I have to be in some kind of specialized treatment or go to jail. I've heard such good things about your evaluations. I've been told they're better than anyone else's. I just wondered if you could evaluate me, and really I don't think I need to be in any treatment right now. I'm in AA, and really, since then I've been a different person. I haven't had a drink since I started the program. You know, even if I have to have some treatment I'd rather have it with you. I think you could really help me, Doc.

Before the conversation was over this client had offered to colead a group with the therapist. This sort of attempt at manipulation should be blatantly transparent except in those instances in which the therapist has unresolved narcissistic issues and is competitive with other therapists. Unfortunately, such situations are not altogether uncommon. Offenders will exploit weaknesses they detect very rapidly, and treatment providers in an area will, accordingly, find themselves split and in conflict with each other.

There are many variations on this theme. If a therapist has any temptation to stray from the straight and humble she may find herself before a parole board (as one therapist did) making claims that a rape/murderer (whose crime involved raping a woman after he had strangled her), was incapable of committing any future crimes. The offender had convinced the therapist of this after a course of "telephone therapy," conversations between the offender and the therapist that were sometimes as short as 15 minutes. The therapist wrote in his report that the client could not commit such an offense again, except in circumstances so bizarre as to be unimaginable. He was also convinced that the client was "cured" of his alcoholism at the level of "psychological certainty" which the therapist defined as at the 95% confidence level. Even if the client did relapse, however, the therapist contended that it would not change his likelihood of committing another murder/rape.

This may be an extreme case, but there are many, less dramatic ways to err in treating sex offenders. Allowing the offender to feed the therapist's narcissism may be the easiest. Unfortunately, such errors can have serious consequences for the community.

RESPECT VERSUS COLLUSION

It is very difficult to extend respect to individuals who frequently lie, con, deny, and minimize behavior that is extremely harmful to small children. The therapist is often hard pressed to respect someone who, for example, has chosen preschool children because they are less likely to resist and unlikely to make good witnesses in court. It is difficult to respect an incestuous father after one has interviewed his 14-year-old who has become addicted to drugs and is suicidal.

Yet the key to the successful rehabilitation of offenders is not ultimately the gadgetry of the plethysmograph, useful though it is, nor the charts and graphs and homework assignments of behavior therapy, essential though they are. The critically important factor is the simultaneous capacity of the therapist to extend respect to people as human beings, to empathize with their pain, and to believe in their capacity to do better in the future while not colluding with sexual abuse a single inch. This author has seen therapists with that capacity, and they are invariably successful with sex offenders provided they are working within an appropriate structure and applying appropriate treatments. Offenders detect very quickly a sense of respect coming from someone very difficult to manipulate, and they then respond as though there were something in them worth respecting. It is this stance that seems to make the difference. Some therapists convey to offenders the impression that they can see in them the admirable person they could have been and still can be, and that all the rest—the lying, the manipulation, and the abusive behavior—can and must be discarded.

This is a very difficult balancing act. The tendency is to fall off in one direction or the other. Those who are able to empathize with offenders often do so by minimizing their offenses and colluding with their rationalizations. Those who do not collude and who do hold offenders accountable for their behavior often are angry and hostile to the offender and make no serious attempt at building rapport. In either case, the therapist's task is greatly eased, but the offender's chance at rehabilitation is correspondingly lessened.

CONFRONTATION

Therapy is sometimes thought to be a process of confrontation and confirmation (Teague, 1979). If so, the process of treating child sex offenders is heavily weighted in the direction of confrontation. Treatment requires continual confrontations.

"No, it would not be a good idea for you to start babysitting again. No, I do not trust you, and I think you would be pretty foolish to trust yourself."

"No, the team does not think you have made sufficient progress to move back into your home."

"Your neighbor has reported that you were seen at your wife's house outside of your visitation hours. What's going on?"

"Give me a break. What do you mean one drink can't do any harm? Drinking is a parole violation, and you seem to be making a serious attempt at getting yourself in jail."

"No, you're not over this. You're never going to be over this in the sense that you can forget all about it. You're going to have to be on guard about this the rest of your life."

However, confrontation does not have to involve hostility, and it must not if it is to be therapeutic. In ordinary settings it normally does, and frequently body language matches the words. Unconsciously, people usually get tense when confronting others, their voices lose all warmth and humor, and body postures become closed and hostile. Natural as the response is, it is counterproductive. The task in treatment is not only to confront, it is to hold the offender with one through the confrontation, and to come out the other side with the message clear but the rapport intact.

There are a variety of ways that therapists do this. Some therapists act more warmly when they confront. They lean forward, their body language is more open and extending, although the message is still the same. The effect is to cut into the stiff formality of a confrontation and to prevent counter-therapeutic defensiveness on both sides. Sometimes acceptance of confrontation can be fostered in the very beginning by making a deal with offenders. "I can't promise you I'll always agree with you. I don't expect you'll always agree with me. I can promise I will always be straight with you. If I don't agree, you'll know it directly from me. Does that seem fair to you?"

Many therapists use humor. "You want to cut yourself off at the knees? This is not my problem. I should worry if you work this hard to get yourself in jail? Why not just go rob a bank and save yourself a lot of trouble?"

"I look maybe like I was born yesterday? In all seriousness you are asking me to believe you went in her bedroom last night to see if she was cold?"

"I hate to tell you this and I certainly don't mean to insult you, but I wouldn't believe that if my grandmother told me."

Another technique is to make a joining comment each time the therapist makes a confrontive statement and thus cut into the ability of the offender to be defensive regarding the confrontive statement.

"I know this is tough to talk about. On the other hand avoiding this is not going to do you a lot of good."

"You know, sometimes we say what we really wish to be true, rather than what is. You say you did not molest her, yet obviously you did. I think you are speaking of your wishes, rather than the reality."

"I'm sure it seems like I'm hounding you, but I can't be of help to you if I don't understand your experience."

"I know this is all difficult, and I'm sure you wish you weren't here, but the last thing that will be useful to you is for you and me to talk bull for 77 years."

"Now you've said that you really don't feel sexually attracted to children, and yet the plethysmograph shows a good deal of arousal to slides of children. Let's take a look at this. Obviously your body is telling you something."

"Well, very often people really don't want to remember things like that. I think you will find your memory improves as therapy goes along."

This latter is also an example of using prediction in therapy. Rather than simply backing the offender into a corner regarding his lies so that he has to lose face to admit the truth, it is possible at times to predict for him, for example, that he will be able to remember more of it as he goes along, that he will come to understand better the role that nonalcoholic factors play in sexual abuse, or that he will be able to see his problems as well as his wife's.

Prediction has two purposes. It makes it easier for the offender to contradict himself without loss of face. It also ties his improvement to his admitting and owning responsibility. Since many offenders are very motivated to be seen as improving and getting through the program, it puts pressure on them to be more honest as a way of demonstrating improvement. It is the therapist's job to make sure the admission, once it comes, is genuine. It is not enough, for example, to admit committing a particular act. The offender must talk about what he did and how he did it, plus what he was thinking and feeling at the time, and how he planned it.

The issue is to help an offender come to terms with his behavior, to look at and own responsibility for the worst in him. It cannot be done without extensive, ongoing confrontation. However, for the offender to accept the confrontation rather than simply grow distant and hostile, it must be done in such a way as to maintain the rapport with him, to hold him, as it were, with one through the confrontation. The holding must be caring and not simply controlling. Therapist and offender must come through the confrontation together with the thread between them intact.

Although this chapter has focused on the differences in treating sex offenders and other clients, many aspects of therapy are the same. Hope is important. Offenders and their families must believe that other families have gone had similar problems and survived as individuals, and when they chose, as families. Offenders must also believe they have a better chance of completing therapy successfully if they work with, rather than against, the therapist. There must be more hope in cooperating than not. The natural tendency of sex offenders, is to withdraw, deny and withhold. They believe, like small children caught in a fire, that if they just hide in the closet and keep quiet, it will all go away.

8

OFFENDER DENIAL

Herman (1981) has written that "denial has always been the incestuous father's first line of defense" (p. 22). Certainly denial is frequently reported by clinicians as a major aspect of an offender's response to disclosure (Abel et al., 1985; Knopp, 1984). However, to date there has been little discussion in the literature of different types of denial. Instead, the implication is often that denial is a binary phenomenon in which an offender either is or is not in a state of denial. Recently the author was asked for a second opinion on a psychological evaluation of an offender in which the offender admitted some inappropriate touching, but denied the extent of the offense as stated by his adolescent victim. The psychologist writing the evaluation used the offender's admission that he had engaged in some sexually abusive behavior (pulling the adolescent girl's underwear down and pulling her pubic hair to "tease" her) as proof that the offender had not engaged in oral sex and other more extensive activities with which the victim had charged him; this assertion was supported by the claim that sex offenders either deny everything or admit the whole truth.

Instead, the opposite is true. Offenders, like icebergs, typically only expose a fraction of the problem initially. This is frequently puzzling to observers, who may be hard pressed to understand why an offender feels that having intercourse with his daughter for six months is so much less objectionable than for the five years the daughter charges. Yet this author has seen offenders who have risked and even accepted incarceration rather than admit to the full extent of the charges. One offender who admitted intercourse with his daughter, but for a shorter period of time than his daughter charged, eventually reversed his story when the treatment team recommended that he be removed from his home for failure to comply with treatment. Upon reversal, he easily told enough details of the abuse to clearly substantiate the daughter's charges. When asked why he had lied about the extent of the abuse for such a long time with such loud and indignant protests of innocence, he was unable to respond. It seemed to him that in some fundamental way what he was admitting to was infinitely less objectionable than what he was denying, even though the sexual activities were the same. Therapists cannot assume because an offender has "no reason" to lie and has admitted parts of the victim's story that his version of events is correct. Offenders make idiosyncratic distinctions in degrees of blame often unintelligible to an outside observer and tailor their stories accordingly.

Denial can be considered more of a spectrum than a single state. In addition there are different components of denial, among them the following: (1) denial of the acts themselves (type and period of time the abuse occurred), (2) denial of fantasy and planning, (3) denial of responsibility for the acts, (4) denial of the seriousness of the behavior, (5) denial of internal guilt for the behavior, and (6) denial of the difficulty in changing abusive patterns.

Figure 8.1 summarizes some of the types of denial in which an offender may engage depending on his responses to the different components of denial as listed above. This chapter will review each of these types of denial and the components of denial as they are manifest in the types.

ADMISSION WITH JUSTIFICATION

Some sexual offenders, most frequently rapists, admit the behavior but justify it. Russell (1975) cites a case of three rapists who told their victim that "she was only getting what she deserved for

	Admission with Justification	Denial of Behavior		Minimizes Extent of Behavior	Denial of Seriousness of Behavior and Need for Treatment	Denial of Responsibility for Behavior	Full Admission W/ Responsibility and Guilt
		Physical Denial With or W/out Family Denial	Psychological Denial				
Admits he committed the acts?	yes	no	no	partially	yes	yes	yes
Describes Fantasy and Planning?	yes or no	no	no	no	no	no	yes
Accepts responsibility?	yes or no	no	no	minimizes	no	no	yes
Accepts Seriousness of Behaviors?	yes or no	no event, no consequences	no event, no consequences	minimizes	no	yes	yes
Feels Guilt or Shame Over Discovery?	neither	neither	neither	shame	shame	shame	guilt
Difficulty in Changing Abusive Patterns?	no desire to	no reason to	no reason to	easy	easy	easy	difficult

Components of Denial

Figure 8.1   Degree of Denial

walking on the street without a man at night." They saw themselves as decent for letting her get away so lightly (pp. 260-261).

Herman quotes an incest offender's comment in a television interview: "In my own mind back then, I thought I was doing her a favor. I made myself feel that I was not doing anything wrong, that I was actually sexually educating her. We never did have complete intercourse. I thought . . . just touching and playing and fondling and all that, that wasn't harmful" (Herman, 1981, p. 22).

This author saw an incestuous father who bellowed "My home is my castle and I'll do what I goddamn well please." Likewise an incarcerated child molester refused to participate in a research project the author was conducting by asking, "Could this project be used to detect child molesters?"

"It could be," I replied.

"Then it's not in my best interest," he stated. "This behavior isn't immoral, you know, it's just illegal."

Such offenders admit the acts. However, they differ on whether or not they take responsibility for them. Some sexual abusers of children maintain, for example, that they were educating the children and/or offering them affection and friendship. Such offenders do not necessarily blame the children for the acts. Others, however, maintain that the child's wearing a nightgown, sitting in the offender's lap, putting her arms around the offender, or running around the house nude after a bath were provocative and responsible for the abuse. This is an equivalent mental process to that of the adult rapist or potential rapist, who declares that rape is justified because women "think they're so high and mighty on a pedestal that nobody can touch them. I would like to rape them to show them that they're no better than any cunt walking down the street" (Russell, 1984, p. 153). Burt (1983) found that rapists "frequently deny all guilt for their acts, and feel no remorse" (p. 144). Whether a projection of anger or a denial of anger and a projection of caring and concern, whether they are oriented towards adults or children, many sex offenders find sufficient justification for their behavior in their fantasies of their victims' thoughts, attitudes, feelings, or behavior, and admit they committed the acts as charged by their victims.

Such offenders rarely appreciate the seriousness of the consequences of the behavior. Ordinarily only those who feel that the victim deserved to be hurt will admit the degree of harm. These are more frequently rapists, whether of adults or children, men who are often aware of being angry when they rape and who justify their behavior by reference to some imagined characteristic of their particular victim or of women and children in general. Clearly, men who tell themselves they are educating the child, comforting the child, being close to the child, loving the child, or satisfying the child's curiosity do not allow themselves to appreciate the destructiveness of their behavior to the child, as this would conflict with the type of denial they employ.

Such offenders may or may not admit to fantasies and planning the behavior, depending on whether they are claiming that the behavior was the spontaneous result of some provocation by the victim. They do not feel guilt over being discovered, as they believe they are not behaving inappropriately, and they rarely feel shame. When they do feel shame, it is over what they have done to their own or their family's status in the community or over some secondary effect of the abuse such as incarceration. They feel no real need to change the abusive behavior, and therefore do not quibble over whether their abusive patterns will be easy or difficult to change.

Recent attention in the literature has focused on the problem of undetected sex offenders. In a study of 6,104 college students, Koss (1985) found that 4.6% of the men admitted a sexually aggressive act since the age of 14 that met the legal criterion for rape, whereas an additional 3.2% reported behavior that met the criterion for attempted rape. Despite this, only 1 of 131 perpetrators defined his behavior as rape. Koss comments that the "perpetrators' primary emotion was pride" (p. 104). Such unacknowledged offenders typically felt that the victim was more responsible for what happened than they were.

DENIAL OF BEHAVIOR: THREE PATTERNS

Physical Denial With or Without Family Denial

Physical denial refers to the denial of the specified behavior on a given day at a particular time and place. Some offenders focus concretely on the details of the alleged abuse and respond, not with an overall denial of the charges, but with an alibi for that particular day. Of these, some will have backup from family or friends for their alibi, and despite strong evidence to the contrary, they will cling doggedly to the alibi.

Terman, 16, was accused of exposing himself to a young woman near his home. The victim reported he said to her, "How would you like to get ahold of this?" while masturbating and exposing his penis. The young woman reported the incident to the police and, based on her description, they picked up Terman for questioning. The victim subsequently picked him out of a police lineup. Terman failed a lie detector test, but despite this and the victim's eye-witness identification, he refused to admit the offense.

Both Terman's mother and stepfather insisted he was with them at a ball game in a neighboring town, some distance away at the time, watching his younger brother play. They insisted he was seen by many observers. The defense attorney repeatedly asked the parents to produce even one witness who could substantiate the alibi. They failed to do so, citing various excuses such as "his friends are too busy" to talk to the attorney. When pressed for the names of witnesses, the parents became evasive and refused to give them. However, even after the court found him guilty, they continued loudly to maintain his innocence, and blamed the conviction on incompetence on the part of the defense attorney. Nonetheless they refused to change attorneys. Terman subsequently refused to cooperate with assessment or treatment.

Paul, 14, was arrested for dragging a young woman into the bushes with a knife at her throat and pulling off some of her clothes before she was able to free herself and run away. The adolescent girl knew Paul, and identified him to the police. Another adolescent male had been with Paul who knew both Paul and the victim and did not take part in the incident. He substantiated the victim's story and identified Paul to the police. Nonetheless, Paul's parents claimed he was with them at the time.

Such offenders do not accept responsibility for the offense, as they either contend it never happened or did not involve them. Since they were not involved in the offense, they neither admit to fantasy nor planning. As there was no behavior, there were no adverse consequences to the behavior. Their response to discovery is neither guilt nor shame, but frequently outrage and righteous indignation. They insist the victim and/or the system is "out to get" them, and that they are the real victims. They admit to no reasons to change their behavior, since they deny any wrongdoing.

When family members support physical denial, the offender is much more difficult to treat, as he is likely to feel pressure from family members to continue the denial, in addition to his own internal tendency to deny. If the family refuses to cooperate with treatment, then the family's collusion with physical denial suggests that the offender should not be allowed to continue living at home. Such offenders must be removed from the source of the support for their deviancy for treatment to be effective. Depending on the circumstances, such offenders may be treated on an outpatient basis while living independently if adults or in foster care if adolescents. They may also be recommended for incarcerated or residential treatment, depending usually on the degree of violence associated with their behavior, and on whether they can be adequately supervised and community safety protected if they are treated in an outpatient setting.

Psychological Denial

Many offenders will deny the overall charge of sexual abuse, without focusing exclusively on the concrete details of a particular day, situation, or event. Rather than saying, "I couldn't have done it because I wasn't there at the time," they say, in effect, "I'm not the sort of person who would do that sort of thing. I am not a child molester; therefore, I did not molest this particular child." They are less preoccupied and focused on a child's memory, for example, of a particular date, and seem to grasp the overall charge better than offenders involved in physical denial, understanding that whether it occurred on June 6th or 7th is not the main point. While their families may support them and also deny the charge, family denial is less pathological than when the family produces a false alibi, since it does not involve outright lying to protect the offender. The latter implies that the family is aware he is guilty. In the case of psychological denial in which the family does not fabricate an alibi, the family often genuinely believes the offender is innocent. Such families are potentially more favorable to treatment than families who lie to protect the offender, since they often support treatment once they become convinced the offender is guilty.

Offenders who deny committing the offense obviously do not admit that their behavior has harmed the child, nor that they fantasized and planned prior to the offense. Such offenders show little evidence of shame or guilt, and like those who deny physically, are often indignant and outraged at the accusations. They see no reason to change an abusive pattern that they deny exists.

MINIMIZATION OF THE EXTENT OF THE BEHAVIOR

Offenders will frequently admit part of their behavior but deny the rest. This happens routinely with offenders who are caught with one victim and who have not been caught for previous offenses with other victims. Such offenders often profess a desire for treatment, but withhold information on the extent of their sexual deviancy because of a fear of additional legal charges. Likewise, additional legal charges may sometimes be brought even with the same victim, if the offender admits that all of what the child stated did indeed happen. For example, the penalties for fondling are often less severe than for penetration; thus an offender may admit to one but not the other.

As stated earlier, however, denial of the extent of the sexual deviancy is common even when legal charges are not an issue. The differences in the story told by offender and victim may not be meaningful to an outside observer even in moralistic terms, as when the offender admits penetration but denies oral sex, or more frequently, admits intercourse but denies the period of time over which it occurred.

Because the offender's insistence on his version of events makes little sense to the clinician unless it is true, it is tempting to believe the offender at the expense of the child victim. Work with offenders suggests, however, that an insistence on innocence of charges that do not differ legally or morally from charges admitted cannot be taken as proof of honesty; the distinctions they make in degrees of blame are often not accessible to others.

Likewise, offenders who minimize the extent of their activities almost inevitably refuse to admit that either sexual fantasies or planning were present, even when the circumstances of the offenses were such that planning was clearly evidenced in the precautions against discovery.

It is, in addition, common for an offender to be arrested for one type of offense, child molestation for example, to engage in but not to admit other types of sexually deviant behavior, for example, rape or exhibitionism. Abel et al. (1985) found that the crossover rate for sexual deviants is quite high. Half of their sample of 89 men who were primarily identified as rapists had also been involved in child molestation, while 29% were also involved in exhibitionism and 20% in voyeurism. Of the 232 men primarily identified as child molesters, 17% were also involved in rape, 30% in exhibitionism, and 14% in voyeurism.

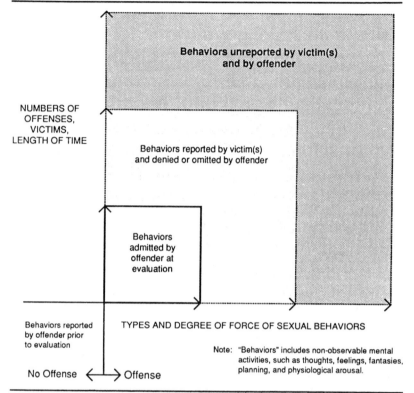

Figure 8.2   Denial, Lying, Minimization, Omissions of Sexual Offenders
SOURCE: Ballantyne (1987).   Copyright © 1987, W. Ballantyne.   Reprinted by permission.

Offenders rarely volunteer information about other types of sexual deviancy unless asked directly. Even when asked they may be less than honest, even when interviewed by experienced clinicians. There is some evidence that confrontation following plethysmograph testing may be more efficacious (Abel et al., 1985). (The plethysmograph, to be discussed in Chapter 12, is a physiological instrument for determining the pattern of sexual arousal.) Without a witness' account, the plethysmograph may be the only successful method for detecting other forms of deviancy for which the offender has not been charged.

William Ballantyne has illustrated the admitted versus the committed but not acknowledged behaviors as follows:

Offenders who admit only some of their abusive behaviors are not assuming responsibility for the totality of their sexual offenses and often equivocate on how responsible they are for the offense they have admitted. In addition, they typically minimize the extent of harm they have caused their victims. When asked directly, they may proclaim loudly that they indeed did do something harmful, but they are unable to specify in what way the abuse was detrimental. They rarely admit deviant fantasies or planning. While they are often distraught and remorseful at discovery, there is often no real sense of internalized guilt. They underestimate the difficulty of change, and feel that simply deciding not to abuse again will be sufficient to prevent relapse.

Denial of the Seriousness of the Behavior and Need for Treatment

Once offenders admit the extent of the deviancy they often still minimize the seriousness of it. It takes considerable empathy to imagine sexual abuse from a child's point of view, and considerable courage to face the extent to which the offenses are not redeemable. The child's experience has been changed in a fundamentally damaging way, and whether or not she recovers, she has been harmed. The residue of the superoptimism found in offenders who minimize the extent of their deviancy is found in offenders who admit it, but imply it was not so bad after all. It was not, one can infer from their comments, such a "big deal." They are quick to believe their victims have recovered, and to see them as "just like they were before all this happened." Denial of the seriousness of the consequences of their behavior protects them from the guilt that such appreciation would entail, and negative affect around the events still consists primarily of shame.

Such offenders are at particular risk to reoffend. The cognitive distortions that justify and give permission for sexually deviant behavior find their root in an underestimation of the impact of sexual abuse on a child. It is a short step from thinking it didn't do her any real harm last time to thinking that one more time wouldn't really matter.

Like the offender who minimizes the extent of the behavior, such an offender believes change will be easy and usually presses for reunification of the family as soon as he has admitted the offenses and has said he was responsible for them. He typically either refuses treatment altogether or tries to abbreviate it. One incarcerated offender was quoted in a local paper as stating that he had refused treatment because he felt the best strategy was "just not to think about it." Treatment would make him worse, since he would have to "dwell on it." When an offender who copes by "not thinking" about the offense is released and finds himself in situations that arouse sexual impulses towards children, he has no coping mechanisms or strategies to rely on in order to resist them. Not thinking about it at that point is likely to be of little help.

Such a refusal to accept treatment should be taken very seriously as an attempt to protect the sexual deviancy by not exposing it to the effects of treatment. At the level of refusing treatment altogether, it is simply a sign of the addictive nature of the disorder, akin to the behavior of an alcoholic who insists he can quit anytime he chooses. Given the highly repetitive nature of sexual molestation, it should not be taken as an indication that the individual will be able to refrain from further sexual offenses. He remains the same person he was while offending, has the same impulses, and has had no intervention that would increase his ability to control those impulses or that would reduce the strength of them. He is expressing the wish that he would not reoffend, but nothing more. For desire to become behavior, treatment is required.

A variation of the refusal to accept the difficulty in changing abusive behavior is the claim of an offender that he has no need for treatment because he has undergone a religious or a moral conversion. Pacht, Halleck, and Ehrmann (1962) have described such offenders aptly:

> The most outstanding of these is a type of resistance in which the patient eagerly grasps onto a psychological or moralistic formula that provides him a rationalization for his behavior. This serves him as a superficial explanation for his difficulties that may also lead him to a conviction that he will not repeat the offense. If an individual states that he is going to stop repeating his aberrant behavior, and holds to his belief on the basis of an alleged change in his morals or an alleged understanding of his difficulties, he sets up a tremendous roadblock to treatment. (p. 806)

The "formula" for many offenders is a religious one, and religious conversions among convicted offenders are common. Such offenders often refuse treatment, insisting that it is both degrading and unnecessary. Instead, they insist that they will rely on God for guidance. The reliance on God or on a recently awakened sense of morality serves only to protect offenders from treatment and, of course, does not reduce the risk of reoffense.

In distinguishing between religious conversions that serve the purpose of evading treatment and genuine conversions that do not, the following should be considered. Those religious conversions that do not have as a primary goal the evasion of treatment will not lead the offender to refuse treatment. Such offenders will take seriously the saying, "God helps those who help themselves," and will attempt to prove their sincerity in asking for divine forgiveness by their behavior in treatment. They will, perhaps, ask for guidance in resisting temptation, but also will ask for help in fulfilling treatment requirements and assignments to the best of their abilities. They will not expect God to do the work of treatment for them, but simply to assist them in doing the work. They will be more aware of temptation rather than less, and will feel they are at risk to reoffend. They will see their religious faith, along with treatment, as crucial in preventing reoffenses that would otherwise be likely. They will not feel that religion gives them immunity from reoffending. In short, the difference in genuine religious conversions and those that serve simply as a method of evading treatment lies in whether or not the individual sees God as helpful to him in changing his behavior through treatment, or whether he sees God as eliminating the need for treatment.

DENIAL OF RESPONSIBILITY FOR BEHAVIORS

Many offenders admit the actual behaviors, either initially or in order to be admitted to a treatment program, and accept their seriousness but deny responsibility for them. Unlike the offenders who admit the behaviors and justify them, these offenders will admit the behavior was inappropriate, but do not take full responsibility. This is sometimes blatant, as when an offender attributes the abusive behavior to alcohol and insists that he needs no treatment at all (as he does not plan to drink again) or at the most needs treatment for alcoholism.

Other offenders are less overt about not assuming responsibility; they will formally say they are responsible for the abuse. However, careful listening to their descriptions of the abuse will detect constant externalization. Blame is placed on their wives' nagging, their wives' lack of interest in sex, their own problems at work, provocation by the child, lack of attention and care from the world in general, excessive care and attention from the child ("she was the only one I could be close to"), and on their own emotional neediness ("I was just so lonely; there was no one I could talk to"). Such offenders find numerous excuses for the behavior, mostly external, but also frequently internal. These excuses have the cumulative effect of reducing offender responsibility. "Yes it happened," the offender says, "but there were a lot of reasons for it; I couldn't really help it." Inevitably, the offender portrays himself as the real victim. The affect is frequently a mixture of self-pity and anger at the world for denying him what should have been freely given him, usually emotional support and sex. The offender does not admit that he committed the offenses because he found them pleasurable sexually, nor does he admit the extent of fantasy and planning that preceded them.

Admission of fantasy and planning is extremely important for this type of offender, as there can be no genuine acceptance of responsibility without it. To recognize and acknowledge deviant sexual fantasies is to admit sexual pleasure in the abuse; to acknowledge planning the offense is to accept the extent the offender groomed and manipulated the child—a recognition antithetical to externalization of responsibility.

An offender who does not truly accept responsibility will minimize the harm to the child, and feels he is the real victim. He will often assure the victim that he has suffered more than she. His suffering is often related to disclosure, and he readily lists what he has lost by public censure: his standing in the community, his job, his freedom, and his family. There is little evidence of internal guilt over the behavior itself.

Such offenders do not typically refuse treatment outright, but instead attempt to obtain a premature termination of treatment, or on termination of treatment, are confident of their ability not to reoffend. While less blatant than the offender who refuses treatment altogether, nonetheless an offender who attempts not to complete treatment or who believes that he is "cured" and no longer at risk is signaling that he has not fully grappled with the reality of his sexual deviancy. Such a stance should call into question all other signs of progress. A little confidence can be a dangerous thing for a sex offender, causing him to relax his vigilance. He is at risk to enter risky situations and not take evasion action early enough to prevent future molestations.

Such confidence does not necessarily involve a conscious attempt to manipulate treatment. Often offenders are euphoric over having current control of impulses that have previously controlled them. While in treatment they are in a carefully controlled environment, often with sufficient rules to keep them from tempting situations. It is easy in such circumstances to overestimate the power of their newly found controls and underestimate the power of their old addiction. This is so particularly if they have managed to persuade their therapists to accept their minimization of the responsibility for the offense(s). If so, they have never fully owned their sexual deviancy, but have been allowed to externalize instead. It is easy to be optimistic about controlling something that wasn't really a problem in the first place.

FULL ADMISSION WITH RESPONSIBLITY AND GUILT

The offender who genuinely does not deny is the offender who admits the extent of his sexual deviancy. His story of the extent of the abuse matches that of the victim. In addition he is able to describe antecedents to the sexually abusive behavior, consisting of previous thoughts and fantasies, and sometimes involving offenses against other victims and/or other forms of sexual deviancy. He acknowledges the extent to which his behavior with that victim was preceded by sexual fantasies of her, the extent to which he planned the abusive behavior, and the various techniques by which he groomed and controlled his victim. He is aware of a current struggle with deviant sexual fantasies and a temptation to relapse. He does not believe change will be easy, and he recognizes an ongoing temptation to backslide. He has fears of molesting again and is nervous about family reunification.

He understands he cannot "undo" the abusive behavior and appreciates the seriousness of the consequences for his victim. He feels guilt for his behavior and the harm it has caused. The depression so frequently seen with offenders arises in his case from an internalized sense of guilt over harm, rather than simply the consequences to him of public disclosure.

CONCLUSIONS

The continuum from admission with justification to admission with guilt is a continuum from more pathological to less. It is not true, however, that offenders jump from one end of the continuum to the other. Typically, offenders either begin with an admission with justification, with physical denial, with psychological denial, or with minimizing the extent of the behavior. If an offender begins with psychological denial, he then typically proceeds to minimizing the extent of the behavior. Whatever the initial stance, offenders rarely move from their initial stance to a full admission with responsibility and guilt in one step. From the point of entry, they will often go through the progression described in the chart. From minimizing they will admit the extent of the behavior, but deny the seriousness of it and the need for treatment. Through therapy, they will begin to accept the seriousness, but externalize responsibility. Finally they will admit the offenses and the seriousness of the behaviors and assume the responsibility for them.

Far from being a binary concept, denial is a complex, multifaceted phenomenon that must be examined carefully in order to assess offenders' progress accurately and to help them move towards full awareness of and responsibility for their behavior.

9

OFFENDER TREATMENT

The usual manner of presenting information on assessment and treatment is to begin with assessment, since this will in practice precede treatment. However this book has reversed the usual order of presentation because decisions regarding treatment techniques and assessment tools cannot be made independently. Insight-oriented treatment will require projectives for assessing intrapsychic dynamics. Behavioral therapy will necessitate the measurement of frequency, duration, and antecedents to specified behaviors. A cognitive program will rely on the assessment of attitudes and beliefs. Therapists treating sex offenders must be clear regarding treatment components in order to choose their tools wisely. This chapter will therefore outline effective treatment techniques for reducing the likelihood of recidivism in child sex offenders. It will be followed by a discussion of one particularly promising technique, relapse prevention; later chapters will address monitoring progress by sex offenders and, finally, methods of assessing them.

An array of good programs currently exist that treat sex offenders. While each program has its own integrity and coherence, there is little reason why a new program cannot be a hybrid, attempting to take the best of each. The techniques employed can be considered complementary rather than contradictory. Programs that specialize in treating pedophiles tend to favor behavioral techniques and group therapy, although the emphasis may vary. Programs that treat only incest offenders often rely exclusively on family therapy. In fact, however, most programs will treat both incest and extrafamilial offenders. Few programs have the resources to treat the two groups separately, and there is no adequate theoretical reason why they should do so. The techniques described in this section have been taken from both types of programs and include group therapy, behavioral treatment, and family therapy. They are recommended for both incest and extrafamilial offenders, and should be tailored to the individual's needs.

Family therapy, group therapy, and behavioral therapy all address different types of problems. Family therapy addresses the nonsexual problems that offenders so often flee from by sexually acting out. Group therapy addresses particularly cognitive distortions. It breaks down the isolation characteristic of offenders, destroys the secrecy, and increases their compliance with all parts of the program. Behavioral therapy decreases deviant arousal patterns and gives offenders tools for self-control. All offenders will require group therapy; most will require behavioral; some will require family therapy. A comprehensive program should have all three available.

GROUP THERAPY

The group therapy outlined in this book is patterned after that of Northwest Treatment Associates of Seattle, Washington, a highly successful specialized program for the treatment of sex offenders. Northwest has been in existence since 1977 and consists of 5 therapists treating approximately 200 offenders at any given time.

Groups can contain between 12 and 16 offenders and regularly meet for two hours weekly. Groups should be held at night, if possible, to avoid interference with work. They should begin on time, and both tardiness and/or absence should be confronted strongly. Repeated tardiness and/or absence from the group should be treated as indicating a poor attitude toward treatment that could result in termination from the program.

Groups should be heterogeneous: Exhibitionists, rapists, child molesters, and other sexually deviant individuals may all be placed in the same group. Homogeneous groups are not only impractical in most rural areas, since few rural settings have enough of any one category for a group, but they also function less well. Pedophiles may see the cognitive distortions that rapists and exhibitionists use better than those of other pedophiles. Rapists may be very clear that child molesting is harmful for children. By mixing offenders there is less risk that offenders will collude with each other regarding attitudes and beliefs they hold in common.

Each group session begins with a "layout." A full layout consists of the following:

(1) person's name
(2) a statement of acknowledgment for the sexual offense: "I am a sex offender"
(3) a reciting of all molestations
(4) a statement of what the individual feels he is capable of in terms of escalating molestations
(5) a reciting of deviant impulses the previous week
(6) a statement about how deviant impulses were handled
(7) a statement of the number of times the individual masturbated and whether to appropriate or inappropriate fantasies
(8) a statement of current sexual activity
(9) what the individual would like on the agenda for that evening

An example might be as follows:

> My name is John Doe. I am a sex offender. I molested my daughter for a period of 6 years. I raped her with my finger and my penis. I also molested my son for a period of two years. I raped him in the anus. I am capable of physically assaulting a child for sex. Deviant impulses— I saw a young boy on the street this week and found myself staring at his buttocks. I punished the impulse with a rubber band (snapping a rubber band on his wrist). I masturbated three times this week, all to appropriate fantasies. I had sex with Judy one time this week. This evening I would like to discuss my autobiography.

Each offender goes through the same layout. While this description sounds time consuming, the time involved can be kept to a minimum in two ways: First, it is the staff facilitator's responsibility to keep the group moving. It is entirely appropriate to tell a member to speed it up, or even to stop an offender who is taking too long. Members can be told point blank to "Come on, let's put some energy into the group. This is too slow. Speed it up."

Second, a full layout does not have to be done every time. It is always useful when there is a visitor or when the group is just beginning. It can be done intermittently at other times, but not necessarily every week. When it is not done, a "partial layout" may be used. In a partial layout, the recitation of offenses, which unfortunately can be quite long, and the statement regarding what the offender is capable of, are omitted. The individual gives his name, acknowledges his deviancy, then goes on to current deviant impulses and the rest of the layout.

Following the layout, the peer leader from the previous week describes what happened in last week's session. Nominations are then accepted for this week's leader. There must be at least two nominations. Each person nominated describes what he would do if elected that week. Discussion follows and a vote. The decision must be unanimous. This often takes a couple of quick rounds, with some members changing their vote after the initial discussion.

The peer leader then conducts the rest of the meeting. However, the staff facilitator is by no means silent. He or she often interjects

(1) to make process comments	"What was helpful about that comment?"
(2) to confront rationalizations and distortions	"What did you do? You just made an excuse."
(3) to hold the peer leader accountable for the progress of the group	"You as the leader set the tone. Let's get going."
(4) to press the group to work harder	"You might be the only one that sees something that keeps a child from being raped."

The group must be confrontive, since the primary purposes of the group are not only to identify and confront cognitive distortions, rationalizations, and excuses for offending, but to signal behaviors that are part of the pattern of reoffending early enough that they may be interrupted before the offender "goes to outlet," that is, reoffends.

The use of language becomes key in the business of detecting hidden agendas and cognitive distortions. Language that minimizes the offense should not be tolerated. Offenders should not be allowed to say they "had intercourse with"; instead they should be required to say, "I raped so and so with my finger, and with my penis."

The staff facilitator and the group members must carefully

scrutinize statements by offenders for their real intent. For example, in one group an offender reported his meeting with his daughter to the group. He told the daughter that he could not come home because his wife did not trust him. The group appropriately pointed out to him that he was not allowed home because he had raped his daughter, not because his wife "did not trust" him; the real import of his statement, the group demonstrated, was to drive a wedge between the mother and the daughter by externalizing the blame for his not being home onto his wife.

In another group, an offender reported that, after discussing it with his wife, he had decided to contact all his previous victims (male children) to inform them that they might have been exposed to AIDS. The offender, interestingly, did not have AIDS. While he lauded this at the time as a humanitarian gesture, reflection would suggest that, given his own negative test for AIDS, his desire to contact his victims was a ploy to get back in contact with them and should be addressed in the group as such.

New members to the groups are considered "candidates" for the group. On their first evening in the group, each man in the group stands up, faces the new candidate and tells him what sexual offenses he has committed. The group then asks the new candidate his offenses. While typical minimizing or denying is met with justifiable skepticism, the new recruit is confronted that evening. He is given several weeks' grace to adjust to the group; then the group asks him again.

Candidates remain candidates for several months before they are put forth for group membership. In that time they have a chance to learn the rules and norms for the group: to admit total responsibility for the offenses; to talk about previous offenses; to describe deviant masturbatory fantasies; to be helpful to other members of the group in their attempts to change; to fulfill their homework assignments, and to follow the rules of the program. When a candidate feels he has met these requirements and is ready to become a member of the group, he applies to the group. After the group discusses the merits of his candidacy, he stands up and approaches each individual in the group from the least assertive to the most assertive (in his opinion) to ask each one for any comments and for his vote. Only members can vote. The vote must be unanimous for him to be admitted; furthermore, staff may override even a unanimous decision of the group.

A benefit of membership is higher status in the group—a

significant benefit in light of the low self-esteem of many sex offenders. In addition, no one can be considered either for reunification with his family and certainly not for graduation until he is a group member.

Group Assignments

Much of the work in a sex offender group is done outside the group. Assignments multiply the therapeutic time by allowing the offender to work on his problems while not in the group. The following group assignments[1] were developed and are utilized by Northwest Treatment Associates:

 (1) sexual autobiography
 (2) index cards (8)
 (3) incentives (40)
 (4) addiction list
 (5) discovery report
 (6) victim reminders (25)
 (7) empathy paper
 (8) reoffense essay
 (9) victim agency
(10) forty adults
(11) chronology
(12) offense questionnaire
(13) bibliography
(14) impact assignment
(15) relationships
(16) questions victims ask
(17) controls
(18) group therapy examination

In addition to the assignments, each candidate should have a list of rules and regulations promulgated specifically for him. All candidates should be required to be drug free. In incest cases offenders should be routinely mandated to leave the home (rather than have the child leave the home). If the spouse objects to this, she should be told that this is unquestionably the shortest route to reunification of the family.

Other rules are individualized and are designed to minimize the possibility of reoffense. For example, a flasher who exhibits from his car may be required only to use his car to go to and from work. He may be forbidden to drive with no destination. He may be required to carpool or to have some one with him in the car at all times. He may be obligated to put his name and address on the outside of his car or on his jogging shirt if he flashes while jogging. Activities that were associated with the offense are often forbidden. An individual who offended while his wife was shopping every Friday night might find himself doing the shopping alone. An individual who offended while his wife worked on Saturday morning might be required to be absent from the house on Saturday morning and to be in some verifiable place.

BEHAVIORAL THERAPY

The chief goal of behavioral therapy is to decrease deviant arousal. This must be done as quickly as possible to reduce the chance of reoffense. While other parts of the program may increase the offender's desire not to reoffend, may clarify for him the error in his thinking, and may point out to him the chain of events that leads to sexually acting out behavior, it is the strength of his basic urge for sexual contact with children, however, that will have a major impact on whether or not he reoffends. Behavioral therapy is designed to decrease that urge to the point where it is manageable, and contains several components:

Boredom Tapes

These are homework assignments designed to reduce deviant arousal by satiation. Most sex offenders have a long history of masturbating to deviant fantasies, i.e., fantasies of sexual activity with children. The pleasure derived from masturbation reinforces and strengthens the sexual impulses toward children and increases the likelihood of molestation. However, the offender's behavior, i.e., masturbating to deviant fantasies, can be used to have the opposite effect. This is done by requiring the offender to masturbate to a deviant fantasy for long periods of time post orgasm, thus causing the fantasy to lose its erotic charge through habituation. While the procedure does not involve punishment, nor even behaviors outside the offender's usual repertoire, it is a difficult assignment for most offenders, since the exercise rapidly becomes significantly boring.

The first step is for the offender and his therapist to decide on an *appropriate* sexual fantasy. This fantasy must involve consenting sex activity between adults of whichever sex the offender chooses. In addition, it must include some expressions of caring and warmth, and some attention to the sexual needs of the partner. The therapist must carefully monitor the offender's "appropriate" fantasy, since, without guidance, child molesters sometimes produce "appropriate" fantasies that are more like rape than consenting sexuality. Having agreed on an appropriate fantasy, the offender then masturbates to that fantasy in the privacy of his home until orgasm or, failing orgasm, for a specified number of minutes, usually 10 or under. He tape-records the fantasy while masturbating. A check on whether or not the offender is masturbating is provided by the presence of sounds on the tape produced by the lubrication. Tapes without any sounds should not be accepted, since offenders often try to circumvent the assignment by not masturbating.

After masturbating to the appropriate fantasy, the offender turns the tape over and masturbates for another 45 minutes to deviant fantasies that he has previously entertained. These fantasies, again, are discussed with his therapist. They should represent behaviors he has actually engaged in, and whenever possible, fantasies he has previously utilized in masturbation. The offender repeats one section of the deviant fantasy continually until all sexual interest is satiated, then goes to the next. The deviant fantasy begins early in the chain of events and includes his emotional state, any environmental stresses, and typical thoughts occurring at the beginning of the chain. (Appendix E contains the instructions and the Boredom Tape Report form given to offenders by Northwest Treatment Associates.)

Staff must decide on an individual basis the number of boredom tapes an individual must make. An average amount is often 2-3 tapes per week for a period of 8 weeks, *after the first tape done correctly.* Tapes are spot-checked by the staff. Tapes that have gaps, that show inappropriate "appropriate" fantasies, that show minimal attention to the deviant fantasies, or that contain no evidence that masturbation was actually taking place are not accepted. Most offenders become motivated to produce acceptable tapes, since only acceptable tapes count toward fulfilling the required number.

Covert Sensitization/Covert Positive Reinforcement

These involve pairing the following:

chain of events leading to outlet----------aversive imagery
chain of events----interruption-------reward scene

The chain of events is one the therapist and client have previously developed that begin with early antecedents of the outlet behavior; e.g., a particular mood, environmental stress, time of day, activity, and so forth. An offender, for example, may find that his change of events begins with anger: a misunderstanding with his boss, anger at his wife, or perhaps with boredom: a rainy Saturday morning when he cannot work outside. The initial emotion may lead to thoughts that he might just see if his daughter would like to go for a ride with him, or, if he is an extrafamilial offender, that a neighborhood child might like to go to a ball game. At this point the offender prior to treatment might not have admitted to himself his ultimate intent, i.e., to molest a child. (See Chapter 10 for a more in-depth discussion of offense antecedents.) These early antecedents (or some aspect of them) are described on tape and then paired with aversive imagery.

The aversive imagery has also been previously elaborated with the therapist, both by utilizing a Composite Fear Inventory (Annon, 1973) and discussing with offenders particularly painful and frightening events in their own lives—surgery, near-drownings, and so forth. The offender will describe on tape some such extremely aversive experience that is likely to elicit negative emotions such as repulsion, disgust, or fear. The sequence thus far might be as follows:

It is early on a Saturday morning. I didn't get called to go into work again. My wife is busy cleaning the house. I don't have anything to do. I wanted to work on the car, but it's raining. I'm getting that caged feeling. I just need to do something. I see Susie playing with her dolls. She's bending over to pick them up and I see her little round buns. They look so little and soft through her shorts. She shouldn't be there playing by herself. A father should play with his daughter. I think I'll see if she wants to go for a ride with me. Yes, that's exactly what I'll do. We could go for a ride down to the lake.

I start to ask her to go with me to the lake. I try to say the words. I'm having trouble breathing. I'm beginning to have an asthma attack just like when I was child. I can't breathe. I can't breathe. I don't have any medicine. My wife is too far away to hear me.

The intent is to pair the attempt to initiate abusive behavior with negative thoughts and feelings that are disquieting so that the negative thoughts and feelings will eventually automatically arise whenever the offender begins the chain of events leading to outlet.

The second category is to pair the chain of events with a self-initiated interruption scene, followed by a reward scene. This is an attempt to train the offender to exit the risky situation. Interruption scenes should be realistic rather than magical; for example, a tape might feature an offender *leaving* a room where he is alone with a child while having deviant impulses rather than staying and not offending. In the example cited above, the offender might follow his description of his desire to invite the child to go for a ride by saying,

That's crazy. If I invite her to go to the lake, I know I'll end up molesting her again. I do need to get out of the house. I'll call up Jack and see if he wants to go fishing. If I'm with someone today, I can't change my mind and come back for her, or try to find anyone else.

Reward scenes can be cognitive ("By God, I made it. I can be in control"); social ("I'm home with my wife and family. I'm not afraid of anyone knocking on the door with something to tell them. I don't have anything to hide"); or material ("I'm having dinner in a restaurant eating this incredible delicious steak and thinking 'no more prison food for me'"). In the example above of the offender and the lake, the offender might conclude the tape with:

It's 7 o'clock. Jack and I are back from the lake. We caught a bunch of fish. Donna is cooking them up for dinner. I'm realizing how good I feel. I'm not afraid. If I'd taken Susie to the lake, I'd be in a panic now, fearful she'd tell, worrying about jail, feeling lousy. I'm feeling terrific.

The therapist makes the first tapes as a model for the offender. It is easy to do covert sensitization tapes badly by producing cognitive descriptions of events that have little emotional impact on the offender. Tapes should be as vivid and speak as specifically as possible to that offender's chain of events and to that offender's fears. The more graphic they are the better. For better or worse, some individuals show a remarkable ability to mimic a sex offender's thought processes. Tapes made by such individuals are unquestionably powerful. Roger Wolfe produced the following example of the aversive portion of a covert sensitization tape as quoted in Knopp (1984, p. 94).

> You are restless. It is about three o'clock in the morning and you cannot sleep. You tell yourself you are going to go to the bathroom. You get up, you go to the bathroom, you urinate, and you continue to stand there. You are thinking, "Little Sally is sleeping in the room next door." You tell yourself, "Maybe I'd better check on her just to see if she kicked her covers off or something." As you are thinking that, you kind of put your hand down on your penis and you feel your excitement. You tell yourself, "She is sound asleep—she won't know if I was in there or not." You go up to her door, telling yourself she is sound asleep and you are just going to check on her, feeling sexual excitement, thinking about touching her, thinking you will just slip up her nightgown a little bit and maybe just look at her, and getting more excited. You are thinking about doing that, with your hand on the doorknob, getting really excited now, really turned on, and you gently, carefully, being really quiet, open that door, you open that door thinking about touching her . . . and you suddenly realize there is something on the floor. There is something moving on the floor in the bedroom. My God, my God, you say it is a snake! There is more than one. There are creepy, crawly snakes all over and you can see their little forked tongues, see their beady eyes. They are moving toward you. You are just terrified standing there, you want to run, but you are just scared. A cold chill runs up and down your body. Your body gets tight. They are moving toward you. God, these cold slimy snakes are moving toward you. One of them is on your toe now.

Covert sensitization is probably best begun when the client is in a relaxed state. Offenders take the tapes home to listen to as homework assignments for a set period of time (e.g., 40 minutes/day). Tapes are changed on a regular basis (e.g., weekly) and later tapes are made by the offenders but spot checked by the staff. The number of weeks is determined individually by the client's therapist, but 10 is probably an average figure.

SOCIAL SKILLS TRAINING

It is not enough to reduce an offender's deviant arousal pattern. Many offenders have poor social and sexual skills with adults, and have sometimes chosen children because they seem less threatening. Abel et al. (1985) found that 40.8% of child molesters as well as 46.9% of rapists had poor social skills. Given the social and sexual nature of human beings, an offender who is unable to meet his social and sexual needs with adults will almost invariably relapse to meeting those needs with children. The finest behavioral modification program to decrease deviant arousal will fail to prevent relapse unless the offender's ability to meet his needs in appropriate ways finds some success. Social and communication skills are key to the offender's ability to initiate and maintain adult relationships.

Social skills training is one area where no therapist should ever have to invent his own curriculum. Social skills packages have been produced for anyone with social skills deficits; some have been created especially for sex offenders. Unlike most curricula in this area, it is not clear that the packages adapted for sex offenders are qualitatively better than social skills packages in general. Social skills deficits are just that, and the deficits that characterize offenders—not knowing how to start conversations, not knowing what to talk about, being unable to maintain eye contact, either being too self-disclosing or totally nondisclosing are generic deficits. Thus a therapist can comfortably choose either a program designed for sex offenders (Abel, Becker, Cunningham-Rathner, Rouleau, Kaplan, & Reich, 1984) or a generic social skills training package (Curran & Monti, 1982). The former is a somewhat limited curriculum and consists of five sessions only, whereas the latter has more curricula, although it has not been tailored to sex offenders.

ASSERTIVENESS TRAINING

Child sex offenders are often either self-effacing or aggressive, but rarely assertive. Abel et al. (1985) found that 40.8% of child molesters had deficits in assertiveness. Self-effacing offenders often identify with and relate to children rather than adults, by whom they are intimidated. Even aggressive offenders are surprisingly unassertive. Abel et al. (1985) reported 46.9% of rapists in their study to be unassertive. The style of aggressive offenders is often to erupt angrily in a way that protects them from any negotiation. Increasing the assertiveness of either group increases the chance that they can interact with adults meaningfully.

The 1984 Abel et al. treatment manual includes 5 sessions of assertiveness training with sex offenders. Again, this is a limited but careful program. Offenders are required to read *Your Perfect Right* (Alberti & Emmons, 1982). Assignments, which are included in the Abel et al. manual, are taken from the Alberti and Emmons book. Those therapists wanting a more extensive assertiveness training program may derive additional exercises and assignments from *Your Perfect Right.*

SEX EDUCATION

While some offenders may lack factual information about sexuality, more common deficits occur in the area of opinions and attitudes concerning sexuality. Therefore a good treatment program will not stress simply the plumbing but values as well. The Abel et al. treatment manual cited above does a particularly effective job in this area. Their program begins by asking offenders to take a sexual myth test anonymously (included in their appendix). The tests are then given to other offenders, and group members then take turns reading the answers, and commenting on them. Other sessions focus on male and female anatomy, on what is "normal" and what is not, on questions group members have about sexual dysfunction, and on sexual communication. Materials include sex education slides (Crooks & Baur, 1987) as well as a text (Strong, Wilson, Robbins, & Johns, 1981) that is provided to each group member. While the Abel et al. program is generally excellent, the short-comings of the text for homework assignments are its language and technical approach. There will certainly be some offenders whose reading levels are not sufficient; in those cases the slides and lectures may be more informative.

Even the slides, however, cover more than most offenders (and most instructors) want to know about the mechanics of sexuality. Therapists may find it judicious to eliminate certain of the complicated charts for many groups. The advantage of the slides is that it is very easy to eliminate unneeded material and concentrate on the anatomical slides and those depicting sexual activity. The slides have a particularly good set of venereal disease photographs, although neither the slides nor the text are recent enough to include material regarding AIDS. A second disadvantage is that the slides do not include any photographs of birth control devices. It is advisable to supplement the material on birth control in the text with actual devices brought into the class.

An obvious source of information regarding sex education is Planned Parenthood, and some sex offender treatment programs have invited Planned Parenthood to teach the section on sex education directly. The advantage of this approach is that it brings experts in the area to the offenders, and while sex offender therapists routinely have some competence in the area of sex education, few consider themselves expert. The disadvantage, however, revolves around the issue of whether or not offenders (a particularly untrusting group of people) will trust an outside person with their own myths and confusions regarding sexuality. A second concern is that many experts in sex education have not had very much experience with sex offenders, and their particular distortions and rationalizations. An alternative is for the therapist to follow a Planned Parenthood curriculum, but conduct the course independently. A local Planned Parenthood Center can usually furnish appropriate curriculum. The preference of the therapist and the availability of local resources are likely to be the deciding factors.

COGNITIVE RESTRUCTURING

A significant barrier to recognizing and neutralizing sexual deviancy is the extent to which the offender rationalizes and defends his behavior. As one offender said, "There's nothing wrong with what I did. It's just illegal, that's all. But there's nothing wrong with it." Such cognitive distortions may wax and wane with the strength of the deviant urges. An offender not feeling any particular impulse to offend at the moment, may be somewhat open to considering that sex offenses against children are harmful to them. However, while feeling a desire to molest a particular child, he may find himself thinking. "It really doesn't do any harm. If he does what I tell him to, that means he wants it." Such thoughts can be considered "releasers," which allow deviant urges to be acted on. Without such rationalizations the offender may have some capacity to resist his deviant attraction and to seek help when his own coping mechanisms fail. With such rationalizations, the offender's ability to successfully resist is undermined. Effective treatment programs, therefore, pay considerable attention to the issue of cognitive distortions. Identifying and effectively challenging cognitive distortions in a neutral setting, as well as teaching the offender how to identify and challenge distortions while under the influence of deviant urges, is an aspect of treatment that cannot be ignored.

Assessment of cognitive distortions may be done with a cognitive distortions scale (for pedophilic attitudes) and a rape myth scale (for rapist attitudes). Details are described in Chapter 12, on assessment. These are difficult tests to fake, since offenders often have convinced themselves of the truthfulness of their distortions. With these tests the therapist can determine which rationalizations the offender believes and utilizes. It is useful also to listen for and record those additional rationalizations and distortions that arise during the course of therapy. These can be added to the tests for future use and can also be utilized in work with the offender.

It is rarely effective for an individual therapist to use arguments against cognitive distortions as a therapeutic technique, although it is entirely appropriate for the therapist to make it clear she does not in any sense agree with them. Trying, however, to argue down an offender is only likely to result in the offender becoming more defensive about his beliefs and more hostile toward authority. Groups appear to have more success. Peers may and should challenge rationalizations for such behavior, and their challenges can be facilitated and encouraged by the group leader.

Equally effective is an exercise in which the offender is asked to challenge rationalizations presented by either the individual therapist or a group member. The offender is to imagine that the other party is about to molest a relative of the offender. Offenders can produce numerous objections to cognitive distortions if they are not producing them. In the role play, of course, the rationalizing party is careful to present arguments to which the offender actually subscribes.

To deal with the problem of offenders "forgetting" appropriate ways of thinking and falling back into cognitive distortions under the press of deviant attractions, many programs ask offenders to write down on index cards a given distortion or rationalization and then a counter thought. An example would be the following:

> Why not look at his buttocks on the street. I'm not doing any harm. He doesn't even know I'm looking. I don't have to go any further. I know I can handle it.

> Stop! That's the kind of thing you always say when you're heading down the road to outlet. First you stare at the kid, then you find yourself fantasizing about having sex with him, and the next thing

you're trying to start a conversation. You can't handle it and you know it. You've worked too hard and come too far to slip back now. Time to go in a store and do a little window shopping until that kid is far away.

Offenders are asked to carry such cards with them and read them at stressful moments or when they find themselves recognizing a cognitive distortion.

RELAPSE PREVENTION

Sexual deviancy can be conceptualized as an addictive behavior that responds to treatment techniques similar to those used with other addictive disorders. The focus of such treatments is neither to "cure" the offender nor to attempt to remove from his psyche all temptation to reoffend. Rather, it is to teach him to manage and cope with ongoing temptation, which may wax and wane in severity in response to both external and internal stressors. Chapter 10 will deal in detail with the theoretical rationale behind this view and with treatment considerations.

Group Versus Individual Therapy

Some aspects of offender treatment appear to lend themselves to either group or individual treatment. Behavioral therapy, particularly, has been successfully conducted on an individual basis (Northwest Treatment) and on a group basis (New York Psychiatric Institute). Likewise, relapse prevention and cognitive restructuring may all be done in individual or group work. Social skills and assertiveness training may be easier in a group because of the ready availability of role players but may nonetheless be used individually as well. The reader conscious of program costs and limited resources might well wonder why individual therapy would even be considered if group therapy appears to be possible. Rural areas, particularly, with a limited number of trained therapists, with major transportation difficulties, and with offenders who may not have the resources for several types of therapy per week might well consider conducting the behavioral treatment in a group setting. However, the difficulties with conducting behavioral therapy in a group setting are as follows:

(1) A large group (12 to 16) following the structure described above would have difficulty finding time to conduct behavioral therapy in a group. The assignments and agendas set by the individual group members easily take the 2 hours allotted per week.

(2) Group members are not likely to progress at the same rate. This appears to be the major weakness of lock-step group programs that allot a specific number of weeks to, for example, boredom tapes. It is not uncommon for an offender to act passive aggressively for the entire number of weeks allotted to that component and to avoid producing a single usable tape.

The major advantages of individual therapy are as follows:

(1) A therapist can get to know an offender better if some individual time is scheduled than if the therapist's only contact with the offender is in a group setting. In addition to behavioral therapy, relapse prevention work (to be described below) and individual progress may be monitored.

(2) In programs that employ individual therapy in conjunction with group therapy, the norm is for the group therapist and the individual therapist to be different people. This allows more than one therapist to have contact with the offender and decreases the chance that an offender will "con" a particular therapist.

(3) In individual therapy failing to do or doing badly a behavioral assignment yields no rewards. The offender has to complete a certain number of assignments after the first one is accepted as correct—before he moves on. This may mean, for example, that an individual spends 16 weeks on boredom tapes instead of 8. While some individualization can take place in a group setting, individualization is more easily accomplished in a one-to-one setting.

Resources differ too much for one to be able to develop one hard and fast structure for all sex offender programs. While a combination of group and individual therapy offers the most intensive program, other structures are possible when either a lack of resources or of trained therapists renders impossible an individual therapist for every offender. This book concentrates on describing components that should be present in some fashion in order to treat sex offenders successfully. The two most effective structures are as follows:

(1) group therapy   2 hrs/wk   confrontation model
    12-16 members

individual	1 hr/wk	behavior therapy relapse prevention monitoring
(2) group therapy 12-16 members	2 hrs/wk	confrontation model
small groups	1-2 hrs/wk	behavioral therapy relapse prevention monitoring
case manager	1 hr/several weeks	

SEQUENCE OF TREATMENT

While a variety of treatment techniques are necessary, their sequence affords latitude, within limits. Those treatment techniques that are the most effective in controlling the behavior in the short run should be introduced first to reduce the chance of reoffense. Thus, boredom tapes are normally one of the first techniques introduced, since they strike at what is often the underlying motivation for offenses, a deviant arousal pattern. Other techniques, such as sex education, can be introduced later.

It is also worth noting that the New York Psychiatric Institute's Sexual Behavior Clinic has found that components of the program that deal with a deviant arousal pattern, such as covert sensitization and boredom tapes, must be introduced first if they were to be introduced at all. Offenders in their clinic were most willing to discuss a deviant arousal pattern and methods to control it when they first entered treatment. If the therapists ignored the issue, offenders were unwilling to reopen it later. The authors also recommended that covert sensitization precede masturbatory reconditioning, as it proved less stressful as an introduction to behavioral techniques (Abel et al., 1984).

In the end, each therapist must order this material as she finds best. It is the author's recommendation to work within a group/individual therapy mode. Ideally, the group begins with boredom tapes, and the individual sessions with relapse prevention. It is useful in the individual sessions to include the spouse. It is very important for her to be aware of the offender's risk factors, as she may be more able than he to detect when he is beginning to slip into his old patterns.

He's in that mood again, and I'm scared. I haven't seen him like this for months, not since it all came out. He's real distant and angry and nothing anybody says is right. I want him to come in and see you. Don't worry. I'll get him there.

Secondly, the spouse can be especially effective in providing information that allows the therapist to discover the offender's chain of events that lead to the offense. She is in a unique position to keep him honest, particularly about those issues in which self-report is known to be unreliable.

"No, I know, dear, you always say you started drinking after Vietnam, but if you remember, you were drinking quite a lot before you left."

With the spouse already involved in the sessions, it is a short step to begin marriage counseling, when that becomes appropriate. After the chain of events has been developed and relapse prevention begun, after the deviant arousal pattern has been addressed via boredom tapes and aversive imagery, it becomes appropriate to teach the offender how to solve the nonsexual problems that he may have avoided facing by sexual acting out. At that point individual sessions may be permitted to alternate weeks with marital, and later, family therapy. By then considerable rapport has often been built with the spouse who understands the goals and process of therapy, and, on many occasions, sees herself as an ally of the therapeutic process.

CONCLUSIONS

In this description of treatment techniques for offenders there has been little reference to helping the offender develop insight into the causes of his behavior. This is because the development of insight has not been demonstrated, by itself, to decrease sexual acting out, even as it has not been shown to control other addictive behaviors. Interestingly, even sex offenders have sometimes commented on this. Field and Williams (1970) reported that their offenders questioned whether, even if a psychoanalytic explanation "were understood and accepted, this knowledge alone would give to him sufficient control over his impulses to avoid the next offense" (p. 29). They termed the results of psychoanalytic treatment with such offenders "disappointing."

The focus on behavioral controls does not mean that either emotion or cognition are ignored in the push to change inappropriate sexual behavior. The emotional states that precede and that occur during the offense are carefully attended to as well as the cognitions that release the behavior at the time and justify it afterwards. Nor is it inappropriate at times to explore with an offender the origins of his need for power and control over children, or of his anger. By itself, however, without behavioral tools to control the deviant urges, such insight-oriented therapy is unlikely to be effective. The insight-oriented therapist who wishes to treat sex offenders must accept the fact that compulsive behaviors respond first and foremost to cognitive/behavioral techniques. Insight-oriented therapies when used alone will produce, in Roger Wolfe's words, "sex offenders with insight."[2]

NOTES

1. See Appendix D for the complete assignments.
2. Personal communication, January, 1986.

10

RELAPSE PREVENTION
A Method of Enhancing Maintenance of Change in Sex Offenders

William D. Pithers, Kennon M. Kashima,
Georgia F. Cumming, and Linda S. Beal

Once upon a time not so very long ago, in a small New England settlement, a group of religiously devout citizens was dismayed to discover, living in their midst, a secret society of witches. The upstanding townspeople felt appalled by the unpredictable spasms that wrested all semblance of self-control from the afflicted. These devout settlers could not understand, despite their best intentions to do so, the etiology responsible for transforming a good townsperson into someone who fell writhing on the ground, uttering the most unearthly guttural sounds, eyes turned backward in the head. One conclusion was patently clear to the unafflicted—"these witches are vastly different from the rest of us." Finally, in their struggle to understand these nonsensical actions, the sound citizens fell upon the explanation that witches were demon-possessed people who had allowed their religious zeal to ebb.

In an effort to free witches from demon possession and also reduce their own distress at the presence of these troubling people in their community, the settlers devised an unfailing and permanent cure— burning at the stake. Although, from the witches' perspective, immolation could hardly be viewed as a reasonable cure, no relapses occurred and the anxiety of the townspeople was effectively diminished.

Over time, we learned more about the nature of the witches' affliction and, in doing so, devised a treatment that more humanely controls their disorder—Dilantin. For the witches of Salem, Massachusetts were not really demon possessed. They were epileptic.

Today's society struggles to understand the incomprehensible actions of sexual offenders. Failing to achieve satisfactory explanations, we react emotionally and fearfully, invoking an account often heard under similar circumstances historically—"these people (sex offenders) are vastly different from the rest of us." Although we do not currently burn sex offenders at the stake, a significant portion of society would seek to remove the sexual aggressor from society permanently.

Sentencing sexual offenders to life in a penitentiary without possibility of parole certainly precludes the potential of relapse. However, such an alternative would be prohibitively expensive and presupposes a uniformity myth that all sexual offenders are similar in the degree of risk they pose to the community. Although sexual aggressors who have murdered or who have recidivated on numerous occasions may warrant life sentences, empirical evidence indicates that many sex offenders can learn, through effective treatment, to control their disorder. Although our understanding of sexual offenders remains rudimentary, increasingly efficacious treatments are being devised. One of these innovative interventions may be Relapse Prevention—a cognitive-behavioral model for enhancing maintenance of change in addictive behaviors.

SEXUAL AGGRESSION: AN ADDICTIVE PROCESS?

Until recently, problem behaviors such as alcoholism, drug abuse, smoking, and compulsive gambling were viewed as independent clinical syndromes. More recently, research has demonstrated that these seemingly diverse problems actually have a great deal in common. Miller (1980) has delineated commonalities identified in addictive, or "compulsive," behaviors. Among the common characteristics of addictive behaviors are: (1) immediate acquisition of short-term satisfaction at the expense of delayed negative consequences, (2) high personal and social costs, (3) an absence of any treatment with proven superior effectiveness, (4) the lack of a single, empirically validated etiology, and (5) the difficulty inherent in transferring initial behavioral changes occurring during treatment into enduring changes after termination. One might also argue that individuals suffering compulsive behavioral disorders are their own worst enemies, frequently setting up circumstances under which relapses occur.

On the basis of these factors, one may consider whether sexually aggressive acts, such as rape or child molestation, can be considered addictive, or compulsive, behaviors. Socially unacceptable sexual acts yield immediate short-term satisfaction for the offender in the form of an explosive release of hostile feelings and decreased tension, but the long-term consequences are profoundly negative and tension inducing. Sexual aggression clearly results in excessive personal and social costs. No treatment model has demonstrated superior efficacy with sexual aggressors. A widely accepted etiology of these disorders has yet to be formulated. Although many treatment programs have been found to induce short-term behavioral changes, prolonged maintenance of change remains relatively unexplored. Rape and child molestation represent prototypes of socially unacceptable behaviors; people who indulge in these behaviors are viewed with contempt by most of society and many professional therapists.

Historically, alcoholics and other drug addicts were once viewed as morally bankrupt. Society formerly incarcerated these individuals for being unredeemably depraved. The moralistic view of addictive behaviors was prevalent throughout the nineteenth century in the United States, reaching its zenith during prohibition (Cummings, Gordon, & Marlatt, 1980; Tongue & Blair, 1975). Even psychiatric nosology implicitly identified individuals with addictive behaviors as being resistant to change by classifying them as personality disorders in the second edition of the Diagnostic and Statistical Manual of Mental Disorders (DSM-II) (American Psychiatric Association, 1968).

It is important to note that as treatments have evolved that offer a more favorable prognosis for addictive behaviors, social and professional attitudes toward these disorders have also changed. Rather than assigning negative personality attributes to substance abusers and incarcerating them, these individuals now are considered to have acquired maladaptive coping behaviors and they receive outpatient treatment. The most recent revision of the diagnostic nomenclature (DSM-III, American Psychiatric Association, 1980) reflects this changed attitude toward addictive behaviors. By removing these diagnoses from the treatment-resistant personality disorders and creating a new category of "Substance Use," the authors of DSM-III implicitly recognize that addictive behaviors are amenable to treatment (Miller, 1980).

Individuals who perform sexually aggressive behaviors currently tend to be viewed as morally bankrupt and refractory to treatment. Even a committee representing the psychiatric profession has advocated incarceration, rather than treatment, of sexually aggressive individuals (Group for the Advancement of Psychiatry, 1977). Perhaps the identification of treatment modalities offering improved prognosis for sexual aggressors will lead to conceptual changes similar to those evoked by the discovery of treatment with improved efficacy for other compulsive behavioral disorders. Specifically, some sexual aggressors, then, may be viewed as individuals requiring treatment, rather than (or in addition to) imprisonment. However, if it is too simplistic to assume that no sexually aggressive individual is worthy of treatment, it would be equally naive to maintain that all offenders deserve psychotherapy. Individuals who have a life-long history of antisocial acts, one of which was sexually aggressive, are not appropriate candidates for sex offender treatment. Individuals who have demonstrated a history of prosocial behavior, with the exception of their sexually aggressive acts, represent acceptable clients for therapy.

PRECURSORS TO RELAPSE

An intriguing pattern emerges when one examines the period of time between a "vow of abstinence" (e.g., smoking cessation, dieting, refraining from alcohol abuse) and the first "transgression" or lapse. In nearly all instances, the initial 90 days of abstinence pose an unusually high risk of relapse into the old behavior pattern. An early meta-analysis of relapse data revealed that nearly 66% of all relapses occur within the first 90 days after the end of treatment

(Hunt, Barnett, & Branch, 1971). The probability of relapse decreased markedly after that period.

Marlatt and Gordon (1980) observed that the traditional interpretation of the similarity in relapse rates across substances had been that the substances were equally addictive. They proposed an alternate conception of relapse rates that maintained that "there may be common behavioral and cognitive components associated with relapse, regardless of the particular 'addictive substance' involved" (p. 6). Analyzing the initial relapses of 311 clients (problem drinkers, smokers, heroin addicts, compulsive gamblers, and overeaters), three high-risk situations—negative emotional states, interpersonal conflict, and social pressure—were found to be the primary determinant of 71% of the relapses, regardless of the substance they abused (Cummings et al., 1980).

It is interesting to note that the first nine months after discharge is the period marked by the highest recidivism rate for sex offenders (Frisbie, 1969). The longer period prior to the relapse of sex offenders may be attributed to the more severe violations of social norms inherent in their acts and the greater penalties imposed for their behavior than for the relapse of a former smoker. Seldom has a former smoker been threatened with incarceration for resumption of this habit (although the smoker's friends may have been sorely tempted by the possibility).

Pithers, Buell, Kashima, Cumming, and Beal (1987) analyzed precursors to the offenses of 136 pedophiles and 64 rapists (see Tables 10.1 and 10.2). In contrast to the analysis performed with substance abusers, which examined the immediate precursor to relapses (Cummings et al., 1980), we looked at multiple determinants of sexual aggression in an effort to identify a relapse process occurring over a longer time. Since these subjects were incarcerated for criminal sexual acts prior to this analysis, the accuracy of retrospective accounts and self-reports is open to question. However, the similarity of results across the subject sample mitigates this concern. Of the subjects, 89% (177) reported experiencing strong emotional states prior to relapse. An intense anger that had been precipitated in a majority of cases by interpersonal conflict was recalled by 94% of the rapists (60). Pedophiles more frequently recalled having felt anxious (46%; n = 63) or depressed (38%; n = 52) generally as a consequence, or cause, of prolonged social disaffiliation. (Since many offenders reported experiencing more than one precursive negative emotion, the sum of individual precursors exceeds 100%.)

TABLE 10.1
Immediate Precursors to Sexual Aggression

Precursor	Rapists (%)	Pedophiles (%)
Anger		
at event	3	3
interpersonal conflict	3	4
generalized, global	88	32
Anger toward women	77	26
Anxiety	27	46
Assertive skills deficits	42	23
Boredom	45	28
Cognitive distortions	72	65
Compulsive overworking	0	8
Depression	3	38
Deviant sexual fantasies	17	51
Disordered sexual arousal pattern	69	57
Divorce	2	2
Driving car alone without destination	17	1
Emotionally inhibited/overcontrolled	58	51
Interpersonal dependence	30	48
Low self-esteem	56	61
Low victim empathy	61	71
Opportunity (e.g., finding a hitchhiker)	58	19
Peer pressure	2	3
Personal loss	6	14
Personality disorder	61	35
Photography as new hobby	0	4
Physical illness	14	6
Planning of sexual offense	28	73
Pornography use	2	7
Psychiatric hospitalization	0	7
Sexual knowledge deficit	45	52
Social anxiety	25	39
Social skills deficit	59	50
Substance use/abuse		
alcohol	42	23
other substances	14	7

In analyzing precursors, a common sequence of changes often occurred that ultimately led to a sexual offense. The first change in the relapse process from the client's typical functioning was affective. They referred to themselves as "feeling moody," "brooding," "not communicating," or "not being a good guy." The second alteration involved fantasies of performing the aberrant sex act. When asked why the fantasy involved sexual aggression rather than

TABLE 10.2
Early Precursors to Sexual Aggression

Precursor	Rapists (%)	Pedophiles (%)
Cognitive impairment (IQ < 80)	9	10
Divorce (more than 5 years before act)	14	15
Exposure to violent death of human or infrahuman	22	2
Familial chaos	86	49
Late sexual experience (older than 25 at initial activity)	0	4
Limited education (< grade 9 completed)	44	26
Maternal absence/neglect	41	29
More than one prior sex offense	14	17
More than one known victim	30	60
Parental marital discord	59	45
Paternal absence/neglect	59	54
Physically abused as a child	45	7
Pornography use (habitual)	14	33
Precocious sexuality (< 12 years at time of first act of penetration not considered abuse)	14	30
Prior arrest for nonsexual offense	44	15
Sexual anxiety	39	58
Sexual dysfunction	11	11
Sexual victimization prior to age 12	5	56
between ages 12 and 18	11	6
Use of female prostitutes	30	8

another form of aggression, one patient stated that he had regarded sexual behaviors as "a safe way to release hard feelings." Fantasies were converted into thoughts, often cognitive distortions or "thinking errors," in the third step of the relapse process. One patient recalled thinking of how his daughter was "getting to be a big girl now" and wondering "what she really looks like." Patients frequently devised rationalizations for their behaviors that minimized the effects of their soon-to-be-committed acts. One incest offender commented, "If she was going to learn how to do it, she needed to learn from someone who knew what he was doing." Cognitive distortions often involved the attribution of inaccurate properties to potential victims, effectively objectifying and dehumanizing women or ascribing adult characteristics to children. As the patients' fantasies and thoughts continued, they engaged in a process of passive planning, cognitively refining the circumstances that would permit commission of a sexual offense. Often, passive planning was accomplished during masturbatory fantasies. In the final step of the relapse process, their plan was manifested behaviorally. Minimal substance use was noted as an occasional immediate precursor to abuse, particularly among rapists.

In this relapse process, the earliest sign of increasing danger involved affect. The relapse process entailed a distinct sequence of functional alterations: affect fantasy thought (cognitive distortion) passive planning behavior. Thus the relapse processes of sexual offenders and other forms of compulsive behavior reveal identifiable precursors that may be addressed during treatment to enhance maintenance of change.

Many theorists propose that sexual offenses, particularly rapes, are "impulsive" acts. While many offenses may appear "impulsive" upon first inspection, we argue that a closer examination discovers a different conclusion. In our analysis of precursors to assaults (Pithers et al., 1987), more than half of all offenders appeared emotionally overcontrolled. Frequently these men left a hostile interaction without expressing their anger. Over time, as they brooded about the incident, their animosity grew. Some offenders in our sample had harbored hatred from a single event for a decade.

Although they failed to express anger at the appropriate moment, eventually their continual amplification of emotion led to an explosive release later in time. Since this outburst, or assault, was so far temporally removed from the instigating event, the behavior might appear "impulsive" to the external observer. In reality, however, the act was not impulsive at all, only delayed.

MISCONCEPTIONS ABOUT THERAPY
MAY PREDISPOSE RELAPSES

A critical issue in all forms of psychotherapy involves the maintenance of cognitive and behavioral changes following termination of treatment. Empirical evidence indicates that psychological treatment modalities are effective in inducing beneficial modifications of behaviors, including those in the sexual arena. Unfortunately, these short-term benefits often fail to become long-term changes. Failure to maintain change induced by treatment is frustrating to both the distressed client and disappointed therapist. However, when the presenting problem concerns sexually aggressive behaviors, rather than less socially troublesome symptoms (e.g., depression), failure to maintain treatment-induced change presents more dire consequences. Obviously, a major therapeutic concern with sexually aggressive clients involves assisting them to maintain changes after termination of formal treatment.

Treatment of individuals who have performed unacceptable sexual behaviors often implicitly communicates the notion that successful psychotherapy results in elimination of attraction to those sex acts or objects. Therapy is construed as a behavioral extinction process and a restructuring of cognitive schemata.

If successful treatment permanently eliminated deviant sexual preferences, relapse rates of sex offenders would be low. Such is clearly not the case. While recidivism rates for sex offenders are lower than those of the general criminal population, repetition of sex offenses is not an infrequent occurrence (Sturgeon, Taylor, Goldman, Hunter, & Webster, 1979). Recidivism data have been used to argue that efficacy of treatment programs devised for sexual offenders has not been proved (Brecher, 1978). Rather than attributing sexual reoffending to ineffective treatment programs, the hypothetical goals of therapy with sex offenders may require examination. Treatment may successfully induce cognitive and behavioral changes in the sex offender, but the client's expectations about the long-term consequences of treatment for sexual deviance may actually increase the likelihood of the client's reoffending. The anticipated consequence of treatment that is most likely to lead to reoffense may be that successful therapy should eliminate fantasies about a deviant sex object or act.

Few therapists who have experience working with sex offenders regard the sexual aggressor as "curable." No existing therapeutic intervention eradicates, across time and situations, the offender's sexually deviant fantasies. However, many sex offenders enter treatment believing that therapy will affect a "cure." When the offender suffered from physical maladies in the past, a quick trip to the physician and ensuing medication usually led to elimination of the disorder. Treatment has been something done to him, rather than an activity requiring his active involvement. Thus the sex offender may enter treatment for sexual deviance with similar expectations about a quick fix that makes few personal demands.

Unfortunately, many treatment programs effectively promote the offender's belief in the possibility of "cure" by failing to prepare clients for the likelihood of lapses (i.e., a return to the moods, fantasies, and thoughts associated with the relapse process). Similarly, institutionally based treatment programs, functioning without associated outpatient follow-up groups, promote the deceptive assurance that treatment ends upon discharge. Clients who leave therapy with such misconceptions are primed for relapse. Fortunately, options exist that enhance maintenance of therapeutic gain.

RELAPSE PREVENTION: A METHOD OF MAINTAINING THERAPEUTIC GAINS

Marlatt (1982) devised an intervention model, "Relapse Prevention," which is designed to enhance maintenance of change of compulsive behaviors. The first stage of intervention entails a detailed analysis of the precipitating situations, cognitions, and affects that have preceded past relapses. Skills training is then conducted to enable the client to recognize and avoid situations that increase the probability of relapse (i.e., risk situations), to provide the client with adaptive coping behaviors that may be employed when risk situations are encountered, and to lessen the negative impact of a momentary lapse during which a trend toward a return of the maladaptive behavior emerges. Given the similarities of sexually aggressive acts and addictive behaviors, Marlatt's model of Relapse Prevention may be employed to enhance maintenance of treatment-induced behavioral changes in sex offenders. Pithers, Marques, Gibat, and Marlatt (1983) modified the Relapse Prevention model for application with sexual offenders. The Vermont Treatment Program for Sexual Aggressors has employed this model for the past five years.

Relapse Prevention (RP) is a therapeutic approach that is geared toward the maintenance phase of behavior change programs. That is, the RP approach is specifically designed to help the client maintain control of a problem behavior over time and across situations. For the sex offender, successful maintenance is the attainment of long-term abstinence in regard to the performance of unlawful sexual acts. Conversely, maintenance failure, or relapse, is resumption of the pattern of sexually aggressive acts that preceded treatment.

Here are several key tenets of the modified RP model: (1) since sexual offenses have some important commonalities with addictions, similar therapeutic techniques may be used to prevent relapse with both disorders, (2) early learning experiences play a major role in the development of a propensity toward sexual offenses, (3) multiple factors contribute to the etiology of sexual deviance (e.g., irrational thoughts, low self-esteem, inability to obtain emotional intimacy, and situational factors), (4) for many offenders, sexual deviance represents a maladaptive attempt to cope with distress, (5) treatment represents a slow, tedious journey in which numerous setbacks occasionally interfere with an otherwise gradual progression of success, and (6) maintenance is a key phase of the change process.

The Relapse Process

What determines whether an individual will successfully avoid relapse? RP proposes that the determinants of relapse are embedded in the following process (see Figure 10.1): First, we assume that the individual experiences a sense of perceived control while maintaining abstinence, and that this perception of self-control continues and grows until the person encounters a high-risk situation. Broadly speaking, a high-risk situation is one that threatens the individual's sense of control and thus increases the risk of relapse.

If an individual in a high-risk, stressful situation is able to perform a successful coping response (e.g., resisting an urge to perform a sexually aggressive act or resolving an argument), the probability of relapse decreases. Successful coping also bolsters the person's sense of control and confidence about facing the next challenging event. This "I know I can handle it" expectation increases as one copes effectively with more and more high-risk situations without relapsing.

But what happens if an individual fails to cope successfully with a high-risk situation? A likely result is a decrease in his or her sense of control, and a helpless feeling of "it's no use, I can't handle it." At the same time, one's expectation for coping successfully with future high-risk situations begins to fade. If these reactions occur in a situation containing cues associated with the prohibited behavior (such as the availability of a potential victim), the stage is set for a probable relapse. This is particularly the case if the person also holds positive expectancies about the effects of performing the pro-

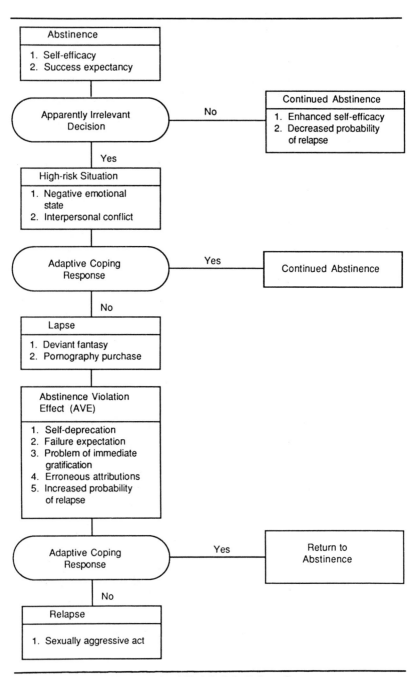

Figure 10.1   A Cognitive-Behavioral Model of the Relapse Process

hibited behavior. A problem drinker, for example, may anticipate the immediate positive effects of alcohol while forgetting about the delayed consequences of drinking. Similarly, a rapist might focus on the immediate effects of performing a sexual assault, such as a feeling of power and release of hostile emotions, rather than keeping in mind the full ramifications of the act.

The combination of being unable to cope with a high-risk situation and having a positive expectancy about the effects of indulging in the prohibited behavior greatly increases the individual's likelihood of crossing the border from abstinence to relapse. At this point, the traditional RP model makes an important distinction between the initial occurrence of the prohibited behavior (a "lapse"), and a complete return to the previous pattern of habitually performing the behavior (a "relapse"). An ex-smoker, for example, who takes one cigarette to cope with a high-risk situation, may or may not continue down the road to total relapse (a return to two packs a day). If an abstaining smoker has been prepared to cope with the initial performance of the prohibited behavior (i.e. smoking one cigarette), the negative consequences of the lapse may be insignificant. However, since even the first performance of the prohibited behavior by a rapist or child molester is totally unacceptable, the traditional RP model has been revised for use with sexual aggressors.

In the orderly sequence of precursors that was found to precede sexual aggression (i.e., affect → fantasy → thought (cognitive distortion) → planning → behavior) it is apparent that the first stage that discriminates most sex offenders from normal individuals is the predominance of fantasies involving sexual aggression. Therefore, for most sexual offenders, the first occurrence of fantasy about performing a sexually aggressive act may be considered the initial lapse. Recurrence of sexually aggressive behaviors is defined as a relapse. Treatment under the RP model for sexual aggressors attempts to teach skills that will enable the client to interrupt the progression of precursors (i.e., affect → fantasy → thought (cognitive distortion) → planning → behavior) at the earliest possible point in order to reduce the likelihood that a sexual offense will recur. After all, the easiest time to stop a speeding locomotive is before it gets started.

Whether or not a lapse becomes a relapse depends on a number of factors, one of which is called the Abstinence Violation Effect (AVE). A major source of the AVE is a conflict between the individual's previous self-image as an abstainer and his recent experience of the prohibited behavior, that is, "If I'm an ex-sex offender, why did I just have a sexual fantasy about that child?" One way of resolving this conflict is to continue abusing children, admitting, "I'm still a sex offender after all." A second source of the AVE is the individual's attribution of the lapse to personal weakness or failure. To the extent that the person views a lapse as a personal failure, his or her expectancy for continued failure increases, and the chances of a full-blown relapse also increase.

In the above discussion, the relapse process is depicted from the point at which a person encounters a high-risk situation. It is important to note, however, that the RP model also examines events that precede the high-risk situation. Although some sex offenders relapse in situations that would have been difficult to avoid or anticipate, the majority appear to set the scene for their own relapse by placing themselves into high-risk situations. This can be done with or without conscious intention on the part of the individual. In some cases, a "craving" or "urge" is experienced and used to justify an indulgence. In other cases, however, individuals engineer relapses with little awareness. For example, an abstinent drinker who buys a bottle of liquor to take home "in case guests drop by during the holidays" is making a choice that we call an "Apparently Irrelevant Decision" (AID).

Through the well-known psychological processes of rationalization and denial, one can covertly set up a relapse by making a series of AIDs, each of which represents another step toward a tempting, high-risk situation. A case study (Marlatt & Gordon, 1985) illustrates this process. On vacation in California, a compulsive gambler (currently abstinent) decided to see the "amazingly blue waters" of Lake Tahoe on his way home to Seattle. Unfortunately, this AID led him across the California-Nevada border into a high-risk situation. By the time he "found himself" in downtown Reno needing change for a parking meter, his relapse was almost inevitable. By putting himself in an extremely tempting situation, the gambler could indulge, claiming he was overwhelmed by external circumstances that made resistance impossible.

The preceding case example of the relapse process leads directly into the RP approach to treatment. While there is very little a gambler can do to avoid relapse in a "Downtown Reno" situation, he can accept responsibility for initiating the chain of events that got him there in the first place. He can learn to recognize the conditions that precede a relapse, and be prepared to intervene before it's "too late."

RP begins by dispelling misconceptions that the client may have regarding the outcome of treatment and describing more realistic goals. RP continues with an assessment of the client's high-risk situations, which are the conditions under which relapse has occurred, or is likely to occur in the future. Also included in the initial assessment is an evaluation of the client's coping skills, since any given situation can be considered high risk only to the extent that the person has difficulty coping with it. In addition to the evaluative techniques unique to RP, we employ procedures described in Chapter 12. After high-risk situations have been identified, an intervention program is designed to train the client how to minimize lapses, and how to keep one lapse from snowballing into a full-blown relapse.

Although the RP maintenance model was devised as a means of enhancing an individual's self-control, it has evolved into a method for facilitating external supervision of a client's adherence to therapeutic requirements. Once an individual's AIDs and high-risk situations have been identified, they may be communicated to a probation and parole officer or social worker responsible for monitoring the offender's behaviors. The probation and parole officer may, in turn, develop collateral contacts with the client's partner, employer, and friends by requesting these individuals to report the presence of any factors related to the client's relapse process. In this manner, the RP model avoids the pitfall of relying solely upon a sex offender's self-report.

RP is a highly cognitive-behavioral approach. In order to avoid exacerbating an offender's intellectualized defenses, the RP maintenance model should not be introduced in therapy until the client has developed emotional and intellectual empathy for victims of sexual assault. Only after recognizing the harm inflicted by their victimizations are offenders sufficiently motivated to maintain the vigilance required by the RP model.

If one abandons the notion that successful treatment must eliminate the client's fantasies about a deviant sex act or object, we may begin to examine some of the cognitive, social, and situational factors that serve as the determinants of risk situations for sexual offending. The combination of these factors determines the probability of relapse. The probability of relapse is a function of the following factors: (1) The extent to which the individual feels controlled by (or helpless relative to) the influence of another individual or group (e.g., criticism from others, anger at others) or by external events "beyond the control" of the individual (e.g., financial hardship, boredom, depression); (2) The immediate availability of a coping response as an alternative to the dysfunctional behavior in a high-risk situation; (3) An individual's expectations about the consequences of the behavioral alternatives in the risk situation; and (4) The availability of victims (i.e., opportunity).

Goals of Relapse Prevention

The overall goals of RP are to increase the clients' awareness and range of choices concerning their behavior, to develop specific coping skills and self-control capacities, and to develop a general sense of mastery or control over their lives. To attain these goals, the RP model includes intervention procedures designed to help the client anticipate and cope with the occurrence of lapses, and procedures designed to modify the early antecedents of lapses. The selection of interventions to be used with a particular client is based on an assessment of his or her high-risk situations and coping skills. That is, while the relapse process appears similar across a wide range of problems, the RP treatment program is not applied as a standardized package, but as an individualized program tailored to meet the particular client's needs.

RP begins by dispelling misconceptions that the client may have regarding the outcome of treatment and by describing more realistic goals. As mentioned earlier, many sex offenders enter treatment expecting that their desire for unacceptable sex acts or objects will be eliminated. In the RP model, although the client participates in procedures designed to reduce his deviant interests and arousal patterns, he is also prepared for the possible return of these problems.

In introducing RP to the client, there is a need to emphasize the development of realistic expectations about the process of therapy and encourage an active, problem-solving approach on the part of the client. Clients are explicitly informed that *no cure exists* for their disorder. They are told that while treatment will diminish their attraction to deviant sexual behaviors, they will discover fantasies about these behaviors recurring in the future at least momentarily. Clients are informed that the return of a deviant fantasy does not signify that they are necessarily going to reoffend. They learn that a critical part of their treatment involves learning what to do when they feel attracted to deviant sexual activity again. Clients are instructed that they will discover a variety of situations in which they make seemingly unimportant decisions that actually lead them closer to offending again, or that take them away from that danger. They are encouraged to develop an ability to recognize these situations and take alternative courses that will reduce the likelihood that they will act out their unacceptable attraction.

Rather than beginning therapy with confrontational techniques designed to "break through the denial system" and force the client to admit responsibility for his crimes, the RP therapist encourages responsibility on the part of the client by fostering an atmosphere of cooperation. This firm, but nonassaultive, approach has several goals. By encouraging the client to serve as his own co-therapist, a sense of objectivity and detachment in the client's consideration of his own behaviors is created. Further, an atmosphere of openness is established in which the client and therapist mutually may begin to explore the problem behavior without the extreme defensiveness that otherwise might be engendered. The absence of a condemnatory confrontation and the focus upon the client's behaviors enable the client to see that sexually aggressive behavior is an unacceptable act that he has performed, rather than an indication of something he is (and always will be), a sex offender. Finally, this nonconfrontational introduction encourages the client, from the beginning of therapy, to play an active part in determining the pace and content of his program.

Assessment Procedures

Since the RP approach to treatment is highly individualized, a thorough assessment of the client's needs is required. The assessment of needs can begin as early as the introductory session, in which the therapist may ask the client to explore the chain of events and decisions preceding his offense. This exploration is the initial step in identifying high-risk situations that the client may face again. In addition to the evaluative techniques described in Chapter 12, the assessment phase of the RP program includes three major tasks: (a) analysis of the client's high-risk situations (including the decisions that created those situations), (b) assessment of the client's skills for coping with the identified high-risk situations, and (c) identification of specific determinants and early antecedents of the client's deviant or aggressive acts.

Assessment of High-Risk Situations. As described earlier, high-risk situations are defined as a set of circumstances that threaten an individual's self-control and increase the likelihood of relapse. Performing an immediate coping response in a risk situation decreases the probability of the problem behavior emerging. If an adaptive coping response is not immediately enacted, the likelihood of relapse increases.

Several methods may be used to identify the conditions, both internal and external, that increase the threat of relapse for a given offender. These include self-monitoring, direct observation, and self-report measures.

Self-Monitoring. Self-monitoring is useful if the offender is still performing the problem behavior (e.g., exposing himself), or still experiencing precursive moods and fantasies (e.g., masturbating to sexually aggressive themes or harboring the seething anger that consistently preceded his offenses). In these cases, assessment should include an assignment for the client to monitor and document these events. For example, the following information should be recorded at the time a client experiences an urge to perform a deviant act: time of day, description of internal events (thoughts and feelings that preceded and accompanied the urge), external situation, and a numerical rating of the individual's consequent mood or feeling. A thorough examination of these self-monitoring records may reveal a pattern of situations in which the behavior most often occurs or is associated with the greatest psychological need.

Direct Behavioral Observation. Direct observational methods can also be used to identify elements of a client's high-risk situations. For example, sexual arousal patterns can be measured by a penile plethysmograph under controlled laboratory conditions. Measurement of the client's relative sexual response to descriptions or visual depictions of various offense situations, themes, and potential victims may reveal high-risk factors that the client has not recognized or reported. Such measurements also provide information about the relative strength of a client's nondeviant sexual interests, information that may be useful later in developing alternatives to relapse.

Self-Report Measures. In many clinical settings, direct observational data are difficult to obtain and the therapist must rely on self-report measures such as questionnaires or structured interviews. In the RP structured interview, clients are asked to provide detailed descriptions of the circumstances associated with past offenses. Again, both the situational and personal (cognitive and affective) antecedents should be identified and AIDs en route to the offense should be explored. Since the concept of AIDs will be new to the client, we suggest beginning with an explanation and a few examples:

> Each of us makes many decisions each day that seem so minor that they could have absolutely no significant impact on our lives. Yet regardless of their apparent irrelevance, some of these decisions profoundly alter the range of behaviors that are subsequently available to us. The cumulative effects of all of these "Apparently Irrelevant Decisions" can be to alter dramatically the major events of our lives. An example may help to clarify this point. Let's take the case of George, an alcoholic who has recently sworn never to drink again. Imagine him walking down a dimly lit city sidewalk close to midnight. As he walks, he reaches into his pocket for a cigarette and discovers that he's out. He anxiously looks around for a store and notices a flashing neon sign up ahead. As he draws closer, he realizes that the sign says BEER. He pauses only a moment to deliberate, deciding that he really needs a cigarette. He enters the bar and goes directly to the vending machine. Reaching for change, he realizes he has none. He asks two men playing pool if they can change a dollar, but both shake their heads. He turns toward the cash register at the bar to get change and hears his name called, "George!" Turning toward the sound, he stares through the drifting blue cigarette smoke and recognizes the foreman of a construction crew he works with. The foreman immediately turns to the bartender and says, "Fill up a brew for George!" Debating only a second, George begins to sip the foaming beer. That was only the first of many he took that night.
>
> Now that you've heard this story, you may be able to see that George made a series of decisions that led up to his final decision to drink beer. At each one of these choice points, George could have made a different decision that would have taken him away from a dangerous situation. Did he really have to have a cigarette? Did he have no alternative but to enter the bar? Could he have refused the beer his foreman bought him? I think you can see that George made a series of decisions, some of which appeared irrelevant to his abstaining from alcohol, but each of which brought him closer to finally taking the drink of beer.
>
> Looking at your decision to sexually abuse a female child in this way, can you tell me the earliest point at which you decided to seek that out?

At this point, the client may provide any of a wide range of responses, none of which should be severely criticized or ridiculed. If the client responds with a statement such as, "I didn't decide, it just happened," the therapist can offer another example (perhaps one closer to home), or proceed with other questions designed to clarify the client's high-risk situations, such as "If you were to become sexually involved with a child again in the future, how might it occur?" or "What particular situations or events would make you feel like raping again?" (Please note the importance of phrasing questions in a way that suggests you expect the client to produce examples of predisposing circumstances.)

Delineation of the client's high-risk situations, and AIDs that led him there, is a process that continues throughout the treatment phase of the RP program. Once the client begins to recall AIDs he has made, the pace with which he remembers them will accelerate. By integrating information from the client's self-monitoring record, direct observational data, and the AIDs that he recalls during a structured interview, the constellation of situations posing a high risk of relapse may be envisioned.

Assessment of Coping Skills. Since a given situation can be considered high risk only to the extent that the offender is unprepared to cope with it, assessment must include measures of his coping abilities. While the most precise method for evaluating the client's preparedness to cope in high-risk situations would be to observe him in a naturally occurring problem situation, this is a rare opportunity in clinical setting. The therapist can, however, use a combination of behavioral and self-report measures to obtain a profile of the client's strengths and weaknesses in coping. These measures include the Situational Competency Test, self-efficacy ratings, and relapse fantasies.

Situational Competency Test. Originally developed by Chaney, O'Leary, and Marlatt (1978) as a treatment outcome measure for alcoholics, the Situational Competency Test has been demonstrated to be a useful procedure for measuring clients' actual coping skills in a variety of high-risk situations. In this test, administered either in a written, audiotaped, or role-playing format, the client is asked to respond to descriptions of common problem situations. For example, the test designed for alcoholics included this item: "You are eating at a good restaurant on a special occasion with some friends. The waitress comes over and says, 'Drink before dinner?' Everyone else orders one. All eyes seem to be on you. What would you do?" The client's response is later scored along a number of dimensions, including the latency and duration of the response, adequacy of the response, and specification of alternate coping responses. A problematic situation is considered to exist whenever the client is unable to formulate a coping response, articulates a strategy that is unlikely to be successful in dealing with the risk, or verbalizes a response only after a prolonged latency.

The Situational Competency Test for sexual aggressors includes a number of frequently encountered high-risk situations, as well as items describing circumstances tailored to the individual client. For example, the test for an adolescent who has offended while babysitting could include this item:

> You are at home alone, watching MTV. You stopped attending outpatient therapy groups for sex offenders six months ago, and everything in life seems to be going well. Since your last offense your family has moved. You're living in a new neighborhood, and you have yet to make many friends. The doorbell rings unexpectedly. Looking through a window before opening the door, you recognize your next-door neighbor. She tells you that she and her husband are ready to go out for dinner to celebrate their wedding anniversary, and their babysitter just canceled. She hesitates awkwardly for a moment, then bashfully asks, "Would you, just this once, watch the kids for a couple of hours?" You realize at that moment that one of her two children is a handsome, little boy, the same age as your last victim. What would you do?

Self-Efficacy Ratings. A second method for assessing the client's coping repertoire involves having the client predict his ability to cope in a variety of problematic situations. Self-efficacy (Bandura, 1977) is the individual's subjective expectancy about his or her capacity to cope effectively in a specific situation. In this assessment procedure, the client is presented with a long list of specific high-risk situations, each of which he rates (on a seven-point scale) according to how difficult or easy it would be to cope with the situation without experiencing a lapse. Again, the assumption is that motivated clients are often the best predictors of their own relapse episodes, an assumption that has been supported by studies of substance abusers (Condiotte & Lichtenstein, 1981).

Lapse Fantasies. For clients with good imagery skills, lapse fantasies can be included in the assessment battery. In this procedure, the client is asked to provide a fantasized account of a possible future lapse. As an introduction to this exercise, the therapist could state the following:

> You and I both hope that a relapse never occurs in your case, and we're going to work as hard as possible to enable you to prevent one.

However, it would be very helpful to our work toward that goal if for just the next few moments you pretend that you're no longer in treatment and that you're having difficulty controlling your urge to rape. I'd like you to sit back comfortably in your chair, close your eyes, and relax by breathing slowly, deeply. Pretend that it's the future; you've been out of treatment now for a couple of years. Throughout most of that time, life has been going well for you. However, lately you have found yourself becoming disproportionately angry at pretty minor frustrations. You recall that under similar circumstances in the past, you found it difficult to free your thoughts from fantasies of raping. I'd like you to imagine a situation that would make it difficult to resist your growing need to rape again. Allow yourself to actually see yourself in this situation. When you can imagine the scene vividly, just allow yourself to start describing your feelings in the situation as clearly as you can.

By reviewing these fantasies with the client, the absence of adaptive coping responses and use of maladaptive coping behaviors can be noted. Occasionally, offenders will become agitated due to the heightened guilt and responsibility they feel as the AIDs and high-risk situations preceding their acts are detailed. It is sometimes necessary to indicate that the intent of recursively detailing these factors is to enable enhanced recognition and coping, not to heighten guilt and induce helplessness. The exacerbation of guilt usually dissipates as the focus of treatment shifts from identifying AIDs and high-risk situations to developing coping strategies for these factors.

Assessment of Determinants of Sexual Aggression. Assessment is not complete until the client and therapist have generated some hypotheses regarding why the client's response to a stressful situation was a sex offense instead of some other (even maladaptive) coping response. That is, although we base this application of the RP model on the similarities between sexual offenders and addictive behaviors, we also emphasize that sexual aggression is a dramatically different response to distress than is drinking a fifth of bourbon or eating three boxes of cookies.

A variety of tools are available to help the therapist and client assess the specific determinants of the client's deviant or aggressive behaviors. The structured interview, for example, can be used to explore the relative importance of a number of common determinants that have been reported by experts in the field of sex offenses. Some of these include: extreme hostility toward women, deficient social and sexual skills, sexual dysfunction, and deviant patterns of sexual arousal (excessive arousal to deviant themes or deficient arousal to nondeviant themes). For this final determinant, the direct measurement methods described previously should be used if available. If not, self-report instruments such as the Clarke Sexual History Questionnaire (Langevin, 1983; Paitich, Langevin, Freeman, Mann, & Handy, 1977) should be employed, along with self-monitoring records, to assess the relative importance of this determinant.

In addition to identifying some of the client's specific determinants, a complete RP assessment should include exploration of "early antecedents," factors in the client's lifestyle, beliefs (views of self, others, and the world), attitudes, needs, and personality structure that appear to be significant predisposing influences. Examples of such predispositions include lack of empathy, cognitive distortions, victim stancing, unrealistic expectations of others, rigid defensive structures, a sense of worthlessness, and excessive power needs. The assessment battery delineated in Chapter 12 enables measurement of most of these early antecedents.

Relapse Prevention Treatment Procedures

Since RP is designed to be an individualized, prescriptive program, it is important to have the client assume a responsible role in determining the pace and content of both the assessment and treatment phases. In some cases the offender may need a number of sessions before he can identify some high-risk situations, and even more time for the next step, recognizing the decisions he made en route to the situations. Usually the best approach is to proceed at the client's own pace, ensuring that he has at least some success at each step of the program. Similarly, the client should have a voice in the selection of specific assessment and intervention procedures. For example, if a client feels that a guided relapse fantasy would evoke unmanageable guilt or dangerous urges, this procedure should be postponed.

Depending upon the actual treatment setting, a number of factors other than client readiness influence the therapeutic process. In the case of highly dangerous outpatient clients, for example, the responsible clinician would forego the luxury of a lengthy assessment period, and begin with interventions designed to reduce immediately the probability of relapse (such as aversive conditioning or psychohormonal therapy). The model presented

RELAPSE PROCESS	RP INTERVENTIONS
	FOR AVOIDING LAPSES
Early antecedents and specific determinants	Lifestyle interventions Relaxation training Reeducation groups Treatment of sexual dysfunction Alteration of deviant sexual arousal pattern Recognition of relapse precursors
Apparently irrelevant decisions.	Stimulus control procedures
High-risk situation	Programmed coping responses Escape strategies Anger and stress management Interpersonal skills enhancement Avoidance procedures
Inadequate coping response	Problem-solving and self-control skills
	FOR MINIMIZING THE EXTENT OF LAPSES
Lapse	Coping with urges Contracting Lapse rehearsals Reminder cards Decision matrix
Abstinence violation effect	Cognitive restructuring Maintenance manuals
Relapse	

Figure 10.2   Treatment Components to Disrupt Relapse Process

here can then be applied to help the client remain abstinent and develop self-control capacities.

In the following sections, a variety of intervention procedures that may be included in a comprehensive RP program are described. Figure 10.2 illustrates how these treatment components correspond to the various precursors of relapse. Since RP is designed to teach clients how to avoid relapse and how to cope with a lapse when one occurs, the interventions are divided into two groups: (a) procedures designed to help the client avoid lapses (or slips); and (b) procedures designed to minimize the possibility of a lapse precipitating a relapse.

Avoiding Lapses

Recognizing the Precursors to Lapses. The first step in teaching a client how to avoid lapses is a straightforward extension of the assessment process: recognizing the chain of events involved in the relapse process that leads to reoffenses. Although identification of high-risk situations and AIDs was introduced as an assessment technique, this process continues throughout treatment. As the client becomes more skilled in observing and analyzing his own behavior, he will discover earlier steps in the chain and more subtle decisions that led to high-risk situations. Continued self-monitoring of thoughts, fantasies, and urges (along with descriptions of the antecedents and consequences of these events) sensitizes the client to recognize important patterns in his behavior. Study exercises, using case examples of the "Downtown Reno Effect," can help the client learn how one can covertly plan an offense by making a series of AIDs:

Jim, a paroled male pedophile, is sitting at home feeling angry and depressed after an argument with his spouse. He decides to take a walk to "cool off." He bursts out the front door, stomping off toward the street, and turns left down the sidewalk. Within a few blocks, he notices a bench at the edge of a vacant park and sits down to rest. His anger has been transformed into a familiar lonely and discouraged feeling. He starts thinking about how hopeless his marriage is, how much his wife seems to enjoy putting him down. He starts thinking, "Maybe she's right, I guess I really am a failure as a man." He remembers how he had looked forward to coming home from prison, all the good times he was sure they would have.

Jim's brooding thoughts are broken abruptly by the lilting sound of children's voices. He gazes up and realizes that a schoolyard is across the street, a steady stream of children approaching the gate, carrying their books, jackets, and lunch boxes. The first few through the gate are boys. They cross the street, run to the center of the park and start playing football. But one of the boys doesn't join the game, instead leaning against a tree and staring down at the ground nearby the bench where Jim is sitting. "Poor kid, he looks as lonely as I feel," Jim says with a sigh, "Maybe I should go talk to him."

These examples can be explored in either group or individual sessions, with the client(s) asked to identify all the AIDs (e.g., going for a walk when he is depressed, leaving home at the time the school day ends, turning left as he started his walk, stopping to rest at the park). After several of these exercises, the client can be given an assignment to think of similar decisions from his own experience, or to work with other group members on identifying the precursors of their offenses.

As a result of these exercises, the client and therapist should be able to identify a discrete point in the relapse process that will be considered the client's "lapse." For most offenders, the lapse will be one of the cognitive steps (fantasy, thought, i.e., cognitive distortion, planning) that precede commitment of an offense. For others, the lapse may be an emotional state (such as intense anger toward a potential victim), a behavior (such as "cruising"), or a combination of behavioral and cognitive events (such as buying child pornography and fantasizing).

Most sex offender treatment programs require clients to identify a "warning signal" that will alert them to imminent reoffenses. "Warning signal" and "lapse" are essentially similar concepts. In contrast to most therapeutic models, however, RP maintains that clients can engage in activities to minimize the frequency of lapses (e.g., identifying AIDs and high-risk situations). In addition, RP proposes that clients can enhance self-control by analyzing lapses, and learning from them, rather than responding to them with alarm. Finally, RP teaches clients specific procedures for stopping lapses from becoming reoffenses. Unfortunately, many other interventions leave clients unprepared to respond adaptively when a "warning signal" is detected. They know they are in trouble, but have no notion what to do.

In the RP model, once a lapse is identified, the client and therapist analyze the situations and decisions that preceded the lapse. Lapses are viewed not as signs of therapeutic failure, but as opportunities to learn. By carefully examining the factors that led to a lapse, an offender may develop enhanced self-management skills.

In spite of this philosophy of RP, clients occasionally believe that they need to maintain perfect control of their behaviors. They may then attempt to maintain a facade of absolute control of their behavior even though they are beginning to feel their self-management skills challenged. The RP model counters this misconception by informing the client that lapses are to be expected and that perfect control of behavior is an unobtainable goal. The importance of sharing perceived lapses with treatment agents is made explicit. When clients share information about lapses, they are reinforced by the therapist's reframing this event as an indicator of therapeutic progress. Clients are informed that recognition of a lapse is a sign that they are actively monitoring their own feelings, fantasies, and thoughts. Having identified a situation precipitating a lapse, the client may identify factors of that situation with which he was unprepared to cope. He may then develop coping strategies to be able to deal more effectively with similar situations in the future.

Stimulus Control Procedures. Teaching the client how to interrupt the chain of events leading to a lapse may begin with some simple stimulus control techniques. To the extent that the client's relapse process includes external stimuli that can be eliminated, he can exercise a good deal of control by simply removing these from his everyday living environment. If, for example, a pedophile's deviant fantasies are elicited by the presence of child pornography, he should remove these cues from his surroundings.

Avoidance Strategies. Along the same line, straightforward avoidance strategies can be useful in the early stages of treatment. A pedophile whose daily drive to work takes him by an elementary school can easily travel another route. As with all interventions, avoidance strategies employed early in the relapse process will be more effective.

Escape Strategies. Since it is unlikely that a client will be able to avoid all cues and situations that might precipitate a lapse, he should also learn some effective escape strategies. These responses are particularly important for the offender who finds himself facing a high-risk situation early in his treatment. That is, until the client has mastered the coping skills necessary to confront successfully a certain high-risk situation, he should be "programmed" to escape. Again, these strategies should be designed for the earliest point in the chain that the offender can recognize. A client who is programmed to get out of situations that precede a lapse is likely to be more successful than one who waits for a "Downtown Reno" situation to develop. For example, in the case of Jim, the pedophile described earlier in this section, an escape response should have been performed when he noticed the school across the street, rather than after he started a conversation with the boy in the park.

Previous research using the Situational Competency Test has

demonstrated that the adequacy of a coping response appears less important in preventing relapse than the speed with which a subject responds in a high-risk situation (Chaney et al., 1978). Thus, the concept of "programmed responses" is critical to the success of escape strategies. A programmed response is one that is performed immediately, as soon as the client recognizes a risk situation. Escape responses can be programmed by having the client overlearn them, by repeatedly rehearsing the behaviors in a variety of situations, to the point that he executes his escape "instinctively" without hesitation. A quick escape may not be an elegant one, and may not be the "optimal" coping skill to employ in a certain risk situation, but it can be effective if the individual gets out of the situation quickly enough to interrupt the chain of events leading to relapse.

Specific Coping Skills. Although some lapses can be prevented by training the client to recognize, avoid, and escape risk situations, successful maintenance also requires the acquisition of additional programmed coping responses and problem-solving skills. Since RP is applied as an individualized program (in both individual and group therapy formats), the content of the skill-training procedures will vary, depending on the offender's needs. The skill-training process, however, remains fairly constant across clients, and is the backbone of the RP program.

Programmed Coping Responses. The development of adaptive coping responses for risk situations always begins with problem-solving sessions. The client initiates the problem-solving procedure by describing his highest-risk situation in detail. Once the situation has been described fully, a brainstorming session is used to generate a large number of potential coping responses. During the brainstorming process, no criticism of any coping responses should be permitted. The important issue is to have the client generate as many behavioral alternatives as he can. After the list of alternatives has been completed, the potential consequences of each option are described to evaluate whether that coping response would have the desired effect of lessening the likelihood of relapse. The most effective, feasible coping response is then selected for performance. Focusing on the thought processes that the client follows in performing the problem-solving strategy is important in providing clues that suggest additional problem areas for further exploration (e.g., an unrealistic approach to life, grandiose expectations, and so on).

While instructing the client in problem-solving procedures, the therapist may enhance the client's learning by modeling both the problem-solving process and the selected coping behavior. If the high-risk situation and the selected coping response are interpersonal (e.g., disagreement with a spouse), role playing may be used to model the appropriate coping behavior. When the problem is intrapersonal (e.g., depression), an internal dialogue of self-statements may be modeled as a coping technique.

The client must then be given an opportunity to practice the selected coping behavior and receive therapeutic feedback. Coaching on the behavior should continue until the client's performance matches the therapist's (or group's) criteria for adequacy. If the client is unable to achieve criteria-level performance after repeated attempts with feedback, it may be necessary to return to the list of alternate coping responses and attempt to use the next best option that the client can be programmed to enact successfully.

Continued practice of the behavior should be conducted throughout the client's treatment. Practice on these behaviors resembles the repetitive drills used by athletic coaches who strive to have their players respond "instinctively" in important situations. These "instinctive" reactions actually result from intensive programming. By practicing over time, the client will perform the programmed coping response in many situations and moods, enhancing generalization.

Interpersonal Skills. Acquisition of effective interpersonal skills is an important part of the RP program for many sex offenders. For some, basic skills necessary for establishing and maintaining relationships with adults are deficient. Others lack dating skill, show deficits in sexuality skills, are unable to communicate effectively, erroneously interpret the meaning of social cues, or are severely inhibited by anxiety in interpersonal encounters. Lack of assertive behaviors is another common social skill deficit that appears as a precursor to relapse. Many sex offenders, particularly rapists, are unable to constructively express feeling to others, and react to interpersonal conflict with unexpressed anger, which is later overexpressed in aggressive outbursts.

Depending on the needs of the individual client, the social skills training component will vary from a brief program of desensitization to an intensive and structured program involving behavioral rehearsal, modeling, social reinforcement, videotaped feedback, and in vivo practice. One such program developed for sex offenders by Abel, Blanchard, and Becker (1978) can easily be incorporated into the skill-training phase of the RP program. The Personal Effectiveness Program developed by Liberman, King,

DeRisi, and McCann (1976) is another excellent source of social skills training procedures.

Anger and Stress Management. Since negative arousal states are common precursors of relapse, skills for managing these affective antecedents are important coping strategies for many offenders. For pedophiles, social anxiety appears to be a frequent antecedent; for rapists, anger is the more common precursor. Our general approach to management of negative arousal states is stress-inoculation training, a cognitive-behavioral program that has been successfully applied to problems of anxiety (Meichenbaum, 1977) and anger (Novaco, 1977).

The stress inoculation program includes three phases: (a) cognitive preparation; (b) skill acquisition and rehearsal; and (c) application practice. The anger management training component, for example, includes the following (from Novaco, 1977):

(1) Cognitive preparation: The clients learn about the causes and functions of anger, their personal anger patterns, when anger becomes a problem, and how anger can be regulated.

(2) Skill acquisition and rehearsal: Three sets of coping techniques are modeled by the therapist and rehearsed by the client. The techniques include cognitive methods (modification of irrational beliefs and anger-instigating self-statements, development of empathic abilities, maintenance of a task orientation, development of coping self-instructions); affective controls (relaxation training, use of competing responses such as humor); and behavioral skills (effective communication of feelings, assertive behavior, task-oriented and problem-solving actions).

(3) Application practice: The clients are exposed to a series of actual provocation stimuli, and practice anger-management skills that are rehearsed with the therapist.

Problem-Solving and Self-Control Skills. A variety of personal problems can contribute to the offender's inability to avoid and/or cope with a high-risk situation. For example, a rapist who is unable to manage his anger when he has been drinking excessively will need to either abstain from, or control, his drinking to reduce effectively the likelihood of relapse. A comprehensive RP program specifically addresses these contributing problem areas, and also provides the offender with a problem-solving strategy that can be used when future problems arise. Mahoney's (1979) Personal Problem Solving approach offers an effective framework for this problem-solving component.

Coping with Urges. As with other addictive behaviors, the performance of sexually deviant acts is typically characterized by some type of immediate gratification (e.g., restored sense of power and control, relief from tension). The negative consequences (e.g., guilt, decreased self-esteem, social disapproval, arrest and incarceration) are typically delayed. Selectively recalling the positive aspects of past offenses, while neglecting the negative aftereffects (for both the victim and himself), increases the probability of recurrence of the deviant act. Positive outcome expectancies for the immediate effects of a behavior become an especially potent force when the client is faced with a high-risk situation and is beginning to feel unable to cope effectively. Under such conditions, the client may experience a strong urge to commit a deviant act.

In order to offset the influence of positive outcome expectancies, we teach the client that his overall response to sexual aggression is biphasic in nature. The initial sense of gratification is frequently followed by a delayed negative effect in the opposite direction. We draw an analogy to the relapsing alcoholic who fondly remembers the pleasant relaxation induced by the first drink but who has selectively forgotten about the torturous hangover produced by the tenth. In order to provide a potent reminder for our clients that positive outcome expectancies are unrealistic, we refer to this phenomenon as the "Problem of Immediate Gratification," or the "PIG" phenomenon.

Individuals who yield to an urge may make the mistaken assumption that this craving will continue to increase in intensity until it overwhelms them, becoming impossible to resist. Therefore, an important point for the client to remember when an urge arises is that it will subside and pass away with time. If the individual is able to endure an urge without engaging in aggression, the internal pressure to respond may become weaker with each succeeding urge.

One might hypothesize how yielding to urges and opponent process theory (Solomon, 1980) could account for the progression in offense severity identified in some aggressors. Opponent process theory holds that novel stimulation evokes an emotional reaction, which the organism attempts to moderate. In response to novel stimulation, the organism enacts an innate process that minimizes (opposes) the emotional state. At any moment, the organism's experience is a sum of the stimulating and opposing processes. In effect, the opponent process protects the organism from stimulus overload.

These interactive processes possess theoretical parameters that change over time. In response to initial exposures to novel stimuli, the excitatory process has a rapid onset and reaches its peak quickly. The opponent process begins more slowly, but eventually becomes stronger than the excitatory reaction and then decays to baseline. After repeated stimulation of the same type, however, the opponent process has a more rapid onset, resulting in quick loss of the excitement.

Imagine an adolescent male who has engaged in voyeurism to counteract boredom. He initially experiences tremendous excitement while secretively observing someone. However, over time the excitement fades rapidly into a familiar feeling of disgusted boredom. Since he has been conditioned to expect excitement when engaging in inappropriate sexual activity, he may increase the frequency of his voyeurism or, perhaps, engage in a more novel criminal sexual behavior in an effort to restore his prior level of excitement. Thus yielding to urges might represent the first step on a progression toward greater problems.

To increase the client's ability to recognize conditions that elicit urges, he can be asked to self-monitor the occurrence of all urges taking place within a selected time period. The client should include the following information in his observation of urges: a description of antecedent events or feelings, an estimate of the intensity and duration of the urge, and any coping response that could have been employed to reduce the likelihood of his acting-out the urge.

As is true with high-risk situations, the first step in learning how to cope with urges is being able to recognize one and label it accurately. The client can then be taught to use self-statements to disrupt the urge. Statements such as "Two minutes of power aren't worth 20 years in prison" may be developed. Inclusion of aversive outcomes in the client's self-statements may enhance their potency in counteracting urges. During treatment, the client may be instructed to visualize himself feeling an urge and then successfully combating it.

Another technique that can assist the client to cope with urges is the decision matrix. In creating a decision matrix, the client is presented with a three-way table ($2 \times 2 \times 2$ matrix) in which the following factors are listed: the decision to perform a deviant act or to refrain from doing so; the immediate and delayed consequences of each decision; and, within each of the former categories, the positive and negative effects involved (see Figure 10.3). The client

	IMMEDIATE		DELAYED	
	POSITIVE	NEGATIVE	POSITIVE	NEGATIVE
TO REFRAIN	1. Increased self-efficacy (+75) 2. Social approval (+20) 3. Respect of spouse (+50) 4. Respect of children (+30) 5. No harm to victims (+65)	1. Denial of gratification (-8) 2. Momentary anger (-30) 3. Frustration (-15)	1. Enhanced self-control (+75) 2. Increased social approval (+35) 3. Respect of spouse (+30) 4. Maintenance of friendships (+40) 5. Avoidance of jail (+45) 6. Less treatment (+5)	1. Denial of gratification (-9) 2. Residual anger (which becomes less in time)(-20)
TO PERFORM	1. Immediate gratification (+20) 2. Release of anger (+15) 3. Sense of power (+30)	1. Social censure (-80) 2. Guilt (-30) 3. Loss of self-respect (-20) 4. Harm to victim (-60) 5. Risk of injury (-10) 6. Possibility of getting caught (-90)	1. Continued gratification (+20)	1. Social censure (-40) 2. Guilt (-25) 3. Loss of self-respect (-20) 4. Identity of offender (-80) 5. Lasting harm to victim (-40) 6. Loss of spouse (-90) 7. Imprisonment (-40) 8. Public disclosure (-40)

Figure 10.3   Decision Matrix for Coping with Urges

and therapist work together to complete each of the eight cells of the matrix, listing outcomes that the client feels would have the greatest impact on his decision making. The client should assign a numerical rating to each of the positive and negative outcomes to illustrate their relative importance. All effects that the client regards as important should be listed in the matrix. The therapist should require that all decision matrices contain factors regarding the harm that sexually aggressive acts inflict upon victims.

Modification of Specific Determinants of Lapses. As was emphasized in the assessment phase, the RP program would be incomplete if it did not address specific determinants of sexual deviance and aggression. Although some of these determinants (e.g., excessive anger/hostility, deficient social skills) have already been covered in the coping skills section, treatments that address the offender's deviant sexual arousal pattern or sexual dysfunction have not been discussed. Since others (e.g., Annon 1974, 1975; Kaplan, 1974; Zilbergeid, 1978) have written extensively on the treatment of various sexual dysfunctions; the only point to be made here is that these dysfunctions should be assessed and treated in a comprehensive program for sex offenders.

The most important "response-relevant" interventions are the behavior-therapy procedures designed to alter those deviant arousal patterns that are critical precursors to relapse for many offenders. The importance of including direct physiological assessments (i.e., penile plethysmography) in interventions with sexual aggressors has been emphasized by many experts in this field (Abel et al., 1978; Laws & Osborn, 1983; Quinsey & Marshall, 1983; Rosen & Fracher, 1983). These therapeutic procedures are detailed in Chapter 12 of this book. As a general rule, however, treatment procedures that are direct, simple, and transferable to the client's home (e.g., masturbatory satiation, orgasmic reconditioning, olfactory aversion, etc.) are employed.

Intervention for Early Antecedents. The final set of interventions that are introduced to help offenders avoid lapses are designed to modify "early antecedents," the global predispositions that have been determined by the client and therapist to contribute to lapses. A wide range of techniques can be included in this component, ranging from didactic sessions on human sexuality to victim confrontations for offenders who lack empathy or refuse to take responsibility for the full extent of their crimes, and cognitive restructuring techniques to correct "thinking errors" that support the offender's interpersonal aggression (Yochelson & Samenow, 1976). "Re-education groups," as described by Groth (1983), may be employed to address the most common early antecedents.

Modification of early antecedents also involves a number of global interventions that are designed to reduce the probability of relapse by helping the offender develop a more positive lifestyle, enhanced coping capacities, and an overall sense of self-efficacy. These procedures stand in sharp contrast to the specific behavioral and cognitive interventions presented in the previous sections, and include "lifestyle interventions" (to attain balance between one's daily ration of "shoulds" in relation to "wants"), life-planning exercises (such as Crystal & Bolles's (1974) program "Where do I go from here with my life?"), the development of positive addictions (Glasser, 1976), and training in relaxation or spiritual centering techniques.

In short, anything that helps the client enhance his overall sense of well-being may be included in his individualized RP program. The inclusion of these global procedures may also help the client feel that change is indeed possible, and encourage him to view himself as a whole, multidimensional person, rather than simply as a hopeless deviant.

Minimizing the Extent of Lapses

Traditional forms of therapy often fail to prepare clients for the possibility of lapses. The underlying assumption is that such preparation is tantamount to authorizing occurrence of a complete relapse. There is general acceptance, however, for the idea that people handle other crises more effectively if they are trained. Children in school take part in fire drills, the Emergency Broadcast System interrupts the airwaves to test its warning signal, lifeboat drills are held on cruise ships, and flight attendants outline emergency procedures prior to airline departures. Many of the training procedures for emergencies have proven so successful that they are no longer optional, but required by law. Preparing a sex offender for the possibility of a lapse into deviant fantasies or thoughts is another example of training designed to prevent an emergency situation from turning into a disaster.

In the RP approach, the therapist informs the client that unacceptable thoughts or fantasies are likely to recur at some point.

By accepting this belief, the client is better prepared to control the negative influence of the Abstinence Violation Effect (AVE) when a lapse does occur.

Several specific RP treatment procedures have been developed to prepare the client to cope with lapses by applying some cognitive and behavioral "brakes" so that the lapse does not "spin out of control" and become a full-blown relapse. A combination of specific coping skills and a cognitive restructuring approach offers the greatest advantage in this regard. First, we need to teach the client behavioral skills to moderate the lapse once it occurs. These coping behaviors can be specified proactively in a therapeutic contract. Second, if these moderating skills are to be successful, we must instruct the client in cognitive restructuring procedures to cope effectively with the various components of the Abstinence Violation Effect. Third, lapse rehearsals may be staged to practice the skills he has acquired to handle the occurrence of a lapse. Finally, an individualized maintenance manual should be constructed to provide the offender with general reference material, specific refresher exercises, and emergency coping strategies to use if all else fails and he is on the brink of relapse. Each of these procedures is discussed in the following sections.

Contracting. The first step to take in anticipation of lapses is to establish a special section of the therapeutic contract that specifically limits the extent to which an offender may permit himself to lapse. The details of this portion of the contract are best worked out in collaboration with the client. The therapist, however, must ensure that the client has not specified a "lapse limit" that is "beyond the point of no return." For an offender whose lapse is defined as masturbating to deviant sexual fantasies, the contract might include the following:

(1) The client agrees to delay beginning masturbating to deviant fantasies for at least 20 minutes after the initial temptation to "give in." This delay is to be used as a time to pause and reflect, to consider the situation, and to see the behavior as a clear choice, rather than as a passive yielding to an urge. A review of the decision matrix would be helpful at this point.

(2) The client agrees that the first lapse will involve a single "dose" of the activity involved. For a rapist whose lapse is masturbating while having violent fantasies, the contract limits this activity to only one such fantasy. The client also agrees to report the occurrence of this lapse at his next therapy session.

Cognitive Restructuring. The principal aim of cognitive restructuring is to counteract the self-deprecating cognitive and affective components of the Abstinence Violation Effect. As described previously, the AVE can play an enormous role in increasing the likelihood that a single lapse will precipitate an actual sexual offense. In the RP treatment model, the client is taught to avoid reacting to the first lapse as an indication of personal failure, and thus to avoid focusing on guilt, conflict, and negative internal attributions ("This just goes to show that I really am, and always will be, a hopeless sex offender"). Instead, the client is taught to reconceptualize the episode as a single, independent event to see it as a mistake rather than as a sign that he has permanently crossed over the border from being in absolute control to being absolutely out of control. Rather than viewing a slip as a disastrous failure in his self-control program, the client should regard a slip as an important indicator of progress in his therapeutic journey. Each lapse is a mistake, an event that provides an opportunity for the offender to learn something about his high-risk situations and deficiencies in his coping and problem-solving skills. It also permits him a chance to remediate these deficiencies and increase his sense of personal control.

The client is informed that he will probably experience at least some degree of guilt after each lapse. Guilt reactions are extremely dangerous since they exacerbate distress that may motivate the client to emit a sexually aggressive behavior in a maladaptive attempt to cope. Clients are taught that guilty feelings are to be expected after lapses, but that these feeling are natural consequences of a transgression, and they will subside after a relatively short time (as long as clients do not reinforce them by relapsing). Knowing that the guilt will rapidly decay and eventually disappear makes it easier to tolerate the feelings without undue consequences.

As an aid in this reconceptualization process, the client can be given a summary of cognitive restructuring material in the form of a reminder card. The client is instructed to carry this card at all times; it can be printed as a wallet-sized card. The card is to be consulted immediately upon each lapse. Items that might be included on the reminder card include (a) what a slip means (a mistake) and does not mean (total loss of control), (b) a description of the AVE and the guilt feelings that accompany it, (c) reassurance that one does not need to give in to negative thoughts and feelings, and that they will subside in time, (d) instructions to examine the slip and identify what may be learned from the experience, and (e) a list of "what to do next" instructions, including the main points of the relapse contract described previously. A list of telephone numbers of therapists, supportive individuals, and treatment-group members should be attached to the reminder card in case the client experiences difficulty coping with the lapse.

Lapse Rehearsal. In this procedure, the therapist makes use of imagery as a means of cognitively representing a range of high-risk and lapse situations. It is similar to the relapse fantasy technique described earlier, but goes beyond imagining a high-risk situation to creating scenes in which the client actually imagines himself engaging in successful coping responses. Although the primary reason for including this technique is to provide practice in ameliorating the effects of lapses, lapse rehearsals also enable the therapist to assess how well the client has learned the importance of AIDs, programmed coping responses, problem-solving skills (for use when specific coping responses have not been programmed), and cognitive self-statements that may turn a lapse into a constructive learning experience. In order to evaluate the client's learning of these skills, the therapist may encourage him to visualize a lapse into unacceptable fantasies, and to "think out loud" how he would handle it. Ideally, the client's account would be along these lines:

> I've just been thinking about volunteering to serve as the supervisor of youth activities for my church group. The thought seemed really attractive to me. I'd be helping the church and the children; I'd be respected by the community; I'd be active and having fun. For some reason though, I felt uneasy about actually doing it. I don't know why. But finally I realized that the decision was what we've been calling "apparently irrelevant." The decision initially didn't seem like such a big deal, but it sure would have put me into an unnecessarily risky situation. I would be better off not volunteering.
>
> Since I didn't have a coping response programmed for the situation, I used the problem-solving strategy that I've learned. I figured out that as a supervisor I'd be alone with a lot of kids. We might even go on camping trips. I couldn't think of anyone who would volunteer to assist me on the job. My main alternatives seemed to be: (1) go ahead and become a counselor; (2) figure out another way I could be with kids in the company of adults, like coaching little league baseball; or (3) just turn down any job that might allow me to be near kids.
>
> I knew I couldn't take the supervisor's position. It just had too many risks for me. I was tempted to think I could handle the risks one at a time, you know, "This will be a good opportunity for me to test

myself, and see if I'm still attracted to kids." But I realized that I was making a "thinking error" to rationalize my desire to be with kids. I really could have set myself up good. The risks never would have ended and one might have occurred when I was feeling down and lonely, which would have increased the risk. Coaching baseball seemed like a reasonable alternative at first. Knowing that other adults were around might keep me in line. My one concern was that some of the parents might start to trust me too much. I could imagine being invited to the parents' house for dinner some evening and seizing the opportunity to ask if they'd mind my taking their boy to a Red Sox game. I know what that opportunity would have led to. So I think I'd better forget about coaching.

You know, for a second when I was thinking about coaching, I could almost see myself alone with a boy from the team, my hands sliding down the little kid's shorts. It terrified me. I've put so much into my treatment only to be plagued by those fantasies again. Even though you said it would happen, I guess I really didn't believe it until it did. But since you had told me that the fantasies would come back at least momentarily, I wasn't so afraid. The first thing I did was tell myself, "This doesn't mean that you're still a sex offender—you didn't know how to stop yourself before, but you do now, so do it." There's a lot of difference between having a fantasy like mine and doing it for real—everybody has some unacceptable fantasies.

I used to fantasize when I was feeling sorry for myself, so I'd better check to see if I'm feeling that way now, and make sure to avoid places where children might be...." These self-statements and ideas worked. I began to feel less anxious. I handled the crisis. I've learned the skills well enough to apply them once. I know I need to keep working on the skills so I can handle myself even better in the future.

Maintenance Manuals

Since the RP treatment model is designed to be an individualized, prescriptive program, each offender should work on developing his own, unique "maintenance manual" for use after the intensive phase of treatment has ended. Depending on the needs of the client, this manual may vary from a pocket-sized spiral notebook that includes his decision-matrix, reminder card, last-minute avoidance strategies and emergency telephone numbers, to a more comprehensive collection of AIDs, coping strategies, imagery and relaxation instructions, self-statements, self-monitoring forms, and diary notes. In either case, the client should be instructed to regularly review, practice, and update the contents of his maintenance manual as his own refresher course for minimizing lapses and preventing relapses. The maintenance manual can be especially valuable for offenders who are in transition from residential to outpatient treatment. In these cases, the manual provides a format for assuring continuity of treatment between institutional and outpatient settings. Maintaining a manual also encourages offenders to remain vigilant for the development of new risk situations.

CONCLUSIONS

Relapse Prevention serves as a comprehensive training program designed to help sex offenders successfully avoid and cope with the problem of relapse. An abbreviated form of the program may be used as a supplemental package, designed to enhance and extend the effects of other treatment approaches. For example, a behavior therapy program to alter sexual arousal disorders may be strengthened by adding assessment of high-risk situations and coping skills, and by training clients to recognize and avoid risky situations, to improve coping and problem-solving skills, and to prepare for the likelihood that treatment may "wear off" (e.g., deviant fantasies and arousal patterns could return). In any case, the basic premise of the RP model is that clients should be prepared; that is, they should be able to recognize AIDs, avoid or effectively cope with high-risk situations, restructure interpretation of urges, and prevent a lapse from creating a full-blown relapse.

No final therapy session is conducted under the RP model. RP is not an activity that a sex offender completes. Clients who assert, "There's no way I'll ever do another rape," are at high risk of reoffending, because they will not remain vigilant for AIDs and high-risk situations. Offenders who believe that their treatment ends with the termination of formal therapy have failed to learn the crucial lesson that maintenance is forever. The client who has adequately learned the RP philosophy will continue his own therapy every day of his life.

11

MEASURING THE OFFENDER'S
PROGRESS IN TREATMENT

Programs must consider carefully their admission criteria and their methods for assessing progress. Reasons for terminating clients who are not making sufficient progress and ways of doing so must also be clearly defined. Although failure to comply with treatment is for many offenders in theory a probation violation, without a written policy on what constitutes a failure to participate the rule may be quite useless. An offender may well continue to deny the offense and to show no motivation or interest in changing behavior he protests does not exist. However, if he has actually been coming to all of the treatment sessions, he is in a good position to argue in court that his attendance has constituted full participation. For programs to use the legal system effectively as an adjunct to therapy and as a way of keeping untreatable offenders off the streets, those programs must be able to demonstrate to an impartial court that the offender was given fair notice of what constituted participation in the program, that he was informed in writing of his failure to participate and given specific written instructions on what he had to change. Documentation that he continued to refuse to participate is critical. Treatment programs must follow a clear written policy regarding termination. This section will focus on methods of monitoring progress and assessing the necessity of termination or the possibility of graduation in group treatment.

Program requirements should be given to the court and the offender at the time that the offender is recommended for treatment. It should be clear these are requirements for participation in the program, not for graduation from the program. A sample written policy might read as follows:

SEX OFFENDER PROGRAM TREATMENT DESCRIPTION

The Child Sexual Abuse Treatment Program is a sex offender treatment program whose purpose is to prevent further deviant sexual behavior by the participants and to give participants the tools required to allow them to continue not to reoffend once leaving the program.

Research and clinical experience have both shown that these goals cannot be met without the active participation of the offender in this program. Changing a pattern of sexual deviancy is a difficult task and cannot be accomplished by offenders who will participate in some parts of the program and not others, by offenders who participate sometimes and not others, or by offenders who participate physically by their attendance but not emotionally by admitting to and working hard to change deviant behavior.

Our policy therefore is only to accept into the program those offenders who are willing to accept responsibility for their behavior and to keep in the program only those offenders who demonstrate an ability to change their behavior.

In order to apply to be accepted in this program as a candidate for admission, offenders must agree to a psychosexual evaluation. This evaluation will include plethysmograph testing. Plethysmograph testing will be explained verbally and in writing to the offender and his informed written consent sought. Plethysmograph testing may be used repeatedly throughout the program. No offender who refuses plethysmograph testing will be accepted into the program.

In addition the offender must agree to the other parts of the evaluation, which include a lengthy psychological test battery, a clinical interview, and access to all previous reports and evaluations. The offender must sign a release allowing the program access to such reports and evaluations, must allow the therapist to speak with previous victims or their families if desired by the program, and must allow the program to speak with other members of his family. The program will contact employers when necessary to monitor progress of the offender. There is no confidentiality within the program, and staff members who treat offenders and those who treat victims, for example, will communicate with each other. In this treatment program, the child protection agency and the Department of Corrections have representatives on the treatment team. They will be privy to information regarding the progress of the offender. The offender must sign the appropriate releases stating he agrees to each of these exceptions to confidentiality in order to be accepted as a candidate.

In addition, each candidate will have specific rules and regulations which are tailored to his circumstances. For example, an offender whose offense involved exhibiting from a car might be required by the program to have a specific destination when driving in order to avoid "cruising" or might be required to have a passenger with him at all times. Offenders must agree to follow the rules and regulations of the program, both those which apply to all offenders and those which apply specifically to them.

All offenders are accepted as candidates only. When the offender's therapy group and the staff feel the offender has made sufficient progress to join the program as a group member, that offender's status will formally change from candidate to group member. This is expected to occur within a few months of entering the program. Until that point the offender is only conditionally accepted into the program. Offenders who deny or minimize the behavior will sometimes be accepted as candidates. No offender will be promoted from candidate to group member who continues to deny the offense. All offenders who continue to deny the offense will be dropped from the program after a trial. The trial will not exceed 3 months in any case.

All offenders, whether candidates or group members, must continue to show progress or be dropped from the program. Evidence of progress will be evaluated in the following areas:

(1) physical participation (e.g., attendance, completion of homework assignments)
(2) accepting responsibility for offenses
(3) intellectual understanding of offense chain and therapeutic techniques
(4) emotional understanding of impact of offenses
(5) attempts to change behavior
(6) assertiveness and willingness to help other group members prevent relapse

All offenders who are being considered for termination from the program will be given a written warning detailing their failure to progress adequately in the program and a sufficient time to correct the behavior, unless the behavior in question constitutes an immediate danger to the community. Those behaviors which do constitute an immediate threat, e.g., further molestation of children or adults or total withdrawal from the program, will be reported to probation and parole immediately.

I understand and agree to all of the conditions outlined above.

Date   Witness   Candidate

_____   _____   _____

Each of the areas of evaluation—physical participation, owning responsibility, intellectual understanding, emotional understanding, attempts to change behavior, assertiveness, and willingness to help others—should be carefully assessed by the staff as to what constitutes progress and what does not.

PHYSICAL PARTICIPATION

Group candidates and members are expected to attend all sessions. Failure to do so is seen as a failure to develop nondeviant priorities. There should be very little more important in the life of a sex offender than successfully completing treatment. Not attending sessions because of conflicting appointments, failure to disclose to his boss and ask for a different work schedule, or inability to secure transportation all must be seen as indicating a lack of motivation. Physical illness to the point of requiring medical intervention is acceptable. Persistent refusal to come to group without bona fide reasons, i.e., verifiable emergencies, should be grounds for dismissal from the program.

All group members are expected to come on time. Coming late to group is a statement of the lack of importance of treatment to the offender, and should be dealt with in the group as such.

All offenders are expected to pay their fees at each session. Again, this is an issue of the priority of treatment. Many offenders who plead hardship and an inability to pay spend their money on other less important items.

An important component of treatment is specific behavioral assignments. Offenders are expected to complete assignments on time. The completed tasks must be of the proper length and deal with the assigned material to the best of the offender's abilities. Offenders who are illiterate should be allowed to use tape recorders. Assignments are facilitated by requiring each offender to buy a notebook at the beginning of treatment. In that notebook he will keep all program materials. This will include program descriptions, copies of releases he has signed, copies of evaluations and progress reports he has been given, a list of all assignments given to him with due dates, assignments he has completed, and any other notes on the group he wishes to take. All notebooks are brought to every treatment session.

OWNING RESPONSIBILITY FOR OFFENSES

A primary goal of any treatment program is to enable offenders to take responsibility for their behavior. Perhaps the single greatest obstacle to treatment is denying, minimizing, and externalizing. Even those offenders who say they take responsibility for their offenses, often say at other times, "I'm not making an excuse, but . . ." and then follow with an excuse. Staff members must listen constantly for whether or not an offender is indeed making progress in actually taking responsibility for an offense as opposed to learning what the staff wants to hear and repeating it back. It is easiest to determine that an offender is not taking responsibility for an offense when he is overt about it. It becomes more difficult as offenders learn the language of treatment and begin to use it. Staff members must listen for what the offender says inadvertently rather than what he says when he is formally addressing the topic.

Attempts to describe the offense as a response to being "lonely," as a way of "loving the child and being close to her," or as "something that just happened—I guess I just wasn't thinking" all should be seen as attempts to evade responsibility. Loneliness can be and has been dealt with nonsexually by adults of both sexes without molesting children. Exploiting and damaging children is not a form of loving them. An offender who insists his offense was not premeditated and has no antecedents in thought or action, should be told that he is extremely dangerous, that impulsivity to that degree indicates a total inability to control the behavior, and an inability to prevent it from happening again. It should be made clear that his progress in treatment is dependent entirely on his ability to find some antecedents in the chain that leads to child sexual abuse.

Constant referral to old childhood injuries during group therapy is not likely to help an offender control his behavior. Like an alcoholic, he may indeed have had reasons he moved along the path to sexual deviancy, but, ironically, tracing the path again is unlikely to help him stop. Like alcohol, sexual deviancy either in thought or action becomes addictive. At the point an offender comes for treatment, he is dealing with the addiction, not only with a childhood no longer present. Attempts to explain away the behavior on the basis of past events must be deflected in the group, so the focus stays on the present sexual deviancy and ways to control it. Family therapy and individual therapy sometimes allow offenders to address childhood issues.

INTELLECTUAL UNDERSTANDING OF OFFENSE CHAIN AND THERAPEUTIC TECHNIQUES

Effective group treatment includes a strong cognitive component. That component does not focus on original causes of behavior or on "insight" into why the offender committed the offenses. It does focus strongly (as described in Chapter 9) on understanding cognitive distortions and on antecedent events in the chain of behaviors leading to sexual acting out. Offenders who refuse to produce antecedent thoughts, feelings, or actions inhibit the therapist from identifying "Apparently Irrelevant Decisions" (leading to reoffense). Such offenders claim a total lack of premeditation or previous fantasy. This is indicative of a lack of progress in treatment.

In addition, treatment includes a variety of behavioral techniques, all of which must be mastered to work properly. Offenders should show progress over time in understanding their own chain of events that lead to "outlet" (reoffense) and in understanding the techniques they are asked to master. Ordinarily a failure to do so is evidence of resistance. An offender cannot effectively utilize a given technique if he refuses to understand it.

However, exceptions to this rule are retarded offenders and extremely anxious offenders. Retarded offenders may have difficulty understanding because of intellectual limitations. They may require more work in individual therapy. Assignments and expectations must be gone over many times and demonstrated explicitly even to the extent of the assignments being made more concrete. Material from such offenders may need to be tape-recorded. Breaking down the assignments into smaller units for them to complete is often productive. In short, failure to master assignments in a retarded offender may not be evidence of resistance, but of confusion.

Occasionally offenders present with extremely high anxiety levels. This sometimes occurs, for example, when the offender has been molesting male children and fears that treatment will reveal, not that he is a child molester, but that he is homosexual. Homosexual panic or anxiety from other causes sometimes results in offenders who are extremely anxious in sessions and have trouble complying with any requests. Frequently habituation to the group reduces the anxiety level. Sometimes relaxation techniques can and should be introduced in the individual sessions to give such offenders techniques to control anxiety. In an extreme case psychotropic medication could be considered.

EMOTIONAL UNDERSTANDING OF THE IMPACT OF THE OFFENSES

Sex offenders must show progress in developing empathy for their victims. This imperative is explicitly addressed in treatment by bringing adult victim advocates and sometimes adult survivors to groups, by assigning readings, by requiring the offender to write the assaults from a child's point of view and by having the offender write an appropriate apology. Most offenders depersonalize their victims and are unaware of their feelings. They attribute to their victims their own rationalizations. "She didn't seem to mind it so much." "She didn't say anything." These are cognitive distortions that interfere with the ability of the offender to develop empathy for the child. The offender must demonstrate through words and behavior that he is making progress in learning that victims have a point of view separate from his own, that he is growing in his ability to determine what the impact of his behavior is on others, and that he is moving toward developing empathy for his and others' victims.

ATTEMPTS TO CHANGE BEHAVIOR

The single most vital issue in sex offender treatment is whether or not the offender can change his behavior. An offender must begin to understand that behavioral change is more than simply announcing, "I won't do it again." Behavior change involves a series of lifestyle changes designed to minimize the risk of reoffending. It involves learning techniques for intervening when deviant impulses arise, and showing a willingness to implement them.

All other measures of progress are secondary to behavioral change. An offender may attend group regularly and promptly, pay for his treatment, say he is responsible for his behavior, demonstrate an excellent understanding of antecedent links in the chain of abuse and of appropriate techniques for interrupting the chain, and cry when the plight of victims is discussed. If, however, he is not changing his behavior outside of group, he remains dangerous to the community. Such offenders may be psychopathic personalities who have learned to manipulate treatment jargon and to mimic desired feelings and attitudes in order to escape from treatment. An incestuous psychopath might, at the same time he is publicly "progressing" in the group, secretly be making unsupervised visits to his victims. An exhibitionist might be cruising daily by a school at 3 o'clock. An extrafamilial offender might invite the papergirl, to whom he has long been attracted, onto his porch to visit. Behavior of this sort should be treated as a red flag that the offender is dangerously close to reoffending. If unchecked or minimized by a staff seduced by an offender's "insight" or by his verbal skills, it will surely lead to sexual acting out.

Such offenders rarely report their own duplicity. When a program learns of such a schism between thought and action, usually through others in the community, it should be taken very seriously and treated as a crisis in treatment. Such an individual might be reduced from group member to candidate. He would surely have tighter rules and regulations imposed involving more supervision. No doubt there would be a meeting involving the treatment team, the offender and his probation officer, to discuss his behavior and the new regulations. His group would surely confront him with lying to them, certainly by omission and possibly by commission. His family would be informed of his changed status and the reasons for it. Persistent refusal to change behavior would be grounds for termination. This would be so despite progress in any other area. When words and behavior differ, behavior is the more accurate indicator of the degree of progress.

ASSERTIVENESS AND WILLINGNESS TO HELP OTHER GROUP MEMBERS

Group therapy implies a mutual responsibility among group members for the progress of all parties. Offenders are often quicker than therapists to pick up on early movement toward deviant behavior and have a choice of either colluding with or confronting it. It is not to be expected that an offender who will collude with deviancy in someone else will confront it in himself. He has little to lose by confronting it in others, and much to change by confronting it in himself.

Once offenders graduate from treatment they will be responsible for detecting and changing any relapse to deviance in themselves. This requires vigilance, assertiveness, and initiative. All of these can be developed and demonstrated in a group. An offender who sits passively waiting for others to speak to him, who has no agenda items, and who does not challenge or confront others is not demonstrating the degree of vigilance and assertiveness he will need in order to monitor movement toward relapse in himself. Offenders should be made aware of and held accountable for helping others in the group by active participation and confrontation.

MONITORING PROGRESS

Offenders will ordinarily be in treatment for two years or more. Following the initial assessment and entry into the group, progress should be assessed formally in three months time. Thereafter a formal review of progress in all areas, by staff and then with the offender, should occur no less frequently than every six months. Events could trigger an earlier review. Concerns on the part of staff that the offender is not making sufficient progress would invite a review; evidence of acting-out behavior certainly would do so. The offender and the staff should communicate their assessment of an offender's progress orally and in writing. The probation officer should attend the meeting and add his assessment.

GRADUATION VERSUS PROGRESS

An offender must demonstrate progress in order to remain in treatment. It is less important how quickly an offender progresses than that he does progress, and that his words and behavior match. In fact, progress that is too quick should be viewed with suspicion, and is often a marker for a words/behavior split. True change is slow and requires effort.

In order to graduate, however, an offender must demonstrate much more than just progress. He must have completed all program requirements. This means that he must first have attended faithfully and promptly, and paid his fees. His homework assignments must have been done on time, have addressed adequately the required tasks, and be of the required length. They must not simply be mechanical responses to requests or attempts at guessing what the program wants to hear. They must evidence thoughtfulness, honesty, and a grasp of the point of the exercise.

The graduating offender must show a clear and convincing understanding of his responsibility for his offenses. He does not make excuses for his behavior either obliquely or directly and will be quick to spot and confront excuses in others. He is aware of his risk factors and can detect thoughts and behaviors that are part of the cycle of reoffending. Most important, he intervenes when deviant thoughts or fantasies arise and uses one of the variety of treatment techniques at his disposal to reduce them. He does not minimize his risk of reoffending, and worries about it. He lives one day at a time and does not ever say, "I'll never do it again." He wonders what it will be like to live the rest of his life knowing that he could reoffend.

He no longer projects his excuses onto the victim, but understands something of the confusion, helplessness, and shame that sexual assault victims feel. He shows genuine remorse for the pain and suffering he has caused and knows he can never make it up or "undo" it. In group he is able to point out to other offenders the impact of their behavior on others, from minor displays of lack of consideration to major offenses. He demonstrates emotional empathy for other people, recognizing how others are hurt by his behavior, sexual and nonsexual. When he talks about not wanting to reoffend he talks not only about the difficulties it would produce for him, but about what it would do to those who love him and to his victims.

Most important, he has made a series of lifestyle changes to minimize risk. He does not put himself in situations that are potentially risky; he removes himself from them when they do arise. He will spontaneously restart some aspect of the program, for example, boredom tapes, when the need demands.

He has learned how to solve nonsexual problems nonsexually, and has adequate social and sexual skills to meet his needs in nondeviant ways. He has become something of a leader in the group, quick to confront, but without a sadistic edge. He is known as one of the most assertive members of the group and helps set the tone for others.

He is not cured. He understands this. He is under control and has the tools and the demonstrated ability to keep himself under control. He has some doubts and he is scared. He is not free from risk. He could reoffend, and some will. However, his risk of reoffense is as low as current treatment techniques can produce.

12

OFFENDER ASSESSMENT

From the discussion of offender treatment in Chapter 9 it is clear that the following information is necessary about an offender in order to adequately treat him:

(1) sexual history—history of sexual fantasies as well as sexual behaviors
(2) arousal pattern—if deviant, with what age and sex of child combined with what degree of force
(3) strength of nondeviant fantasies
(4) attitudes and knowledge regarding sexuality
(5) chain of events leading to sexual acting out
(6) cognitive distortions regarding sexually deviant behavior
(7) particulars of the offense for which he was charged
(8) degree of denial
(9) degree of empathy for victim
(10) degree of antisocial behavior—extent to which sexual acting out is part of an overall pattern of criminal or sociopathic behavior
(11) attitudes towards women
(12) social skills
(13) assertiveness
(14) aggressiveness
(15) strengths and problems in marriage

(16) family problems
(17) personal/developmental history
(18) alcohol use/abuse
(19) personality traits correlated with sexual abuse: externalization, psychopathy, depression

With this information a therapist is in an excellent position to tailor treatment to a particular client's deviancy, as well as to know which clients not to treat. Knowing which cognitive distortions an offender holds, for example, allows a therapist to focus on those particular cognitive distortions; likewise, knowing that a particular client was aroused to violence with no erotic component alerts a therapist to a client too dangerous to treat on an outpatient basis.

What is striking, however, about this list of required information is that the routine mental health battery of tests generally applied to mental health clients is unlikely to address them. A typical battery might include the following:

(1) Wechsler Adult Intelligence Scale
(2) Rorschach
(3) Thematic Apperception Test
(4) Bender-Gestalt
(5) Clinical Interview

These tests not only do not address most of the issues listed above, they also provide information that is largely irrelevant to the treatment of sexual deviancy. It is not the intention of this manual to find fault with these tests for other clients in other contexts. Their durability attests to the amount of useful information that therapists derive from them. However, a moment's reflection will illuminate their limitations with regard to sex offenders.

INTELLIGENCE

Intellectual level does not appear to be correlated with sexual deviancy. Offenders range from the retarded to the brilliant. Most offenders fall in between. Nor has the presence of learning disabilities been demonstrated to correlate with sexual acting out. Thus IQ and/or the presence of specific learning disabilities are usually irrelevant variables in sex offender treatment. It is true that an offender with limited cognitive capacity must have things explained more slowly and more concretely than a more intellectually competent person, but most therapists are able to identify someone who is not understanding the material without recourse to an IQ score. Certainly, when working with truly retarded offenders, a therapist may wish to be clear about the extent of the deficits. There are indeed cases in which a therapist is unsure how much an offender is understanding. In situations where, for example, a retarded offender may be pretending to understand for fear of being embarrassed, an IQ test could be useful. For the majority of cases, however, it will be of little utility.

PROJECTIVE TESTING

The primary difficulty in using projectives with offenders is that offenders can be found who have many different personality types. The single personality type that appears to be found with more frequency in child sex offenders is the antisocial personality. Abel et al. (1985) found that 29.2% of his sample of rapists and 11.6% of his sample of child molesters met DSM-II criteria. Virkkunen (1981) in a summary of the literature suggested also that antisocial personality disorders are frequently found in child molesters. With such offenders, molesting children or assaulting adults is part of a general pattern of lack of concern for persons and property, manifested also by a history of other criminal behavior.

With that exception, most psychiatric and personality characteristics of offenders appear to be causally unrelated to the process of offending. Depression, for example, is frequently noted clinically among offenders; however, it appears in many cases to be related to the effects of discovery. With regard to other personality traits, it may be of academic interest to note unconscious themes and strivings, but it is of little practical consequence if the task is to minimize the risk of reoffense. Both an offender with obsessive-compulsive defenses and one with hysterical traits may respond to a treatment program that treats them alike in regard to their sexual deviancy. They may also respond to psychotherapy that is designed to reduce one's degree of compulsiveness and the other's degree of hysteria, but such a program will not reduce the likelihood of reoffense. Lanyon (1986) has commented that intrapsychic difficulties have not been shown to play a causal role in the development and maintenance of the deviant sexual behavior and ... although they may hamper treatment, they are not the root of the disorder and do not necessarily require treatment for the sexual problem to be alleviated. (p. 176)

BENDER-GESTALT

From the Bender-Gestalt Test a therapist may justifiably infer whether or not the offender has difficulties with perceptual motor skills. However, the test has not infrequently been used to extrapolate to fields far removed from these fields. This author listened to a psychologist testify in court that his client's poor performance on the Bender was a justification for not taking the plethysmograph since, we were to infer, he would not have the coordination to masturbate. This author has also read a psychological report in which the psychologist claimed his client was unlikely to have committed the sexual offense for which he was charged, since he was not impulsive in copying the designs. The author of the report felt only men who were impulsive committed sexual offenses, and accepted a lack of impulsivity on the Bender-Gestalt as indicative of a general lack of impulsivity.

Both types of arguments are inappropriate. First, a client who has sufficient perceptual motor coordination to open doors and otherwise function in the world has enough coordination to masturbate. Second, there is little evidence that impulsivity on the Bender-Gestalt correlates with impulsivity outside the perceptual motor realm. Third, many sex offenders plan their offenses and are more careful than impulsive. Even when sex offenders commit sexual crimes impulsively, they are often not impulsive in other ways. Offenders can be found who are teachers, principals, psychologists, doctors, and so forth, all of whom hold jobs that do not permit seriously impulsive behavior.

CLINICAL INTERVIEW

The clinical interview is used with sex offenders, but without the degree of confidence one ordinarily assigns to it. A client entering therapy for depression, anxiety, or marital or family difficulties can be expected to be relatively honest with his/her therapist. The client is experiencing distress and is seeking help in alleviating it. It would be as foolish to lie extensively to a therapist regarding the distress as it would to show a physician the wrong part of the body. Certainly, not all clients know exactly what is wrong, nor do they initially trust a therapist enough to share, for example, information regarding an affair or their homosexuality. There is, of course, a universal tendency for people to try to make themselves look good (except for depressed clients, who may be biased in the opposite direction) and it is simply human to try to elicit the therapist's sympathy for how right one is in certain situations and how wrong/unfair/blind another party is. Still, the client has no systematic reason to lie directly, and the clinical interview may be used to obtain a reasonable sample of the individual's experience and history with occasional distortions, as earlier noted.

The clinical interview with a sex offender, particularly before he has begun the process of treatment, must be assigned a different degree of weight in the overall assessment. He is typically afraid to tell you, and even himself, the truth. He has been hiding his sexual proclivities, often for decades. In all likelihood he believes that a sex offender is the "scum of the earth" and that if he admits to the extent of his deviancy his world will collapse. He will be sent to jail; you and the world (including himself) will find him disgusting; he will lose his family; he will lose his job; he will never get another job; he will have no future; no one will ever care for him again.

Still, there seems to be something deeper here as well. Even if the offender could be convinced that none of these disasters would be realized, it is this author's opinion that many sex offenders would nonetheless lie. Magical thinking may be at work here, whereby *if they say it isn't so, it isn't so.* For many, sexual deviancy does not occur when they commit the act, it occurs when they admit it. A sex offender is not a sex offender until he tells you he is. He really is, in some sense, a wrongly accused innocent until he says the words, "Yes I did do it."

Even a cursory reading of the literature should inform the novice sex offender therapist that a clinical interview cannot be trusted, especially one conducted prior to treatment. In a study by Abel et al. (1985), objective measures of sexual arousal (via plethysmograph) and self-report coincided in only 30% of their sample (7 cases) *even when complete confidentiality was elaborately guaranteed.* The remaining 70% of the sample (17 cases) were confronted with the discrepancy. Of those, 70% (12 cases) then admitted to additional deviant sexual arousal patterns. Thus a full 49% (12 cases) of the entire sample revised their report after a single experience with objective assessment and subsequent confrontation. This is particularly striking, since these were volunteer subjects whose admissions would not have been reported to the authorities. A clinical interview is thus utilized in working with sex offenders, but as much for a check on the offender's level of denial and to obtain information unrelated to the sexual deviancy as to obtain reliable information.

WHAT IS USEFUL

The following is a list of psychological tests that address issues that are relevant to understanding and treating sex offenders. The only absolutely essential one is the plethysmograph, because it is the only objective one. All other tests, with the exception of reports from outside sources, rely on self-report. These tests either measure sexual deviancy or issues relevant to treatment, e.g., social skills, cognitive distortions, and empathy. They represent the most adequate tests this author could discover at this time. With the exception of the plethysmograph and the Minnesota Multiphasic Personality Inventory (MMPI), chosen for the extensive research that has been done with the MMPI on sex offenders, most of these choices are ultimately arbitrary, although the categories they represent are not. The reader who has found a better social skills scale or a better cognitive distortions scale should use it. However, whatever the choice, some good social-skills and cognitive-distortion scales should be included. No doubt this recommended assessment battery will be revised over time as more experience with sex offenders and better tests permit a further refinement of tools.

ASSESSMENT BATTERY FOR SEX OFFENDERS

Abel and Becker Cognitions Scale
Attitudes Toward Women Scale
Burt Rape Myth Acceptance Scale
Buss-Durkee Hostility Inventory
Clinical Interview

Family Adaptability and Cohesion Evaluation Scale (FACES)
Interpersonal Reactivity Index
Michigan Alcohol Screening Test (MAST)
Minnesota Multiphasic Personality Inventory (MMPI)
Multiphasic Sex Inventory
Penile Plethysmograph
Previous Reports and Evaluations (Offender's Statement to the Police,
    Victim's Statement, Presentence Investigation)
Social Avoidance and Distress Scale
Wilson Sexual Fantasy Questionnaire
Optional Tests:
Abel and Becker Sexual Interest Card Sort
Adult Nowicki-Strickland Internal/External Control Scale
Fear of Negative Evaluation Scale
Jackson Personality Inventory

Abel and Becker Cognition Scale

This scale measures many of the cognitive distortions many sex offenders hold that allow them to rationalize their behavior (Abel et al., 1984). It consists of 29 items chosen from statements offenders have actually made in treatment. It is a surprisingly good measure, because those offenders who hold cognitive distortions are often unaware of them. They have persuaded themselves that their behavior is not harmful, and will often try to persuade others as well. Thus they admit to the distortions. For example, a pedophile may well strongly agree with the statement that "A child 13 or younger can make her (his) own decision as to whether she (he) wants to have sex with an adult or not." By asking offenders to fill in the questionnaire reproduced in Appendix F, the therapist can focus treatment around those distortions that a particular offender actually believes. The scale is used clinically and is not formally scored.

Attitudes Toward Women

This scale has 15 items that measure attitudes towards a number of aspects of the female role, including vocational, educational and intellectual aspects as well as interpersonal relationships (Spence & Helmreich, 1978, 1972). The interpersonal realm covers dating, sexual behavior, and marital obligations. Subjects indicate their degree of agreement on a four-point scale from "agrees strongly" to "disagrees strongly."

Much of the research to date with this scale has concentrated on nonoffending populations. Spence and Helmreich (1972) report data that suggest that women score higher (less conservatively) than men, that college students score higher than parents of the same sex, that undergraduate psychology students score lower than graduate psychology students but are higher than engineering students, and so forth. All of these findings suggest that the scale does indeed measure traditional versus more egalitarian attitudes towards women.

Koss divided male college students into the following categories: (1) sexually assaultive, (2) sexually abusive, (3) sexually coercive, and (4) sexually nonaggressive (Koss, Leonard, Beezley, & Oros, 1981, 1985). Sexually assaultive males were those who had obtained intercourse through the use of or threat of violence. Sexually abusive men had applied force to obtain fondling or had attempted, but not completed, intercourse through the use of force. Sexually coercive males had employed verbal manipulation (e.g., threats to end the relationship, false promises), whereas sexually nonaggressive males admitted only to consenting sex. Koss et al. used a 25-item version of the Attitudes Toward Women Scale and found that highly sexually aggressive males subscribed to more conservative attitudes towards women than did less sexually aggressive men. (Appendix G contains the scale.)

Burt Rape Myth Acceptance Scale

A measure of rape beliefs should be included in an assessment of child molesters because of recent research indicating that many sex offenders engage in multiple paraphilias (Abel et al., 1985). The Burt Scale is a 19-item questionnaire designed to measure acceptance of rape myths (Burt, 1980, 1983; Burt & Albin, 1981). Items are scored on a 7-point scale ranging from "strongly agree" to "strongly disagree." Research indicates that the greater the amount of sex role stereotyping, adversarial sexual beliefs, and tolerance of interpersonal violence, the higher a subject's agreement with rape myths (Burt, 1980).

Koss et al. (1985), using an early version of the Burt Scale, found that sexually assaultive males differed from sexually nonaggressive males in their acceptance of rape myths. Koss used an early version of the Burt Scale. Burt (1983) found that the higher rapists scored on the Rape Myth Acceptance Scale, the more likely they were to justify violence in clinical vignettes (Burt, 1983). In a study of the general population she found that the more individuals subscribed to rape myths, the less likely they were to define a sexually coercive situation as rape (Burt & Albin, 1981).

Check and Malamuth (1985) gave college males a pornographic rape portrayal and then later a newspaper account of an actual rape. They measured the individuals' self-reports of their own likelihood of raping and correlated these with scores on the Rape Myth Acceptance Scale. Findings indicated that men who scored higher on the Rape Myth Acceptance Scale were more likely to perceive the victim's experience in the pornographic rape depiction as positive, more often felt that the victim in the newspaper account was responsible for the rape, and more frequently subscribed to the belief that women secretly wished to be raped and to the belief that natural tendencies in men as well as the behavior of women were responsible for rape. In addition, such males were more likely to self-report a higher likelihood of raping women. Check and Malamuth cited other research that has substantiated the connection between rape myth acceptance and aggressive behavior, including actual aggression under experimental conditions (Check & Malamuth, 1985). (The scale is included in Appendix H.)

Buss-Durkee Hostility Inventory

This scale contains 66 true/false items that measure the following seven aspects of hostility: negativism, resentment, indirect hostility, assault, suspicion, irritability , and verbal hostility (Buss & Durkee, 1957). Subscale totals are obtained along with an overall hostility index. Anger and hostility appear to be more frequently components of rape than of child molestation (Groth, 1979), and have been little studied in regard to the latter. However, in their study of paraphiliacs (Abel et al., 1981) found that 58% of their sample of child molesters used unnecessary force in the commission of the offense, compared to 71% of rapists. Injuries resulted to 42% of the children, as opposed to 39% of the adult rape victims. Peters (1976) found that physical force was used on 46% of their child victims of sexual assault. Thirty-seven percent of the children were subjected to forcible rape, that is, intercourse through force or the threat of force. Likewise, Abel et al. (1985) found that 50.6% of their sample of rapists also molested children, whereas 16.8% of their child molesters committed rape. Because of the degree of overlap between rapists and child molesters, the reports of excessive force used in a significant percentage of cases of child molestation, and the well-known association of anger and rape, a measure of hostility and assaultiveness is advised. (The measure is found in Appendix I.)

Clinical Interview

A clinical interview should first of all cover information about the present sexual offense, other possible offenses of the same nature, and other sexual deviations that have not previously been revealed. Many sex offenders have multiple deviations but do not volunteer them. Second, the interview should focus on the client's feelings and beliefs regarding his deviant sexuality and his feelings and beliefs regarding the victim's reaction. Finally, an interview should cover the client's personal and family history. Personal history is not covered in any of the other questionnaires or tests. It is better to decide on a format for the clinical interview and use it uniformly, as it is easy to overlook vital information. See Groth (1979) for a more detailed description of a comprehensive clinical interview.

Family Adaptability and Cohesion Scale (FACES)

This is a 20-item scale that assesses family adaptability and cohesion (Olson, Portner & Lavee, 1985). One set of 20 items is used to measure perceived family functioning and a second set with identical content but slight wording changes is used to assess ideal family functioning. Responses range from 1 ("almost never") to 5 ("almost always").

The scale identifies four levels of family cohesion from extremely low cohesion to extremely high. These are labeled "disengaged," "separated," "connected," and "enmeshed." Adaptability likewise falls into 4 levels from low to high, termed "rigid," "structured," "flexible," and "chaotic." By combining all possibilities, a set of 16 different family types is generated. Of these 16, 4 fall into the moderate area on both scales and are thought to be more functional for families. Eight types are extreme on one dimension and moderate on the other, and are considered midrange types of families. Four types are extreme on both scales.

FACES is one of the more adequate scales of family dysfunction and is, in addition, very easy to use. Family dysfunction, while not etiologically responsible for child sexual abuse, is a barrier to control of sexually abusive behavior and should be addressed in treatment. FACES allows the clinician to assess objectively the degree and type of dysfunction. Research on families of runaways, of alcoholics, of adolescent juvenile offenders, and of sex offenders has found that they fell more often into the more extreme ranges on FACES than did control families (Olson et al., 1985). The scale and manual can be obtained from the author.

Interpersonal Reactivity Index

This 28-item index measures four dimensions of empathy: perspective taking, empathic concern, fantasy, and personal distress (Davis, 1980). Responses are made on a five-point scale from A ("does not describe me well") to E ("describes me very well"). Perspective taking measures the ability to assume cognitively the role of the other. Empathic concern measures feelings of warmth, compassion, and concern for another. Fantasy addresses the ability of the respondent to identify with characters in fiction, including movies, novels, and plays, whereas personal distress addresses anxiety and negative emotions resulting from feeling the distress of another. This last scale shows a negative correlation with perspective taking.

The strength of this particular scale is its ability to divide the generic term "empathy" into a cognitive and an emotional component; there are two scales for each. Davis (1983c) demonstrated correlations between the subscales and measures of social competence, self-esteem, emotionality, and sensitivity to others. Perspective taking was related to social competence and self-esteem, and was less correlated with measures of emotionality than were other subscales. Empathic concern scores were less related to social functioning and more related to emotional sensitivity to others. Empathic concern was also correlated with the Mehrabian and Epstein empathy scale. The role of individual differences in empathy has also been demonstrated (Davis, 1983a) and found to be dependent on variability in empathic concern rather than perspective taking. Finally Davis (1983b) found that variations in empathic concern were correlated with the viewing of and contributing to a muscular dystrophy telethon.

The difference in perspective taking and empathic concern may be particularly important in dealing with sex offenders, since clinically at least, some offenders give every indication of being able to take the perspective of the child but use that ability to manipulate the child, lacking any type of empathic concern for the effects of the manipulation. A preliminary study is in process to determine whether or not sex offenders do score as high on perspective taking as controls but lower in empathic concern. (Appendix J contains the scale.)

Michigan Alcoholism Screening Test (MAST)

The MAST (Selzer, 1971; Skinner & Sheu, 1982) is a 25-item true/false questionnaire. Interestingly, it asks no questions regarding the quantity of alcohol consumption, as previous studies found answers to such questions vague and not discriminatory. Instead, it focuses on questions regarding interpersonal problems over or while drinking, social, physical, or job-related consequences of drinking, and attempts to control drinking.

Alcoholism has repeatedly been shown to correlate with sexual aggression. Virkkunen (1974) reviewed research that found alcoholism rates of 50% to 80% in sex offenders. Peters (1976) and Rada (1976) reported that approximately half of their samples of offenders were drinking at the time they committed the offense. Abel et al. (1985) found that 30% of their group of child molesters indicated that drinking alcohol increased their attraction to children, whereas 45% of the rapists stated that alcohol increased their desire to rape. Abel et al. concluded that, "alcohol appears to be a particularly dangerous drug for paraphiliacs to use" (p. 198). Given the correlation between sexual aggression and alcohol as well as the potentiating power of alcohol, a measure of drinking behavior should be included. (The scale may be found in Appendix K.)

Minnesota Multiphasic Personality Inventory (MMPI)

The MMPI is the most widely known and best researched personality instrument used with sex offenders. It consists of 566 true/false items that produce 4 validity scales and 10 clinical scales. Clinical scales are currently designated more frequently by number than by name to lessen the possibility that unintended meanings will be attributed to them on the basis of common interpretations of scale names. Nonetheless the scales retain some degree of similarity to their original names, which are as follows:

(1) hypochondriasis
(2) depression
(3) hysteria
(4) psychopathic deviate
(5) masculinity-femininity
(6) paranoia
(7) psychasthenia
(8) schizophrenia
(9) hypomania
(10) social introversion

Research on the MMPI has sometimes found a 4-8 MMPI code to be the predominant mean profile of some types of child sex offenders. Armentrout and Hauer (1978) found child rapists to have an 4-8 profile, as compared to incest offenders, who did not. Likewise Panton (1978) found child rapists to have a 4-8 profile, but did not find that profile in nonviolent child molesters. In subsequent research Panton (1979) found incest offenders to have a 4-2 code mean profile. Some research (Hall, Maiuro, Vitaliano, & Proctnor, 1986; Langevin, Paitich, Freeman, Mann & Handy, 1978; Quinsey, Arnold, & Pruesse, 1980; Toobert, Bartelme, & Jones, 1959) has found no differences in mean 4-8 profiles when comparing sex offenders with other types of offenders; for example, offenders against persons or property in a psychiatric hospital (Quinsey et al., 1980) or prison inmates not convicted of a sex crime (Toobert et al., 1959). However, differences in those studies that did and those studies that did not find a 4-8 profile may in part be explained by the methods of data analysis. In a 1986 study by Hall et al. of 406 incarcerated offenders, the highest mean elevations were on Scales 4 and 8. However, this was true despite the fact that only 7.1% of the offenders had a 4-8 or an 8-4 profile. Most of the offenders had multiple-scale elevations, with 67% having three or more. Even though scales 4, 8 and 2 had the highest mean ratings, no subject had these three scales elevated exclusively. While only 7% had no scale elevations, Hall found considerable diversity in the profiles. He found his population to be "a more varied and heterogeneous group than they were initially proposed to be" (p. 496).

The MMPI can validly be used to determine the psychological profile of a given offender. Scores on the depression and psychopathy scales will be of particular interest to the treatment-oriented clinician. However, there is no evidence at present that the MMPI can be validly used to determine whether or not an individual is a sex offender. Although this author has seen psychological reports that attempt to "prove" an individual's innocence of a particular charge of child molestation on the basis that he did not have a 4-8 profile, the literature cited above suggests that this cannot be done.

Unlike many of the instruments described in this section, the MMPI cannot be used by anyone who is not a clinical psychologist. It can be administered and scored by others with ease, but must be given to a psychologist for interpretation. The complexity of interpretation of this particular test requires specialized training.

Multiphasic Sex Inventory (MSI)

The Multiphasic Sex Inventory (Nichols & Molinder, 1984) consists of 300 true/false items. These produce 20 clinical scales and a sexual history. The clinical scales are as follows:

Type of Scale	Number
validity	6
sexual deviance	3
atypical sexual behavior	5
sexual dysfunction	4
sexual knowledge scale	1
treatment attitudes	1
	20

The Paraphilias (Sexual Deviation) Subtest, consisting of the Child Molest Scale, the Rape Scale, and the Exhibitionism Scale is considered the backbone of the MSI. These scales measure cognitions and behaviors thought to be common to child sexual offenders, and thus are considered by the test's authors to measure "universal" aspects of molestation.

The Paraphilias (Atypical Sexual Outlet) or P(ASO) consists of five scales: Fetish, Obscene Call, Voyeurism, Bondage and Discipline, and Sado-Masochism. These are considered along with the scales on sexual dysfunction, sex knowledge and belief, and sex history, to measure individual differences among sex offenders. The P(ASO) is designed to assess behaviors that, although often a cause for clinical concern, rarely result in legal action against the offender.

The validity scales included a Parallel Items Scale (identical items to a subset of the MMPI), Sex Obsessions Scale, Social Sexual Desirability Scale, four Lie Scales, of which only the relevant one is used (child molestation, rape, exhibitionism, and incest), a Cognitive Distortions and Immaturity Scale, and a Justification Scale, which measures the degree to which the offender justifies his behavior.

The authors caution that the MSI cannot be used as a test of whether or not an individual is a sex offender since "no test, no device, has the power to pick out a sexually deviant person from any other person in a crowd" (Nichols & Molinder, 1984, p. 3). The test is to be used following discovery. Nonetheless, validity studies found significant differences on the clinical scales in the expected directions between untreated sex offenders and normal college males. Notwithstanding, posttreatment means on the sex offender's clinical scales increased dramatically, in some cases doubling, indicating greater deviancy in the posttest than in the pretest. At the same time, scores on the validity scales went down on the posttest, in the direction of less lying and less defensiveness. On the posttest they approached the scores of the college population. Thus, although sex offenders scored very differently from controls, even when untreated, the effects of treatment were such that the offenders admitted to more deviancy after treatment than before, while their defensiveness and deception decreased.

The validation research on this test is quite promising, and indicates generally that this test measures reliably what it was intended to measure. In addition, the manual is extremely well written and offers a short but highly accurate course on sexual deviancy. The test can be obtained from the authors (Nichols & Molinder, 1984).

Penile Plethysmograph

The plethysmograph is currently the most valid and reliable method for determining sexual preference. It consists of a small transducer that the offender places on his penis while in a room alone. He sits in a chair with his pants down to the point that clothes are not touching the transducer. The transducer is connected to a recording device in another room, which charts changes in the tumescence of the penis as detected by the transducer. Instructions are usually given by a therapist through a microphone connecting the two rooms, thus ensuring as much privacy as possible for the offender. Prior to the session the therapist has calibrated the equipment and set up the stimulus. The stimuli can be either slides, audio tapes, or video tapes. Slides are considered the weakest stimuli and videotapes the most arousing. A particularly effective combination appears to be the use of slides to determine the age and sex of child the offender finds arousing, and audio tapes to determine the degree of force.

The slides cover preschool children through adolescence plus both sexes of adults. The degree of force generally ranges from consent (manipulated consent in children, and genuine consent in adults) to the rape of children and/or adults (application of a degree of force necessary to perpetrate the abuse), and finally to sadism (use of force beyond that necessary to obtain compliance).

Research has repeatedly shown the plethysmograph to be useful. It has been shown to differentiate rapists from nonrapists (Abel, Blanchard, & Becker, 1978; Abel, Blanchard, Becker, & Djen-deredjian, 1978; Barbaree, Marshall, & Lanthier, 1979), to determine an individual's interest in sexual sadism (Abel, Blanchard, Barlow, & Mavissakalian, 1975; Abel, Blanchard, Becker, & Djenderedjian, 1978; Abel, Barlow, Blanchard & Guild, 1977), to identify child molesters with an inclination towards child rape (Abel et al., 1981), to separate recidivists from nonrecidivists (Quinsey, Chaplin, & Carrigan, 1980) and to measure response to treatment (Quinsey, Bergersen & Steinman, 1976; Quinsey et al., 1980). It remains the most practical and objective method for determining sexual prefer- ence in an individual whose self-disclosure may be suspect.

Nonetheless there are limitations in the ability of the plethysmo- graph to detect sexual deviancy, and these limitations fall on the line where preference meets behavior. The plethysmograph is a test of an individual's sexual preference; it cannot determine whether an individual has acted or will act on it. It is entirely likely that individuals exist who have an abnormal sexual preference but sufficient internal controls to refrain from indulging it (Finkelhor, 1984).

Conversely there is no proof that *all* sex offenders have a deviant arousal pattern, and various terms—situational, opportunistic, regressed—have been used to describe offenders thought to commit sexual crimes, in the absence of a consistent sexual preference for children. Sufficient empirical data have not been amassed to answer the question of what percentage of sex offenders have a deviant arousal pattern, and results of research to date have been equivocal (Abel et al., 1981; Murphy et al., 1986; Quinsey et al., 1979).

In conclusion, the presence of an abnormal sexual preference does not guarantee that an individual has committed a particular crime, nor any crime at all, while the absence of a deviant arousal pattern conversely does not prove an individual is innocent of a particular crime. Misuse of the plethysmograph in either direction will surely lead eventually to limitations on its use, thus depriving treatment professionals of one of the few ways of validly determining an offender's sexual preference.

Previous Reports and Evaluations

All previous reports relating to the sexual abuse should be obtained. These frequently include the following:

> victim's statement to the police
> offender's statement to the police
> presentence investigation
> probation and parole report

A permission form must be signed to obtain the above; an offender should not be accepted into treatment who will not sign it. Previous mental health evaluations should also be obtained, if possible, but these are often less useful, since the offender may not have admitted to his sexual deviancy or been evaluated for it.

Social Avoidance and Distress Scale

This is a 28-item true/false scale (Watson & Friend, 1969). It was designed to assess an individual's desire or effort to avoid social interactions with others as well as the extent of personal distress present in social interactions. Validation studies have found that high scorers do avoid social situations and are anxious when in them. They are described as "clearly isolated and often fearful" (Watson & Friend, 1969, p. 457).

In a summary of the literature on social-skills deficits, Howells (1981) reported consistently positive findings. Assessment and remediation of social-skills deficits are important to therapeutic success, since newly acquired or strengthened sexual arousal to adults cannot be realized without sufficient social skills. (Appendix L contains the scale.)

Wilson Sexual Fantasy Questionnaire

The Fantasy Questionnaire (Wilson, 1978) consists of 40 items, each describing a sexual activity. Respondents are asked to rate how often they fantasize about these themes in the daytime, how often they fantasize about them during intercourse or masturbation, how often they dream about such themes, how often they have acted them out in reality, and whether they would like to act them out in reality. For each category respondents are asked to fill in a number from 0 ("never") to 5 ("regularly").

The scale covers a wide variety of sexual activity, from sado-masochism to object fetishes. Since fantasies often are used in the chain of behaviors leading to sexually abusive behaviors, knowledge of the offender's sexual fantasies is essential in developing covert sensitization tapes. (Appendix M includes the scale.)

OPTIONAL MEASURES

Abel and Becker Sexual Interest Card Sort

The Abel and Becker Card Sort contains 75 items measuring sexual arousal in 15 categories: adult male, adult female, heterosexual pedophile, homosexual pedophile, male incest, female incest, rape, sadism, masochism, frottage, voyeurism, exhibitionism, tranvestism, male gender identity, and female gender identity. Arousal is measured on a scale from "extremely sexually repulsive" to "extremely sexually arousing."

This is a self-report test and therefore most useful with offenders who are honest about their sexual proclivities. With other offenders it is useful as a measure of denial when combined with the plethysmograph. Since response categories are similar, it affords the therapist an early opportunity to begin to confront the offender. For example, the discrepancy between the offender's self-report of arousal to female children and the more objective readings of the plethysmograph afford a chance for a therapist to point out the difference between the two, and to explain that the penile plethysmograph permits a direct measure of sexual arousal, while self-report often encompasses what one would like to be true.

In addition, while offenders who are being less than honest rarely give high ratings to any of the categories, the relative differences may be interesting. An exhibitionist, for example, who denied any arousal to exhibitionist items, scored several of the voyeur items as less repulsive and a few as neutral, compared to the "extremely repulsive" ratings he gave all other items on the test. (The Abel and Becker Card Sort is found in Appendix N.)

Nowicki-Strickland Internal/External Scale

The Nowicki-Strickland (Nowicki & Duke, 1974) is a locus-of-control scale that consists of 40 statements to which the subject responds with "yes" or "no" depending on whether he believes them to be true of himself or not. Low scorers tend to believe they are responsible for what happens to them; average scorers tend to locate control either internally or externally, depending on the situation; high scorers tend to feel that they have little control over their fate.

A measure of locus of control may be useful with sex offenders, given the degree to which they externalize responsibility for the sexual assaults (see Chapter 8 on Denial). However, it is unclear at present whether or not the externalization characteristic of sex offenders is specific to sexual deviancy or part of a larger pattern of denying responsibility. The Nowicki-Strickland measures locus of control generally, and is not focused on sexual issues. For this reason it is suggested as an optional scale. Further research will be needed to determine whether or not an externalization scale that only deals with sexual offenses will need to be developed. (Appendix O contains the scale.)

Fear of Negative Evaluation

This is a 30-item true/false questionnaire that measures anxiety over evaluations by others, expectations of negative evaluations, discomfort over evaluations, and avoidance of them (Watson & Friend, 1969). It can be used clinically as an indication of how sensitive an individual is to criticism and how avoidant of situations in which such criticism is possible. Correlational research has indicated that high scorers tend to be defensive, dependent, and self-effacing.

This scale is recommended because of the literature suggesting that child molesters, particularly, are avoidant of social interactions. Abel et al. (1985) found that 45% of a sample of child molesters and 50.6% of the rapists had below-average skills in assertiveness. Overholser & Beck (1986) found that child molesters displayed more fear of negative evaluation than did rapists or non-sex-offender inmate controls. Howells (1981) concluded that pedophiles saw adult relationships in terms of dominance and submissiveness, and found "adults overbearing, whereas children are viewed as non-threatening and easy to relate to because of their submissive status" (p. 74). Excessive concern about evaluation by adults along with a belief that children are more tolerant may be a factor in a pedophile's preference for children. (The scale is contained in Appendix P.)

Jackson Personality Inventory

The Jackson Personality Inventory[1] is a 320-item true-false personality inventory consisting of 16 scales, each with 20 statements. It typically requires approximately 40-50 minutes to administer. The 16 scales are as follows:

anxiety
breadth of interest
complexity
conformity
energy level
innovation
interpersonal affect
organization
responsibility
risk-taking
self esteem
social adroitness
social participation
tolerance

value orthodoxy
infrequency

The last scale, infrequency, is a validity scale. As can be seen, a number of these scales are particularly relevant to the assessment and treatment of sex offenders, among them conformity, interpersonal affect, responsibility, risk-taking, social adroitness and social participation.

The chief disadvantage of the Jackson Inventory, other than its size, is that it was designed to be primarily used with normal and not pathological populations, its norms being based on "normal" college students. Frequent uses are in counseling, personality research, and in business and industry.

However, sex offenders include in their ranks many "normal" members of society who function well in nonsexual areas and who do not have any other psychiatric disturbance other than the sexual deviancy. Thus it is felt that this test can be taken by sex offenders and its results may well enlarge our understanding of them. Certain allowances will need to be made. Working-class men, whether sex offenders or not, are likely to register as low in tolerance and high in value orthodoxy as compared with a sample of middle-class college students.

The fact that this is a well-constructed test with well-defined scales that show little correlation with each other makes it particularly attractive.

Relationship of Measures to Evaluation Questions

The relationship of these measures to the evaluation questions can be seen in Figure 12.1.

CONCLUSIONS

The strengths of the measures in this section are that they address issues that are relevant to the assessment of sexual deviancy, particularly the nature, extent, and severity of the deviant behavior. Each measure can be justified on the basis of its contribution to core issues that must be addressed in treatment. The measures also contain very little extraneous information, e.g., IQ or intrapsychic variables.

Tests and Measures

Clinical Dimensions	Abel & Becker Cognitions Scale	Attitudes Towards Women	Burt Rape Myth Scale	Buss-Durkee Hostility Inventory	Clinical Interview	FACES	Fantasy Scale	Interpersonal Reactivity Index	MAST	MMPI	Multiphasic Sex Inventory	Plethysmograph	Previous Reports	SADS	Optional: Abel & Becker Card Sort	Fear of Negative Evaluation	Jackson Personality Inventory	Nowicki-Strickland Scale
Sexual History					X					X	X							
Sexual Arousal Pattern					X		X			X	X	X						
Sexual Attitudes & Knowledge			X		X						X							
Chain of Events					X													
Cognitive Distortions	X		X		X						X							
Particulars of the Offense					X								X					
Degree of Denial					X						X		X					
Social Skills														X		X	X	
Assertiveness/Aggressiveness				X														
Attitudes Towards Women		X	X															
Marital Strengths & Problems						X												
Family Problems						X	X											
Personal History					X													
Alcohol Use/Abuse					X				X									
Personality Traits										X							X	X
Empathy								X										

Figure 12.1 Application of Tests and Measures to Relevant Clinical Dimensions

Although the battery is a lengthy one, the bulk of the time needed is spent in filling out the tests. All measures are easily scored objectively, and some, like the Jackson, were designed with ease of scoring a key design factor. It may be argued that it is too wearing a battery for offenders to complete. However, sexual molestation against children is a crime for which men can, and do, serve lengthy prison terms. It is unlikely that a few hours spent taking psychological tests can be considered cruel and unusual punishment.

The main weakness of this battery lies in its limited interpretive powers. While some tests, such as the MMPI, have been used extensively with varied populations, others have been normed exclusively on college students. Some offenders are middle class and college educated, while others are not. There are few working-class norms available. In particular they are not available for the Jackson Inventory, the Social Avoidance and Distress Scale, and the Fear of Negative Evaluations. This is a serious weakness, as it is difficult to determine without adequate norms whether an offender's score differs from the middle-class norms because of his sexual deviancy or because of his social class.

The compelling argument for using these tests despite the lack of norms is that tests are not available that both address the relevant issues and that have been normed on an appropriate comparison group. Research in this area would be a great service to the field.

Finally, while these tests are useful in describing an offender's personal and sexual characteristics so that treatment may be focused and informed, none of the tests described in this chapter can determine whether a particular individual did or did not commit a particular sexual crime. It would be a misuse of these tests to try to use them in that manner. A finding of guilt or innocence of a charge of child molestation must be made on the basis of the available evidence. That evidence, in the end, frequently consists of a child's testimony, and the finding of the court depends on whether a court does or does not believe that testimony. (See Chapter 14 for a discussion of children's credibility.) It would no doubt be useful to be able to collaborate a child's testimony with relevant psychological tests; however, at present this cannot be done. An individual may have all of the characteristics frequently associated with sexual deviancy—poor social skills, little empathy for others, a belief in rape myths and cognitive distortions on child molestation, stereotyped views of women, personal aggression, alcoholism, and a deviant arousal pattern—but still not have committed a particular sexual crime, or any crime.

This is not to imply that the battery can only be used after a finding of guilt. Frequently prosecuting attorneys request a psychosexual assessment of an offender before agreeing to a particular plea bargain. The disposition that the prosecuting attorney's office is willing to accept may differ depending, for example, on the presence or absence of a deviant arousal pattern, the presence or absence of alcoholism, the degree of personal aggressiveness and its relationship to the offense, and the degree of honesty in admitting to and accepting responsibility for the offense. However, clinicians should be particularly cautious when utilizing this battery before a finding of guilt or innocence by the courts; clinicians should not attempt to replace the function of the court and make a determination of guilt or innocence on the basis of this battery or any test battery. Clinicians should be forewarned that various parties in the legal system often try to use a psychological report to ascertain the guilt or innocence of a particular party. Care in the wording of psychological reports and a clear understanding of the limitations of psychological tests are recommended.

NOTE

---

1. Available from Research Psychologists Press, Goshen, NY 10924.

PART IV

SPOUSE AND VICTIM ISSUES

13

SPOUSE AND VICTIM TREATMENT

Although offender treatment is crucial in preventing remolestation, treatment of the spouse and child is also essential, since it contributes both to their own healing and to the rehabilitation of the offender. In both intrafamilial and extrafamilial abuse, the spouse can be key in identifying the chain of behaviors leading to sexual acting out and in intervening to interrupt the chain. She forms an important external barrier to reoffending, whether or not the offender's victims are in the home. Though the child's treatment is focused primarily on her own recovery, in the process she should learn assertiveness and communication skills that should make remolestation by an intrafamilial offender more difficult. Extrafamilial offenders generally have little opportunity to remolest the same child after discovery.

SPOUSE TREATMENT

The spouse is often the member of an offender's family most reluctant to engage in treatment. Offenders are routinely mandated into treatment by the courts; having no choice, they are not difficult to engage, at least superficially. One or both parents will often seek treatment for the child (accepting the fact that the child needs help). However, many spouses see a recommendation of treatment for themselves as a sign that someone believes they are at fault and their acceptance of treatment as an indication that they agree. "I told him that this is his problem. I have nothing to do with it."

Alternately, many spouses break up the marriage upon hearing of the incest and do not wish to be further involved with the offender. Other spouses deny the offense took place, while still others side actively with their husbands and blame the child. None of these groups is easy to engage in treatment. The group that most often accepts treatment readily is the group of spouses who do believe the offense took place, do not blame the child (although they may be conflicted and confused), and are hopeful of reuniting the family. They will cooperate with treatment if they believe it is the most direct way to reunite the family safely.

It is ideal to have a group for spouses. Spouses can supply more support to each other than can an individual therapist. The presence of other women who have been through the same ordeal and who have survived affords women in the early stages of treatment a vivid sense of hope. When they listen to other spouses, they can see the futility and inappropriateness of taking all the blame and responsibility for the situation on themselves. They can see in other women's doubts of their womanhood a mirror of their own doubts and, by confronting them in other women, begin to take the first steps toward confronting them in themselves.

Spouses are often reluctant to commit themselves to staying with a group, however, and time-limited groups may be easier to get started than ongoing groups of indefinite duration. Eight weeks is a reasonable minimum amount of time for such a group.

A spouses' group will focus on the spouse's feelings and understanding of the situation, but it will also serve as an educational forum to teach the spouse about the dynamics of both offending and victimization. Northwest Treatment Associates, again, has an excellent spouses' group; much of what follows was developed by Florence Wolfe. The following issues should be discussed in all spouses' groups.

Offender Dynamics

What are offender traits?
Why do men commit sex offenses?

What is the particular chain of events that preceded the partner's sexual acting out?

How much can you trust your partner?

What should you look for as signs he may be on the road to reoffending?[1]

Name one way your partner manipulated you.

Ask your partner to name 3 ways he manipulated you.

Victim Dynamics

What does sexual assault do to children?

What is the child feeling?

What questions do victims ask?

Why don't victims come to their mothers?

How to handle a child after discovery so that more damage is not done.

Why not to make minimization comments.

How not to make minimization comments.

Why excessive contact with the offender while he is out of the home can be damaging.

Speakers may also be brought into the group. The following is a list of speakers some of whom will be appropriate only in certain groups, depending on the issues that the members confront:

a feminist attorney—on the spouses' legal rights

a victim counselor—on stages of recovery

a battered women counselor—for those spouses who have been battered

an adult-survivor counselor—for those spouses who were abused as children

a rape counselor—for those spouses who have been raped

a budget counselor—offenders being out of home often cause a financial crisis

a family counselor—on reunion

Spouses who feel they cannot exist without their husbands' financial and/or emotional support are particularly difficult to treat. Such spouses often want to "bury the past" as quickly as possible, usually without examining it, and "get on with" the future. For them the incest is an emotional powder keg that, if tampered with, might destroy the entire family.

"It's over now. Why does she have to keep talking about it? It's not going to do any good. Why can't she just forget about it and go on?" They often object strenuously to the husband being out of the home and feel the sooner things "get back to normal" the better.

The most effective way to deal with such spouses is to convince them that they will not get the family back together unless they cooperate fully with treatment. Such spouses should be told bluntly that the fastest way to reunification is for the husband, not the child, to leave the home. They may be told also that the husband is changing and that they must too, in order to keep up with him.

"We're going to get your partner healthy. It won't work if you're not healthy also. He's going to grow, and you have to too if you want him to be with you." Predictions regarding the future may be employed. "How you act now may well determine if you ever see your grandchildren." In each case the therapist is not arguing with the spouse about what she should want, e.g., what's best for the child, but is using what she does want—her husband (and frequently the children)—in order to engage her. In those cases where the spouse rejects the children entirely, the case can still be made that her husband's progress through the program, and ultimately his chances of graduating rather than being ejected and going to jail, can be dramatically improved by her cooperation.

VICTIM TREATMENT

Group treatment for sexually abused children has been frequently recommended and well described in the literature (Berliner & Ernst, 1984; Blick & Porter, 1982; Knittle & Tuana, 1980; Lubell & Soong, 1982; Sturkie, 1983). Unquestionably, group treatment is an effective method for treating victims. Groups reduce isolation and facilitate peer relationships in a manner not possible in individual therapy. However, group therapy is sometimes not possible because of limitations in the number of victims seeking treatment at any one time, particularly in the younger age groups. Group therapy for preschoolers has been less utilized for developmental reasons, and group techniques described in the literature are most frequently appropriate for late middle childhood and adolescent victims. For these reasons this section will focus on individual therapy with younger children, primarily preschool children through middle childhood.

The question often arises as to whether individual therapy with sexually abused children differs from therapy with nonabused children. In fact, therapy for sexually abused children should be as specific to the dynamics of sexual abuse as is therapy for offenders. It should address in a hierarchy of importance the particular fears and dilemmas that such children face.

Below is a discussion of seven issues that it may be important to address in therapy with sexually abused children. It is suggested that they be addressed in therapy in approximately the order in which they are presented here. While the order should not be considered invariant, there can be little doubt that safety is the initial and dominant issue for most children. Likewise, the helplessness that child sexual abuse engenders in the child should be an early concern. By contrast, later issues such as education and assertive skills arguably could be put in any order. What is important is to have a plan regarding which issues to cover along with an appropriate order for addressing them.

Perception of Safety

Children do not feel safe following the discovery of child sexual abuse. Adults, who have a broader knowledge of the world, may know that a particular child is not at risk for remolestation. The offender may be in jail. The child's parent may be in an excellent position to prevent contact with an offender not in jail; a babysitter's employment, for example, may be abruptly terminated. A spouse may separate from her husband, or he may be required to move outside the home. These measures may ensure the actual safety of the child, but the issue for most children is the perception of safety, both day and night. A child who feels safe during the day may not feel safe at night or may be plagued by nightmares. Because very young children, in particular, may believe that dreams are real, nightmares may be a serious source of suffering for a child. Of course, the first consideration must be a child's actual safety, but therapists must also pay attention not just to whether the child is safe, but whether the child feels safe.

Janet was a 4-year-old girl sexually abused by another 4-year-old girl. The activity was labeled sexual abuse rather than sex play between two children because of the type of activity and the degree of coercion involved. Cindy held Janet down and inserted a variety of sharp objects in her vagina over a period of 6 months. Cindy's mother had known about the abuse but had not taken any definitive steps to stop it. Janet's mother discovered the abuse when Cindy walked into the living room where the two mothers were sitting and asked her mother to open a broach for her. Her mother refused, saying she knew what she would do with the sharp pin. When Janet's mom inquired, Cindy's mom said only that Cindy liked "to play doctor." Thinking her daughter was in danger in getting a "shot," Janet rushed into the room in time to find her daughter lying on the floor with her head wedged between her bed and a bookshelf, tears running down her cheeks, her pants down, and Cindy sitting on her legs trying to force a sharp toy into her vagina.

Cindy had never molested Janet at the nursery school they both attended for a few hours a day. The nursery school was carefully supervised. There were no places to hide. After the nursery school was alerted to the problem, there was even less chance of abuse occurring there. Nonetheless, Janet had nightmares each night when school was due the next day. She bit her nails and whined on the days school was in session. When she was sick for two weeks and did not attend school, the nightmares and the regressive behavior stopped.

Cindy's mother refused to take her daughter out of the nursery school, and the school refused to compel her to, so Janet stopped attending, a decision supported by her therapist. The school's argument, that both children could attend, because Janet was safe, was beside the point. Janet did not feel safe, and no amount of adult logic would make her feel so.

Connie was a 6-year-old girl playing outside her house with her 4-year-old brother when two men came walking down the railroad tracks. One of them, quite possibly drunk, walked over to the little boy, grabbed his arm, and tried to pull him away. Connie grabbed her brother's other arm, yelled at the man to let go of her brother, and started pulling in the opposite direction. The man had a bottle in one hand, and let go with the other hand to pull out a knife. When he did so, Connie pulled her little brother away and into the house, yelling for her mother, who was in the back of the house. The description Connie gave the police was sufficiently accurate that the police recognized the man, and felt there was little doubt that she was telling the truth. It was highly unlikely that the man would return, and the mother's supervision, although never lax, became even more strict. Still, Connie did not feel safe. After all, if she could be grabbed in her own front yard, there was little reason for her to believe the man wouldn't come in her room one night. Connie's dog had been killed a few days before the stranger approached her. Connie believed, correctly or not, that if her dog had been there he would have frightened away the strangers.

An appropriate response was to get Connie a new dog, one that could sleep on her bed at night and "protect" her. While in this case the parents might well choose a protective dog, there are cases where it simply does not matter whether the dog is a Doberman or an amiable spaniel accustomed to licking every stranger's hand, so long as the child believes the dog will protect her. There may perhaps be children who prefer a watchdog-goldfish; if so, the fish would be a wise investment.

Nightmares plague many sexually abused children. As the offense retreats in time and the child begins to trust it will not reoccur, the nightmares generally recede. However, such dreams can be problematic and painful for a time, and there are sometimes ways to shorten their duration and to diminish their power.

Roberta was a 4-year-old girl, sexually abused by an older child. Because of her developmental level, her nightmares were not about the offender, but about "monsters." Roberta equivocated during the day as to whether she thought the monsters were real or not, but at night they were real. Her therapist suggested that when she was a little girl she had a friend named Caspar the Ghost who was very scary indeed to other people, especially monsters, whom he terrified witless, but who actually was very nice to little girls. Caspar was available, she said, and frequently came into people's dreams when they asked him to. He was just part of the child's imagination, and not real, but then, so were the monsters. Caspar really didn't like it when monsters scared children and he would be happy to drive them away. The little girl decided to employ Caspar, who worked out well.

Is this a magic bullet for nightmares? Of course not. For every child who finds Caspar, or a mythical lion, or even a policeman to be useful, another child will find them to be useless. Angie was nine and troubled by intense nightmares about the offender, her stepfather who had raped her forcibly and repeatedly. She screamed at night for him to get away from her. Since he had been arrested and jailed, and since his removal had seemed to provide some sense of safety for her, the therapist asked her if she had considered calling up a policeman in her dreams. The therapist explained that, since dreams came from the imagination, people could sometimes call up things from their imagination to help them. "No," she said. "Why not?" the therapist asked surprised. "I'm not sure I want a policeman in my dreams," she replied.

None of this is to suggest that the issue of the actual safety of the child is unimportant. The actual safety of the child is a necessary, but not sufficient, condition for the child's recovery. The child needs to feel safe, as well.

Empowerment

From the very beginning the therapist should focus on the issue of empowerment. For most children, sexual abuse is a profound experience of helplessness. Adolescents are fully cognizant of being manipulated, either by threats or bribes. Young children are less aware of subtleties, and may not know, for example, that a father who tells them he will go to jail if the child tells is manipulating them. Still, offenders are often less subtle and are frequently directly coercive with young children. One offender, a physician, told his middle-childhood daughter he would kill her much-beloved mother if she told. The manipulation and coercion are paired for children with a discomfort, found even in preschoolers, with the type of touching offenders seek. Only the very youngest children escape the knowledge that they are doing something wrong and that they are being manipulated and controlled. More typically, the child who approaches therapy has behind her a long history of having her will usurped, her exit blocked, and her ability to communicate her distress impaired. Even when she tells, she becomes at best not the master of her fate, but an element in someone's protocol. It is not up to her, nor can it be, to determine what happens next, or what disposition the offender is to receive. If the child did not have a background of abuse, her lack of power within the legal system would not be necessarily traumatic. A sexually abused child entering the legal system is entering a system over which she has little say following an experience in which she had no say.

How can a therapist empower a child? First, during the sessions themselves, it is possible to replay the sexual abuse with action figures or dolls, while changing the ending. The child can "punch him out," or get her mother, or call the police. In the beginning the therapist can play the part of the child, but children quickly want to do it themselves. It does not matter in this play that the child's solutions may be fanciful—a four-year-old punching out a 6-foot adult male is not realistic. Realistic assertiveness training can take place at a later time in treatment. What does matter at this stage is to break into the child's feeling of helplessness and hopelessness, and, at least on a fantasy level, provide the child with a sense of efficacy.

Expression and Ventilation of Feelings

Even the most repressed child has feelings regarding child sexual abuse. Anger is almost invariably a component, although not always the dominant one. Particularly in incest cases, where the child may be very attached to the father, fear of loss may take precedence over the anger. While badgering children into sounding or acting angry when they do not believe themselves to be angry is always inappropriate, providing the opportunity for a child to express anger in a primarily nonverbal way can be helpful. Children should be invited, not pressured, to express their anger. Those children who resist ventilating anger when afforded the chance in a nondemanding way should be allowed to engage in other activities. Such children will nonetheless understand the message that it is acceptable to be angry, that often other children have been angry in this situation, and that it is entirely understandable if they become angry later.

There are numerous ways of facilitating the expression of anger. The therapist may have a throwing wall for clay. Covered with acrylic paint, the wall can be easily cleaned. Children can throw clay at human profiles and pretend the profile is whomever they wish. Likewise, a wall may be painted with acrylics for drawing. Most children have wanted to draw on walls at some point. Such a wall allows a child to draw lifesize images if she wishes, which she can then shoot, draw over, erase, or throw clay at as she chooses. These activities are simultaneously empowering and ventilating.

On a smaller scale, playdough and clay can be used very effectively. The therapist can make a playdough model, anatomically correct, of the offender, which she then smashes with her fist, verbalizing at the same time, "You'll never hurt this little girl again. Take that. And that. It's goodbye to you," and so forth. Children often respond with remarkable gusto. One child, an 8-year-old girl, carefully took off her shoes and socks, folded the socks neatly, put them inside the shoes, and then jumped up and down on the playdough offender yelling wildly! It is best to explain, even to younger children, that this is OK, because it is only playdough and not a real person, and that it would not be OK to do that to a real person, even to someone who had been mean to them.

Other forms of expressive therapy can be used as well. Paint, magic markers, and pencils are all appropriate. Children can be encouraged to draw their families, their homes, the offender, the sexual abuse, and so forth.

Playdough and clay can be used to reenact the offense. The therapist can, with the child's help, make anatomically correct models of the offender and the child. She can then ask the child to show with the figures what the offender did. This technique can be employed partly as a way to help the child learn to communicate what happened, thus reducing her isolation, and partly as an opportunity for sex education. The therapist can ask whether the penis was standing up or not, and show what she means with the clay. A prepubescent child may have had no real understanding of why the offender's penis was erect, where it went, why it hurt so much, or what mechanically happened between them. One child eventually reduced all the extraneous parts from the figures ending up with a tube she labelled a vagina, and a cylindrical object she called a penis. She would then repetitively insert the "penis" into the "vagina" over and over again. Playdough and clay have the advantage over anatomically correct dolls of allowing such manipulation and also of allowing the child to smash the figures if she should choose.

Sandtray work is an expressive medium that also lends itself to the treatment of abused children. A sandtray resembles a sandbox with two exceptions: first, the bottom is painted blue so that the child can create lakes and rivers just by parting the sand, and second, instead of pouring and scooping accessories, the sandbox has small figures, buildings, animals, and vehicles, roughly in scale, from which a child can create a world. Ellie Breslin, a therapist with the Child Sexual Abuse Treatment Program in San Jose, California, has identified four different worlds sexually abused children create from the sand: (1) the dysfunctional, chaotic world, (2) the dyadic, aggressive world, (3) the isolated world, and (4) the functional world. Her thesis is that play changes during successful therapy from dysfunctional or isolated to functional. The significance of the appearance of the dyadic aggressive world in this context is less clear; this world is also found in the play of nonabused middle-childhood children. Children of that developmental level generally favor pure heroes and villains over the flawed protagonists of adulthood. The significance may well lie in the choice of content; the good/bad guys may be chosen from their own personal experience. More affect and more anguish may be seen to accompany the play than would be the case for nonabused children playing their version of cops and robbers.

Education About Sexual Offenses

Children typically have little information about child molestation and have trouble making sense of it. A child particularly needs to know that she is not alone, and that this has happened to other children. She needs to be told that some adults choose children for sexual partners instead of adults. It should be made clear that this is inappropriate, since adults should restrict their sexual activities to other, consenting adults. She can be told that children cannot drive cars or drink alcohol, and that sex with adults is not OK for children either. Abused children need to know that the adult, not the child, is the one who made the mistake, since he is the grown-up, after all. In addition, these children often wonder if their bodies are OK, and need to be reassured that the abuse did not change their bodies in any way. It did not make them incapable of bearing children, nor did the abuse leave any physical scars. Where physical injuries did result, the child needs to have them explained, usually with drawings, and to be reassured as to the ultimate prognosis. Abused children frequently worry that others can tell they have been sexually molested by looking at them. This fear is not restricted to younger children; a college senior who said she "knew better," nonetheless asked seriously whether anyone could look at her and tell she had been sexually abused. Male victims often worry whether others will think they are homosexual and worry over whether the fact that they were sexually abused means they are homosexual. Children need to know that, while sexual abuse may make them feel different, it does not make them look different, nor does it change sexual preference.

Books and film strips can be very helpful in imparting information to children. A particularly good book for younger children is *Something Bad Happened to Me* (Sweet, 1981). For teens, *Top Secret* (Fay & Ferchinger, 1982) is excellent and covers date rape as well as incest and rape.

Sex Education

Few young children have had an adequate sex education. It is still commonplace for parents to postpone discussions of the "plumbing," and to avoid mentioning sexual activities until children are in late middle childhood or early adolescence, by which time the information is seldom needed. Younger children who have been sexually assaulted are thus left in a confusing situation. Quite often, as mentioned above, they do not understand exactly what happened to what. They have sometimes no names for body parts and, particularly in the case of little girls, may be totally unfamiliar with male anatomy. They rarely know what an erection is. Thus their emotional confusion is compounded by cognitive confusion. "What was that sticky stuff that came out of him?" "Why did that thing stand up like that?" "Why did he turn red and look so funny?" Little girls may be unaware of having a vagina. "Where did he put that thing?" "Was it in my 'pee-pee'?"

Although children have such questions, they rarely volunteer them. If a therapist initiates sex education with such children, with either books or slides, children will raise their concerns, often in the form of statements. "Sticky stuff came out of him."

Every child who has been sexually assaulted needs some type of sex education. It may range from a simple naming of male and female body parts for a preschooler and talking about special and private parts, to slides of bodies and of intercourse with a child in middle childhood, to charts and graphs for a teenager. A combination of slides with age-appropriate books can be very effective. The slides may be altered by leaving out slides that are too difficult for a younger child to understand. The Crooks and Baur series recommended in Chapter 9 may be used by deleting slides as necessary. The recommended text, however, is too complicated for children, and should be replaced with an age-appropriate book. *The Touching Book* (Hindman, 1985), for example, is appropriate for late preschoolers through middle childhood.

Assertiveness and Communication Skills

Children need to learn realistic ways of being assertive and saying no. Fortunately, assertiveness training has been adapted for children. Excellent resources for this material are the personal safety curricula developed for school systems. For kindergarten through 8th grade, Geraldine A. Crisci's (1983) *Personal Safety Curriculum* is effective. The primary flaw in this curriculum is that the "As If" stories, although employing an excellent device, focus more on interactions with strangers than on interactions with acquaintances or family members, which are by far the more frequent. For high school students. *No Easy Answers* (Kent, 1982) is a particularly inspired curriculum that employs educational and problem-solving approaches to sexual dilemmas. Therapists treating child sexual abuses cases would be advised to obtain these curricula and to utilize those parts that seem relevant to the developmental level of their child and to the child's situation.

Guilt, Trust, and Ambivalence

Certain issues are continuous throughout therapy and are not confined to discrete phases of treatment. They must be considered whenever and however they surface. They may emerge during sandtray play, while stomping on clay figures, or just in conversation.

"He was my stepfather. That's the whole thing, don't you see? He was my stepfather," one child said solemnly while watching sex education slides. "Do all men do this to little girls?" she added. It was apparent she did not entirely believe the therapist's negative answer.

These issues are sometimes as confusing for the adult therapist as for the child, not because the adult does not understand these issues, but because it is difficult to recapture the point of view of a child. Children need reliable adults in the world, and a child may find it more frightening to think that adults are untrustworthy than to think that she deserved to be abused. A child has no sense of efficacy at all in regards to an untrustworthy adult, whereas the condition of deserving abuse is a form of efficacy. A child can at least imagine that she might change and thereby no longer be abused. This issue of helplessness and efficacy is perhaps one reason so many rape victims have in the past insisted the rape was their own fault, precipitated by dress or action. Although the culture of sexism was the major impetus for this belief, it has been surprising the extent to which rape victims have sometimes clung to such beliefs despite much input to the contrary. It may be less frightening to think one caused the rape and thus that one could prevent it next time than to think it was entirely random and thus could happen again, without warning, at any time or place.

For children, the sense that the adults close to them are at least not malevolent is a vital one. In the context of the preadolescent's view of the world: a world of heroes and villains, a dualistic world wherein ambivalence is primarily expressed over time—loving someone from their toes to the top of their heads today, hating them ferociously when angry tomorrow—the notion that adults can be *somewhat* trustworthy, *partially* responsible, *sometimes* in control, is difficult. Children find it easier to love or hate adults who wear appropriate hats, white or black. Certainly children want to believe that the adults close to them, particularly family members, wear the white hats. The black hats are reserved for strangers.

For a sexually abused child, a parent may be wearing a black hat, or even more confusing, a white and black hat. A total stranger may stop the abuse. What color hat is the stranger wearing if he puts daddy in jail? What color hat is the child wearing? She is told she did the right thing by reporting the abuse, but her mother cries constantly, and her siblings say it was all her fault. When there is a bond between the child and the offender, as there so often is in incest cases, the fact of sexual abuse forces the child to deal with and to try to assimilate an ambivalence foreign to her developmental level. Her ability to accept ambivalence seldom lasts very long. The child usually resolves the ambivalence one way or the other, either by "forgiving" the father and allowing herself to love him again, without admitted reservation, or by rejecting him, and deciding she would prefer he never came home again. The latter resolution is particularly difficult in situations where the child's bond to the mother is important to the child, and the mother's bond with the father is important to the mother.

The adult resolution, to be aware of loving and hating him at the same time, of being relieved he's gone, and wanting him home again, of being glad the abuse is over and yet feeling guilty for reporting him, is a difficult and sometimes impossible task for the child. Instead, the child often expresses ambivalence over time, and may feel polar opposites toward her father during the course of therapy. This means that while the child is encouraged to ventilate her suppressed anger and rage initially, the therapist should always leave the door open for other emotions.

"I knew another child whose father molested her, and she was so angry and then later she didn't feel so angry. Sometimes people just stay angry and sometimes they don't. You'll have to see how you feel."

"You know, lots of kids don't feel angry at first. And then later some of them get really angry, so angry they could yell. And some still don't feel so angry. You'll have to see how you feel."

The important task is to make the child aware that if different emotions arise, they will be understood and accepted. This stance is sometimes difficult for the therapist, who, having no bond with the offender, may stay quite angry with him over the abuse of the child. At its worst this dynamic can cause the therapist to see the child's abrupt change of heart as a "betrayal," a "reneging" on her earlier stance. The child, reading on some level the therapist's reaction, will now feel guilty about betraying the therapist, and will often not share with her therapist her reemerging affection toward her father. Thus one child who acted as though she were quite angry toward her father in therapy wrote plaintive letters to him in secret, letters that the defense attorney used to try to influence the sentencing.

CONCLUSIONS

Perception of safety, empowerment, expression and ventilation of feelings, education about sexual offenses, sex education, assertiveness and communication skills, guilt, trust, and ambivalence are all important issues to address with a sexually abused child. By addressing them explicitly in a sequence that supports the emerging needs of the child, the therapist can remove impediments to the child's own natural ability to heal and thus can aid and abet the child's own process of recovery from sexual abuse.

NOTE

1. See Partner Alert List in Appendix Q.

14

VICTIM IDENTIFICATION AND BEHAVIOR OF SEXUALLY ABUSED CHILDREN

To what extent can sexually abused children be identified by their behavior? Because children frequently do not reveal abuse, several authors have suggested "laundry lists" of behaviors and/or symptoms thought to indicate abuse in the absence of a verbal report. However, such lists are generally too nonspecific to differentiate sexual abuse from other clinical problems. If we consult the research from the past 25 years we find that children's symptoms can be divided with few exceptions into "internalizing" and "externalizing" symptoms, regardless of the stressor. The exceptions, those behaviors and/or symptoms that are suggestive of sexual abuse, are discussed in this chapter, one of the most telling being the verbal report of the child. Because children are frequently not believed when they report sexual abuse, the literature on the incidence of false reports will be examined along with those developmental characteristics of children that explain low rates of fictitious reports. Finally, this chapter will list the characteristics of a fictitious sexual abuse report that suggest it may be false.

REPORTING OF CHILD SEXUAL ABUSE CASES

Studies of adult victims have found that only a small percentage of sexually abused children reveal the abuse during childhood. Finkelhor (1984) claims that adult-incidence studies find that less than half of the adults revealed the abuse, and that only one in five ever came to the attention of authorities (p. 232). His own research found that 19.2% of a sample of 530 college women and 8.6% of 266 college males were sexually abused as children. Of those 63% of the females and 73% of the males did not reveal the abuse to anyone (Finkelhor, 1979, p. 67). When children do reveal the abuse, the reports are not necessarily forwarded to the authorities. A Finkelhor study of 48 Boston parents whose children had reported abuse to them found that parents differentially reported the abuse to outside agencies depending on their relationship to the offender. Of those parents whose children were abused by a stranger, 73% reported the abuse. When the offender was an acquaintance, only 23% did so. However, when the offender was a relative, none reported the abuse (Finkelhor, 1984). Thus, even when children reveal the abuse to parents, parents by no means universally report the abuse to the authorities.

In Russell's classic study (1984) only 5% of the 647 cases of child sexual abuse were ever reported to the police. The 5% (30 cases) consisted of 4 cases of intrafamilial abuse (2% of the total) and 26 cases of extrafamilial abuse (6% of the total). Donaldson (1983) found that 70% of her sample of 40 adult survivors had not told anyone about the incest as a child; for the 13% who told their mothers, the abuse nonetheless continued. Studies of specialized populations sometimes find even lower rates of reporting. In a study of street prostitutes, of whom 61% were the victims of child sexual abuse, Silbert (1984) found that 91% felt "there was nothing she could do, no one she could tell" (p. 253), whereas 3% had reported the abuse to the police and 1% reported it to professionals.

It is likely that reporting rates are now increasing as a result of increased media attention to the problem of childhood sexual abuse and of increased attempts by parents and teachers to educate children and encourage them to report sexual advances by older children and adults. In Vermont, for example, the number of substantiated sexual abuse cases jumped from 88 in 1980 to 607 in 1985. As the survey in Chapter 1 of older incidence studies of sexual abuse indicates, there is little reason to assume that the overall quantity of abuse itself is actually increasing. However, the 1985 rate of 607 cases represents only .4% of the population of children in Vermont in that year, whereas incidence studies of sexual abuse in children, based on accounts by nonclinical samples of adults, range from 8% to 38% with more methodologically adequate studies finding higher rates. Thus even the higher reporting rates currently in evidence do not begin to reflect the actual incidence of child sexual abuse. It remains something children speak of only infrequently and evidently with the greatest reluctance. When they do so, either to friends or relatives, their revelations are sometimes not relayed to the authorities.

It is particularly ironic, then, that they are so often not believed by the legal system when abuse is reported. This author has personally seen numerous cases in which courts discounted the testimony of a child, ranging from a 14-year-old boy who told of molestation by his father (and who was sent home with the same father following the hearing) to a 4-year-old girl who spoke clearly and articulately of her abuse by her father. Her descriptions were both spontaneous and childlike. ("It hurt; I said, 'daddy, stop,' 'cepting he didn't.") The judge, however, believed the argument of the psychiatrist for the defense, who had not interviewed the child but who testified nonetheless that her story reflected an Oedipal fantasy.

Behavioral Indicators of Child Sexual Abuse

Because children so frequently conceal child sexual abuse and because the unsupported testimony of a child in court is often discounted, investigators have sought behavioral indicators of abuse that might be used to detect children who have not reported as well as to add credibility to those who have. Behavioral indicators have, in addition, been particularly sought after, because child sexual abuse, unlike child physical abuse, infrequently leaves physical signs (Kerns, 1981). Numerous "laundry lists" of behavioral indicators, composed partly of symptoms and partly of behaviors, have been formulated. The question arises, however, as to the specificity of the lists.

A range of behaviors and/or symptoms have been suggested. McCown (1981) suggested pediatric nurses consider the following as indicators of sexual abuse, if the child:

(1) arrives early at school and leaves late
(2) is nervous, aggressive, or has disruptive behavior toward adults, especially toward the parents
(3) runs away
(4) uses alcohol or drugs
(5) shows sexual self-consciousness, provocativeness, vulnerability to sexual approaches
(6) is sexually promiscuous
(7) withdraws from social relationships
(8) has an appearance of mental retardation
(9) demonstrates regressive behavior
(10) acts out aggressions
(11) establishes poor peer relationships and is unable to make friends (McCown, 1981, p. 26)

While the author does not feel that the above behaviors are sufficient for a diagnosis of child sexual abuse, she does state that several indicators in combination "warrant serious consideration of the possibility" (McCown, p. 26).

Blythe and Orr (1985), physicians publishing in *Indiana Medicine,* reported that sexually abused infants and toddlers may have irritability, sleep difficulties, feeding disturbances, and "altered leveling activity" (p. 13). The authors state that toddlers and some preschoolers may show either regressive or aggressive behavior, a precocious understanding of sexuality, and may display inappropriate sexual activity. Other preschool and some school-age children may have excessive fears and phobias, may alter their behavioral patterns suddenly (withdraw, become depressed), may have sleep difficulties (nightmares, sleep terrors, difficulty sleeping), and may also evince age-inappropriate understanding of sexuality. School-age or adolescent children may experience a sudden drop in grades, may arrive at school early and leave late, may have few friends and may withdraw from school and social activities. Finally, adolescents may be promiscuous, may run away from home, may turn to prostitution, and may attempt suicide.

Sgroi, Porter, and Blick (1982) in Sgroi's excellent handbook for mental health providers list the following behavioral indicators:

(1) overly compliant behavior
(2) acting-out, aggressive behavior
(3) pseudomature behavior
(4) hints about sexual activity
(5) persistent and inappropriate sexual play with peers or toys or with themselves, or sexually aggressive behavior with others

(6) detailed and age-inappropriate understanding of sexual behavior (especially by young children)
(7) arriving early at school and leaving late with few, if any, absences
(8) poor peer relationships or inability to make friends
(9) lack of trust, particularly with significant others
(10) nonparticipation in school and social activities
(11) inability to concentrate in school
(12) sudden drop in school performance
(13) extraordinary fears of males (in cases of male perpetrator and female victim)
(14) seductive behavior with males (in cases of male perpetrator and female victim)
(15) running away from home
(16) sleep disturbances
(17) regressive behavior
(18) withdrawal
(19) clinical depression
(20) suicidal feelings (pp. 40-41)

Sgroi did not state that these behaviors alone could be used to identify child sexual abuse and has stated that "Although the presence of some of these indicators may be helpful, they are not conclusive" (p. 40). They are included here because they represent one of the more complete general lists of behavioral indicators.

Finally, Justice and Justice (1979) found that younger children were likely to show bed wetting, hyperactivity, a change in sleep patterns, fears and phobias, compulsive behavior, learning difficulties, compulsive masturbation, precocious sexuality, including early sex play and an unusual degree of curiosity about sex, separation anxiety, and seductiveness (p. 166). Older incest victims were more likely to evince the following:

Blurring of generational lines. . . .
Father jealous of daughter's being with peers and dating
Father overpossessive of daughter
Father often alone with daughter
Favoritism by father toward daughter over other siblings
Siblings jealous of daughter chosen by father
Daughter depressed
Daughter has poor self-image
Daughter withdrawn
Daughter uninvolved in school activities; grades may fall
Daughter secretive
Daughter excessively seductive
Physical cues (pp. 165-166)

Despite the considerable overlap on the various lists proposed to indicate sexual abuse, the reader must be impressed by the diversity of symptoms presented. Regressed, withdrawn, depressed behavior is often found in the same list with aggressive, acting-out behavior. Fear and avoidance of males are noted along with promiscuity and seductiveness toward males. Nervousness and symptoms of anxiety coexist with pseudomature behavior. Poor school performance, an inability to concentrate, and withdrawal from school activities are found along with coming to school early and leaving late. Sleep disturbances, enuresis, poor peer relationships, lack of trust and other somewhat less severe symptoms are found along with suicidal feelings, running away, and alcohol and drug use. Finally McCown (1981) includes "an appearance of mental retardation" (p. 26), although this particular symptom does not appear to overlap with those on other lists.

BEHAVIORAL INDICATORS OF OTHER PROBLEMS

It may be that all of these symptoms have been and can be found in sexual abuse victims. To note the diversity of symptoms reported is not to quarrel with their accuracy, but merely their specificity. Child clinicians will no doubt note the overlap among symptoms of child sexual abuse and other childhood stressors. Wallerstein and Kelly (1980) found among their sample of children from divorced families that aggression, depression, guilt, fears, anxiety, sleep disturbances, somatic complaints, withdrawal from school and peers, a drop in school performance, role reversal, and even sexual concerns, sexual preoccupation and sexual provocativeness were common. Nor is divorce the only stressor to produce widespread symptom formation in children. Children of alcoholics are reported to show role reversal, pseudomaturity, acting out behavior, guilt, anger, depression, poor school performance, poor self-image, and alcohol and drug abuse; later in their twenties they show depression, loneliness, fearfulness, anxiety, difficulty with intimacy, and alcohol abuse (Black, 1981). Even learning disabilities have associated behavioral symptoms, which may include aggression, withdrawal, social isolation, lying, defensiveness, immaturity, low self-esteem, in addition to the academic failure characteristic of the group (Meyer, 1983; Silver, 1984). Hyperactive children are thought to exhibit aggressiveness, excitability, mood swings, poor self-image, irritability, social problems, school difficulties and attention-seeking behavior, in addition to attentional difficulties, distractibility, and impulsivity (Taylor, 1986; Wender, 1987).

INTERNALIZING VERSUS EXTERNALIZING SYMPTOMS

There is another approach to the diversity of children's behavior. Studies of children's symptoms have for at least 25 years yielded information that children's responses to stress can be categorized most successfully into two broad-band factors, often labeled internalizing and externalizing (previously labeled personality problems and conduct problems). Internalizing symptoms include those that represent a turning inward of stress; most frequently items such as depression, anxiety, nail-biting, withdrawal, and school failure are included. Externalizing symptoms are those that turn stress outward and result in acting-out behaviors, which typically include aggression, destruction of property, and disruptiveness.

Studies that support the division of children's symptoms into two broad types can be found from the beginning of research in this area. In an early factor-analytic study of children's symptoms Himmelweit (cited in Eysenck, 1953) found two major factors, the first indicating general maladaption and the second personality problems versus conduct problems. Later, Peterson (1961) used the same terms to describe his major factors: conduct versus personality problems.

In a comprehensive 1966 study, Achenbach analyzed case histories of 300 male and 300 female child clinical cases. His analysis covered two levels of specificity and yielded a number of specific or narrow-band syndromes. Several of the factors were similar for both sexes: aggressive behavior; obsessions, compulsions, and phobias; somatic complaints; and schizoid thinking and behavior. There were additionally several factors that loaded for one sex but not the other. Further analysis found that many of these narrow-band syndromes could be grouped into broad-band syndromes, which Achenbach termed *internalizing* and *externalizing*. Aggressive behavior, for example, was found to correlate with the externalizing factor whereas somatic complaints, compulsions, and phobias correlated with the internalizing factor. Schizoid thinking and behavior did not correlate with either.

Achenbach and Edelbrock (1978) completed a thorough review of the literature on children's-symptom checklists derived from mental health workers, teachers, and parents. They concluded that broad-band factors similar to those previously called internalizing and externalizing (called in the 1978 review "overcontrolled" and "undercontrolled") could be found in studies of all three. They have since written (Achenbach & Edelbrock, 1984) that the apparent diversity in studies of children's symptoms is more apparent than real; they argue that further analysis of studies that have found different narrow-band syndromes shows that

> narrow-band syndromes of hyperactivity, aggression, and delinquent behavior covary to form a broad-band grouping of "undercontrolled" behavior. Conversely, narrow-band syndromes of anxiety, depression, somatic complaints, and obsessive-compulsive behavior covary to form a broad-band grouping of "overcontrolled" behavior. (p. 233)

Based on these concepts Achenbach, has developed the Child Behavior Checklist (Achenbach & Edelbrock, 1983) unquestionably the best normed children's behavioral checklist currently available. The checklist yields both specific syndromes such as Depressed, Social Withdrawal, Aggressive, Delinquent, Sex Problems, Somatic Complaints, and Schizoid or Anxious as well as two broad-band factors, Externalizing and Internalizing.

Externalizing and Internalizing symptoms can be found in children who have been sexually abused, just as they can in other children under stress. Abused children typically become either withdrawn, depressed, removed from school interests and activities, or they become angry, aggressive, and disruptive. Friedrich, Urquiza, and Beilke (1986) found that 35% of the males and 46% of the females in their sample of sexually abused children were significantly elevated on the Internalizing Scale, while 36% of the males and 39% of the females were elevated on the Externalizing Scales.

To observe that the symptoms produced by children under stress are similar regardless of the type of stressor is not to imply that the experience of sexual abuse does not differ, for example, from that of living with divorced parents or of coping with a learning disability. It is important, however, to recognize that either of the latter situations can produce, for instance, a general reaction such as depression. However, even symptoms that seem more specific such as going to school early and staying late can be associated with other problems, such as parental alcoholism. With few exceptions sexual abuse cannot be inferred from behavioral problems. Those exceptions are described next.

BEHAVIORS CLOSELY ALIGNED WITH SEXUAL ABUSE

Behaviors that are rarely found with any other stressor than sexual abuse, or are found significantly more often in sexual abuse include the following: (1) specifically sexual symptoms, (2) somatic symptoms with sexual content, (3) physical symptoms, (4) running away from home, (5) bizarre degree of jealousy and possessiveness on the father's part, and (6) verbal reports of sexual abuse. None of these are routinely associated with any other clinical syndromes in the literature, nor are they found as general psychiatric symptoms with sufficient frequency to appear readily in factor analytic studies of children's symptoms. Of the behavioral indicators cited in the previous lists, approximately three quarters of those listed are general symptoms that could be associated with a variety of problems, while only one quarter are symptoms more specifically associated with sexual abuse.

Sexual Symptoms

Sexually abused children show a variety of sexual symptoms that range from a preoccupation with sex to fear and avoidance of any aspect of sexuality. While it is true that children of divorce may also be preoccupied sexually, particularly when their parents are beginning to date and take new sexual partners, the quality of the concerns are different. Preadolescent and adolescent children of divorce often mimic their parents' dating behavior and affect a maturity beyond their years. The sexual preoccupations and concerns of abused children often lead more directly to sexual acting out and can be found even with very young abused children. Preschool and some middle-childhood children may masturbate excessively and even publicly. The masturbation is often not the intermittent and casual masturbation of the nonabused child, but a driven and compulsive masturbation that may preoccupy much of the child's waking time. It is frequent for nonabused preschool children in day care to masturbate, for example, at nap time, as they rock back and forth on their bottles or hold their genitals. It is part of a self-soothing process of going to sleep. It is unusual for a nonabused child to masturbate throughout the morning while other children are playing and to prefer masturbation to play, but it is not unusual for a sexually abused preschooler to do so. In addition, the masturbation of abused children frequently involves toys or objects, and may include inserting the objects in the vagina or rectum.

Sexually abused children may act out sexually with animals, attempting to poke objects in an animal's rectum, for example, or carefully examining the rectums of all the neighborhood pets. Nonabused children are typically not fascinated by rectums. The sexual abuse of animals by children is so unusual for nonabused children that it should always be viewed with concern.

Sexually abused children may similarly act out sexually with stuffed animals in a preschool setting or at home. One 2-year-old compulsively and repetitively flipped a stuffed animal on its stomach in his day care, then mounted it from behind and made copulating movements. He was preoccupied with this daily to the exclusion of other forms of play.

In addition, abused children may act out the abuse sexually with other children, usually their own age or younger. Parents and clinicians are frequently called upon to decide whether a particular type of sexual behavior by a child is merely "exploration" or instead a possible indication of sexual abuse. Where there are proponents of the view that any sexual behavior on the part of a child is simply "exploration" and not cause for concern, there is a difference in the young child who asks to look at another's "pee pee" and offers to "show you mine if you'll show me yours" and the 2-year-old girl who forces sharp objects into another child's vagina against her will (as described in Chapter 13). Exploration can be distinguished from abuse in terms of the following characteristics: type of activity, force, and age difference.

Type of Activity. Nonabused children look at each other's bodies. They may want to see where "pee" or babies come from. They often "play doctor," but "playing doctor" has as many elements of shot-giving and broken-bone-fixing as it does attention to genitals. Young children, after all, do not usually receive internal examinations, and "playing" doctor usually involves undressing and looking, at the most. Sexually abused children, by contrast, may engage in oral sex, anal intercourse, vaginal intercourse, insertion of objects in the vagina, and mutual masturbation. Whenever two young children are engaged in a type of sexual activity that is not typical developmentally, e.g., oral sex, it is important to determine who started the game as a way of potentially identifying an abused child.

Force. Nonabused children do not typically force other children to engage in sexual activity. A child who is holding down, threatening, physically harming, or tying another child while engaging in sexual behavior is likely to be a victim.

Age Difference. Children "explore" when they are very young and with children their own age. A child significantly older than another child (5 or more years) who is engaging in sexual activity with that child is possibly modeling an age and power difference she has experienced.

Sexually abused children may also approach adults sexually. This typically makes adults sufficiently uncomfortable that they simply reprimand the child, often without exploring the meaning of the behavior. Adults, especially if they are teachers, day-care providers or other nonfamily caregivers, may be fearful enough of a false accusation of sexual abuse that they do not report the behavior to the child's parents. Such behavior may include, but is not confined to, trying to touch or smell an adult's genitals, coming up behind an adult who is bending over and simulating copulating movements from the rear, climbing on top of an adult in bed or on a couch and simulating intercourse, rubbing or touching an adult's breasts, suggesting "French" kissing, or even somewhat more subtle behaviors such as rubbing a teacher's knee while staring sadly into her face.

While the sexual behaviors described in this section may all be symptoms of sexual abuse, an aversion or extreme fearfulness in situations in which a child's genitals may be exposed or touched may also be suggestive. Some sexually abused children are fearful of diapering, baths, and showers and often grab their genitals and yell "don't hurt me" or "no touch" at such times.

Somatic Symptoms with Sexual Content

While many clinicians believe that chronic abdominal pain may be an indicator of sexual abuse, it is simply too frequent a symptom in middle childhood and has too many other causes (Barr & Feuerstein, 1983) to be reliable as a marker. However, bizarre physical symptoms with sexual content are sufficiently uncommon to cause concern. One 10-year-old girl with diabetes used her blood-testing needle to draw blood from her finger and smear it on her underpants. She continued this over a period of time. When outpatient tests failed to reveal a cause for the repeated bleeding, she was scheduled for an inpatient admission and a DNC. The night before the admission she confessed to her mother that she had faked the symptoms. Although this child never admitted directly that she had been sexually abused, she hinted repeatedly of "something happening" with a babysitter who had "forced" her to "do some things."

Physical Signs

Physical indicators of sexual abuse include red or swollen genitals, blood in the child's underwear, repeated fissures in the anus, any tear in the vagina, constant rashes in the vaginal area when a child is past the age where diaper rashes are common, complaints that the genital area hurts or itches, bruises on the upper thighs or in the genital area, "hickies" anywhere, and vaginal discharges. Obviously, any evidence of venereal disease or even an unusual amount of concern on the child's part as to whether she could have venereal disease, be pregnant, or have AIDS, may be indicative of sexual abuse.

Paternal Jealousy

Incestuous fathers occasionally display an inordinate amount of jealousy of their daughters, refusing to allow them to date, warning them that males are only interested in "one thing," monitoring their phone calls, and attempting to keep them home and away from after school activities. The degree of jealousy and paranoia distinguishes this behavior from simply a conservative approach to childrearing. Such fathers do not try to limit their daughter's dates or social contacts to appropriate contacts; they try to eliminate them. These fathers show an unjustified amount of affect around these issues, and their behavior may border on the paranoid. While this behavior is primarily associated with adolescents, fathers of young children may also be paranoid and/or extremely angry about the possibility of sexual contacts between younger daughters and other men. One 3-year-old reported that her 15-year-old babysitter had sexually molested her. Her father became extremely irate, and thought, he later confessed, of shooting the babysitter. He called the police instead. When they came, the daughter said, in effect, he only did to me what my father does. The father subsequently admitted that he had been sexually abusing his daughter. In his case, his reaction to the sexual abuse of the babysitter was not unusual for a nonabusing father and could not be taken as an indication of abuse itself, but it does serve to illustrate the degree of anger that perpetrators may have toward other individuals who might seek to have sexual or even social relations with their victims.

Running Away from Home and Prostitution

While running away is not an infallible sign of child sexual abuse, it appears to occur far more frequently in abused populations. Herman and Hirschman (1981) found that 33% of the women in her sample who had been victims of incest ran away, as compared to 5% with "seductive" fathers who had not committed incest. Meiselman (1978) found that 50% of the adult survivors of incest in her sample had left home before the age of 18, compared to 20% in her control group. Reich and Gutierres (1979) found that 55% of the sexually abused delinquent children in their sample were charged with offenses related to escape, as opposed to 5% who had records of offenses related to aggression. Thus, the sexually abused children were charged with delinquent acts because of their attempts to escape the abuse, not because of antisocial behavior. Even when the population studied consisted of drug addicts, the results were similar. Benward and Densen-Gerber (1975) found that 23% of their incest group had left home prior to age 14, as compared to 11% of the nonincest group. By age 16, 52% of the incest group had left home, as opposed to 39% of their nonincest group.

The association of incest and running away may explain the connection sometimes reported between prostitution and child sexual abuse (James & Meyerding, 1977; Janus, Scanlon, & Price, 1984). Silbert (1984), for example, found that 61% of a sample of women street prostitutes were victims of sexual abuse. Two-thirds had been abused by either their natural, step-, or foster fathers. The association may be partially due to a devaluing of sexuality as a result of the incest, but is also likely to be due to the fact that young adolescents, living on the street without either the necessities of life or job skills to obtain them, have few practical alternatives for survival. In Silbert's study, 96% of the women were runaways before they were prostitutes. In a 1981 report on this sample, Silbert and Pines stated that 89% of the women said "Needed money; was hungry" (p. 410) when asked why they began prostituting.

Verbal Report

By far the most reliable indicator of sexual abuse is a verbal report by the child. This report may range, according to the age of the child, from a 2-year-old who points to her vagina as she says "Daddy hurt me," to the 4-year-old who says clearly that her father touched her "pee pee" with his hand and that it hurt, to the adolescent who can describe exactly what was done to her. Often in their reports children reveal details too sophisticated or too graphic to be the results of any sex-education course. The preschooler who says with a puzzled look, "White stuff came out of him," or "he peed in my bottom" can only be speaking from experience. Sometimes the reports may be explicit. Frequently, however, children begin by hinting, "What would you do, mom, if dad were doing something bad to me?" "What if somebody was doing to me like what was happening to that girl in the movie?"

Occasionally children who are being abused at home, may make up wildly improbable stories of being raped repeatedly by strangers, at a time and in a setting where it was not possible. Before dismissing such claims as entirely false, it is wise to look further to see if perhaps real abuse may be occurring that is simply too close for the child to report. In order to protect family members, a child may sometimes report the abuse as occurring elsewhere by an unrelated person.

Lying. Children are frequently accused of lying about sexual abuse, routinely by defense attorneys and men charged with abuse, and increasingly in the media. While sexually abused children who have the misfortune to have divorcing parents can expect the most difficult time, all abused children who report can expect to have the question raised. It is inevitably a component of a court trial, and, in the final analysis, all cases in which the offender does not confess rest on the credibility of the child. In this situation child sexual abuse victims undergo the sort of difficulties previously experienced by rape victims, who, until a few years ago, were routinely put on trial to test their veracity and to examine their previous sexual experiences.

This unwillingness to believe children has a long history. L. Thoinot (Thoinot & Weysse, 1911) devotes an entire chapter in his book *Medicolegal Aspects of Moral Offenses* to the problem of false accusations in child and adult sexual abuse cases:

> Nothing is more common in this matter than complaints that end in being dismissed: it can be said that in France from 60 to 80 per cent of the accusations made are recognized as unfounded . . . Taylor says that for one real case of rape brought to trial before the English courts there are at least twelve false accusations. If it is the same everywhere, if everywhere the number of false assaults exceeds, and by a good deal, the number of real assaults, it is because these false assaults obey certain psychological laws that are bound to exist, and, in fact, are nowhere absent. (p. 223)

Thoinot goes on to distinguish in children and adults between conscious lies and unconscious lies. Both children and their mothers may produce either. As an example of a false accusation he cites the following:

> A shirt merchant was called before the judge on a charge of indecent assault on a child of ten years. He protested his innocence in indignant terms and affirmed that he had not quitted his place of business at the time at which the assault of which he was accused, was said to have taken place. The deposition of the child was there, clear and precise; she repeated it in all its details and the parents confirmed her statements. The magistrate, moved by the attitude of the merchant, a perfectly honorable man, stopped the proceedings and let the affair go no further. (p. 231)

No doubt, with legal criteria such as these for the dismissal of cases, it is easy to see why up to 80% of the charges would be viewed as unfounded.

There is little empirical evidence to support the supposition that children frequently lie about sexual abuse. Jones and McGraw (1987) found an 8% rate of fictitious accounts of sexual abuse in their study of founded and unfounded child protection cases. Of these, 26 cases (6%) were fictitious claims by an adult that a child had been sexually abused. In only 8 cases (2%) did the child allege the abuse. These eight fictitious allegations were made by a total of five children, one of whom made three separate allegations, and another child made two. Four of these five children were disturbed adolescents who had in fact been sexually abused by an adult in the past, although the current allegation was fictitious. In a separate phase of the study, 717 cases were reviewed that were seen at the Kempe National Center between 1983 and 1985. Of the total, 21 cases (3%) were thought to be fictitious according to criteria elaborated by Jones and McGraw. Of these 21 cases 9 fictitious accounts (1.3%) were alleged by adults, 7 (1%) were mixed cases, in which it was impossible to determine whether the adult or the child had originated the charge, and 5 (.79%) were fictitious accounts produced by a child. In both these studies then, false claims of sexual abuse made by a child occurred in less than 2% of the cases.

Peters (1976) found 6% of reports to be fictitious, although there is no information on whether the child or another adult alleged the abuse. Horowitz, Salt, Gomes-Schwartz, and Sauzier (cited in Jones & McGraw, 1987) found 5% to be so. Katz and Mazur (1979), in their critique of studies that looked at false reports by adults charging rape, found 2% to be the most reliable figure.

The widespread belief that children lie about sexual abuse has its origins in adult fearfulness about false accusations and not in child development. To understand why lying about abuse is so infrequent, it is necessary to look at developmental stages in children and at why, when, and how children lie.

Lying and Developmental Considerations. Children at all ages lie to get out of trouble. The lies they tell consist predominantly of denial, "No, I didn't break the cabinet; no, I don't have any idea how it happened. No, I wasn't fooling around with the basketball in the kitchen." They rarely make up stories to explain the broken cabinet, missing cake, or stolen money. They typically rest their case on the flat statement that they had nothing to do with it, and "why do you always pick on me when something goes wrong?"

Preschool children frequently report monsters, and other creatures of ill renown they fear. The line between reality and fantasy is thinner in the preschool years than later, and a strong belief in monsters under the bed and bathrobes turned into monsters by the flick of a light switch permits children to go screaming into their parents' room in the night in a state of panic. Even so, children rarely report that they actually saw the monster, but that something, a closed closet door, the empty space under the bed, the scratching of a branch against the window, caused them to think about monsters that could be there. The child's imagination invents the possibility of creatures, and the child does not have the logical capacity to determine that they could not exist. Even preschool children, however, are extremely accurate reporters of things that touch their five senses. They do not typically report that they smelled things that were not there, that they touched things that did not exist, or that they saw or heard things not present.

More than one case of child sexual abuse has been determined on the so-called Santa Claus defense. The defense attorney asks the child whether or not she believes in Santa Claus, the Easter Bunny, and the Tooth Fairy. The preschooler says yes, and the defense claims the child is incompetent to testify because she cannot separate the real from the unreal. This defense, and a court's acceptance of it, indicates a lack of understanding of child development. Santa Claus and the Easter Bunny are cultural myths that are systematically taught to the child. The entire culture colludes with this myth-making, to the extent of producing men in red suits whom the child can see and on whose knees she can sit. To know that this is a giant cultural fraud is indeed beyond the capacity of the child, but does not reflect negatively on her ability to report accurately what touches her five senses. She is indeed telling the truth about men in red suits, and it is the culture that has taught her the meaning of the event. To use the child's trust in what she has systematically been taught by her parents, by books, in cartoons and movies, and by department store Santas as an indication that she is unable to accurately report whether someone sexually assaulted her is to confuse the abstract with the concrete, a cultural lie with a personal one.

While preschoolers are also presumed to lie because they are angry with someone, in fact this sort of lying is generally outside the cognitive capabilities of the preschooler. To understand the meaning of sexual abuse in this culture, and to foresee what will result from a false report of sexual abuse, is to have a capacity for abstract thought that does not occur until adolescence. Preschoolers simply cannot de-center sufficiently to look at things from different perspectives. They are not capable of the "what-if" type of thinking required. Only in adolescence, with the development of abstract thinking, the observing ego, and its associated imaginary audience (Elkind, 1984), can children de-center sufficiently to take the perspective of other people on sexual abuse and to strategize such sophisticated ways of getting someone "into trouble."

In middle childhood the line between reality and fantasy is very firmly drawn, partially because the capacity to make the distinction has been so recently acquired. Children who once believed fervently in monsters repudiate them, and, although nighttime may cause regressions, they are generally aware of what is fantasy and what is not. They are still too concrete to appreciate that a false report of sexual abuse is a strategy for revenge, sharing with the younger age group an inability to reason abstractly and plot imaginary scenarios. They do not falsely report sexual abuse as an exaggeration of a normal fear, partially because sexual abuse is not a normal fear at any age.

Bauer (1977) found in his study of children's fears that preschool children were overwhelmingly afraid of ghosts and monsters, while middle-childhood children feared bodily injury and physical danger. The type of bodily injury and physical danger described by the children in their dreams involved physical rather than sexual assaults: "'They want to cut off my head.' 'That he would kill me.' or 'Guess he would have choked me or something'" (p. 146).

In general, whereas younger children fear monsters, children in middle childhood fear "bad people": kidnappers, murderers, and burglars. The following are answers that first and fifth graders gave to the question of what they fear most.

Typical first-grade responses:

> My dog groaning at night, and being in the woods camping in a tent. An my sister groaning at night too. My dad snoring. I think it is a monster. An owls hooting. My sister scares me when I'm asleep by tapping me and then making funny faces.

> When there is noises when I am sleeping and I don't know what they are. Sometimes of the dark. When my dog licks me when I am asleep, I don't know who it is. To get kidnapped. you could never get back to your parents, you should only get picked up by your parents. Falling off a bridge. When my dog groans. A bear. Nothing.

> Being in the woods alone at night. Being picked up by someone I don't know. Going off the road in a car and dying. Spiders. When a car is going really fast across a bridge, maybe it could fall off. Being kidnapped.

As can be seen, first graders are divided, with some clinging to the monsters of yesteryear and others moving into more of the concrete fears associated with middle childhood. Fifth graders have left the world of monsters behind and are caught between the more concrete fears of middle childhood and the more abstract fears made possible by formal operations and the abstract thought characteristic of adolescence.

Typical fifth-grade responses:

Death, war, kidnapped, and water. Death because, what is it like? What does it feel like? Do you know you're dead? Kidnapped because, will I ever be found? Will I be killed? War because, what is it like? Will the world blow up? Water because, when I'm swimming will I suddenly sick? Will I drown?

Water, heights, and AIDS. (Other diseases don't scare me much.) Getting killed by other people. I usually don't mind snakes that much. I'm afraid of war, and things that could happen to me later in life.

Killer (crazy people) I hear about them on the news and in the papers. There's even someone walking around killing women in Hartland, Vermont. I hate to think someone would do something like that to me or my friends.

While middle childhood children fear kidnappers, it is not sexual assault that troubles them, but being separated from their parents and killed. They most certainly do not spontaneously report being afraid of sexual assault from acquaintances, family friends, or relatives. They have little reason to exaggerate their fear into a false report of sexual abuse, since it is not a fear in the first place. Secondly, even for those fears children genuinely do have, they do not falsely describe them as occurring; thus, for example, they do not tell their parents that they were kidnapped or that someone attempted to murder them.

It is only in adolescence that children even have the cognitive capacity to manipulate a false report of sexual abuse in order to obtain revenge for a real or imagined slight. While there have been occasions when they have done so, the occurrences are rare, partly because it is so highly embarrassing to most adolescents to have to talk about sexuality with strangers. There is considerable peer pressure in adolescence not to be different from peers, and being sexually abused is extremely stigmatizing. An adolescent who reports sexual abuse runs a gauntlet of peer pressure, frequently of family pressure, and certainly of public exposure. There are easier ways to make a point.

Nor do adolescents, any more than younger children, particularly fear sexual abuse. While they still fear being knifed, murdered, kidnapped, and robbed, they also add the abstract fears their age entitles them too. Sample eighth grade fears are as follows:

Nuclear war, scary movies, getting murdered, being kidnapped.

I am most afraid of AIDS and breaking a bone.

A nuclear holocaust.

Sexual abuse at the hands of acquaintances, friends, or family is not something that children of any age spontaneously fear. Nor is there any evidence that children falsely report their fears as realities beyond the preschool years, where there is some confusion over monsters in the dark. The charge that children manipulate accusations of sexual abuse in order to harm adults is totally erroneous for children younger than adolescents because they do not have the cognitive capacity to do so. Adolescents are cognitively capable of taking such a stance, but emotionally the overwhelming thrust of development is against it, as it makes the adolescent not only feel different from other adolescents, but also appear different in public. It requires an adolescent to discuss explicit sexual details with strangers, e.g., policemen, lawyers, judges, at the age most difficult to do so. The self-consciousness of adolescents regarding sexuality is legendary.

Custody Fights and Fabricated Charges. It is currently the fashion to suspect all charges of child sexual abuse when they occur during the divorce process. This is an unfortunate turn, given that many allegations of child sexual abuse made during a custody fight are nonetheless true. In a study by Jones and Seig (cited in Jones & McGraw, 1987) there were more cases in which a custody fight coexisted with a true report of child sexual abuse than cases in which a custody fight coexisted with a false report. As reported in Chapter 4, Mian (1986) found in a study of 125 sexually abused children under the age of 7 that 67% of the incest victims came from families who were separated or divorced at the time of the report compared to 27% of the children reporting extrafamilial abuse.

Incest is frequently reported only after the offender has moved out of the home, because children fear retaliation if they report earlier. In addition, many offenders molest children for the first time during the break-up of a marriage. Revenge against the divorcing spouse has been cited by some offenders as a motivation. For others, the period of the marital break-up is a period in which the offender is particularly vulnerable. If sexual molestation is a temptation while under stress, he may act out, particularly since he is often alone with his child. On visitations there is no spouse to interrupt the abuse. Finally, not everything that is labeled a custody fight is one. In one sexual abuse case, the defense persisted in labeling the issue as a custody fight. In reality, the divorce had occurred three years previously, and no changes in custody had been sought by the mother. The first time her daughter reported sexual abuse at the hands of the divorced father during visitation, she ignored it through fear of her ex-spouse, who had physically abused her during the marriage. After the second report from her daughter she did call the authorities. Although the mother remained fearful throughout the court process the father would kill her, she was nonetheless labeled by the defense as a vindictive spouse who had initiated a charge of sexual abuse in order to harm her ex-husband.

Assessing the Accuracy of Sexual Abuse Reports by Children. While still rare, there are false reports of child sexual abuse. In those cases there are often indicators within the testimony of the child. Jones and McGraw (1987) cite several dimensions along which accurate and inaccurate reports can be distinguished: explicit detail, unique or distinguishing detail, age-appropriate words and sentence formation, a child's perspective, affect during the reporting, affective and behavioral sequelae, the progression of the abuse, secrecy, and a precocious understanding of sexuality. In my experience, the following are particularly useful guides.

Detail. Adults rarely give young children enough details to make a lie convincing. Frequently a young child repeats a set phrase, such as "Daddy did something bad to me," and is unable to elaborate. The child cannot always answer where it happened or (even with allowances for a child's sense of time) when it happened. Work with adult survivors supports the concept that explicit details of sexual abuse, including the surroundings, are often remembered for decades and are frequently vivid (Silver, Boon, & Stones, 1983). This is not to imply that every child who cannot produce vivid details has manufactured a report, but that the level of detail and the type of detail are important considerations for the purposes of assessing validity. Physical sensations ("it felt sticky and yucky") and particular odors or tastes associated with various types of sexual activities are not typical of adult-fabricated reports. When questioned, older children who are producing a fictitious report may be angered by being asked for details.

Level of Description and Evidence of Spontaneity. Adults rarely explain things at exactly the right language level for a child. Descriptions of sexuality that are consistent with an adult's understanding but not a child's are suspicious. A child's descriptions should be concrete, should emphasize what was done to the child using language and sentence structure appropriate to the child's developmental level. In a case described by Jones and McGraw (1987), a fictitious report by a 5-year-old used language appropriate to a 3-year-old. She had in fact been sexually abused at age 3 by a different man.

There may be spontaneous comments about the abuse that do not sound rehearsed, for example, the comment cited previously, "It hurt; I said, 'daddy stop,' cepting he didn't."

As times goes by, a lie may either stay exactly the same, a rigid, parroted statement that is often in adult language or includes adult judgments, or it may become extremely grandiose. Flights on airplanes, Satanic happenings, and numerous abusers may be included. When the list of abusers continues to grow and includes numerous people not in the same family and not connected with each other—family members, plus day-care providers, plus other unconnected adults—it is appropriate to question the charges. At this point, if the child is young enough, she may genuinely have confused herself and may no longer be clear about what happened.

Affect. In false reports there is often an absence of affect around the revelation and an absence of the sense of puzzlement many children have about it. False reporters do not ask questions, such as whether all men do such things to little girls, or other comments that would indicate the child is trying to process and to make sense of the experience. Likewise, they do not find it difficult to talk about the experience, and frequently repeat the tale in an almost cavalier manner. True reporters often refuse to discuss the incidents with a new investigator, are often embarrassed and ashamed, and often won't look at someone when discussing it. This is not inevitably true; some children have been interviewed enough times to habituate to the experience. At the minimum, however, shyness and difficulty in discussing details of the offenses should not be taken as evidence against their accuracy.

Progression. An absence of a progression of the offense, as cited in Sgroi et al. (1982), is also an indication that the charge may not be genuine. Offenders almost inevitably begin abuse slowly and progress to more intrusive behaviors. Fortunately, some children are now reporting early enough that they may be reporting the first contact; if so, it is usually inappropriate touching as opposed to intercourse. Intercourse by a drunken father is an exception, as an inebriated offender may progress immediately to penetration.

Secrecy. Secrecy is a difficult element on which to base firm generalizations. While many offenders do explicitly threaten or bribe their victims not to tell, many others, particularly with young children, apparently do not feel the need to do so. It is not unusual for a young child, particularly, to state that the offender never said anything about not telling. Thus, while an absence of explicit instructions regarding secrecy does not invalidate a child's story, the presence of the type of instructions regarding secrecy offenders frequently use would support it.

CONCLUSIONS

In identifying sexual abuse, the verbal report of the child remains the most common significant piece of evidence. Physical symptoms such as VD are extremely reliable, but also rare. Certain other symptoms inappropriate sexual behavior, somatic complaints with sexual content, paternal jealously, and running away from home are all specific enough to sexual abuse to be highly suggestive. Other frequently cited symptoms such as depression, poor school performance, aggressive behavior, and/or regressive behavior, for example, are far too general and are found with too many other childhood traumas to be useful.

False child reports of sexual abuse are rare and occur in perhaps no more than 2% of the cases (Jones & McGraw, 1987). False reports in general, which include charges fabricated by adults as well as false reports by children, may total up to 8% of all cases. Despite the rarity, it is extremely important to determine when a child is lying, both to protect the accused, who is not guilty, and to protect those many children who are telling the truth and whose chances of being believed are severely damaged by fictitious allegations by others. Criteria by which false accusations can be distinguished from accurate reports include the extent and type of detail, the level of language and presence/absence of spontaneous statements regarding the abuse, the affect of the child, the progression of the offenses, and the statements regarding secrecy.

15

CONCLUSIONS

Finkelhor (1984) has suggested four preconditions for child sexual abuse: (1) the motivation to abuse, (2) overcoming internal inhibitors, (3) overcoming external inhibitors, and (4) overcoming resistance by the child. The dynamics of sexual abuse as developed in this book and the types of therapies needed to treat offenders and their families can be subsumed under this general model. Figure 15.1 illustrates the relationships.

The offender's motivation to abuse, most certainly the necessary condition without which abuse would not occur, was discussed in Chapter 3. Offenders against children sometimes have a deviant arousal pattern that makes them sexually attracted to children; stress may, but need not, be a contributing factor. Evidence at present suggests there are also men who molest children who do not have a deviant arousal pattern, but for whom the molestation is a form of acting out in response to nonsexual problems. A deviant arousal pattern responds only to behavioral treatment, while nonsexual problems will response to either individual, marital, or family therapy.

The internal inhibitions that should be present for offenders include empathy for the child and a rational appreciation of the

Finkelhor's General Preconditions	Specific Preconditions	Therapeutic Techniques and/or Goals	Types of Therapy
1. Motivation	A. Deviant Arousal	Boredom Tapes Covert Sensitization	Behavioral
	B. Avoidance of Non-sexual Problem	Social Skills Training Assertiveness Training Resolution of Individual and Family Issues	Group/Family/Individual
2. Overcoming Internal Inhibitions	A. Cognitive Distortions	Group & Family Confrontation Relapse Prevention	Group/Family
	B. Lack of Empathy	Assignments in Group; Group Confrontation; Family & Victim Confrontation	Group/Family
	C. Apparently Irrelevant Decisions	Relapse Prevention	Group/Family/Individual
3. Overcoming External Inhibitions	A. Belief in Ability to "Get Away with It"	Close Monitoring of offender by Probation & Parole; monitoring of child by child protection agency; therapist & child willing to disclose	Coordinated System Response to insure certainy of reporting & legal proceedings
4. Overcoming Child's Resistance	A. Child afraid, isolated, unassertive &/or unaware of sexual abuse dynamics	Knowledge of sexual abuse; close relationship with mother; awareness of offender's risk factors; close relationship with therapist & other abused children	Family (mother/child) child group; child individual

Figure 15.1 Relationship of Finkelhor Model of General Preconditions to Specific Preconditions, Therapeutic Techniques, and Types of Therapy

harmfulness of the behavior. These are lacking in child sex offenders, who instead rationalize their behavior in ways described in Chapter 9. They show little true empathy for their victims and find it difficult to separate the point of view of the child from their own (see Chapters 9 and 10). Motivated to molest children and without sufficient internal inhibitions, they make the Apparently Irrelevant Decisions discussed in Chapter 11 on Relapse Prevention that lead to molestation. These issues of the offender's motivation and his internal inhibitions can be addressed in group therapy. They can be addressed in family therapy as well, a beneficial consequence being the alerting of the family to the thinking patterns that signal the beginning of the abusive pattern. Family therapy, however, cannot replace group therapy, because the family will be unable to confront the offender as strongly as a group can, nor will a family adequately understand his point of view or be as aware of his attempts to manipulate other people.

External restraints are partially the responsibility of a unified system. The offender must know that incarceration will be the response to further abuse, and that his compliance with treatment conditions will be monitored carefully by the Department of Probation and Parole. He must also know that the mother and child have developed a sufficiently close relationship to make further abuse likely to be reported. The relationship between the child and her therapist should reinforce his concern. An increased likelihood that the child and her mother will report further molestations will decrease the likelihood of their occurring. An aware and empowered mother is particularly important. Sexual abuse thrives on secrecy and power. A knowledgeable and assertive family offers a significant deterrent. Many offenders will remolest if they believe they can get away with it; few will molest if they believe they cannot.

The child's ability to resist sexual abuse is increased by knowledge, both of sexual abuse in children and of her offender's risk factors in particular. She should know how and whom to alert if the offender, for example, begins to drink or to "just visit" in her room. A close relationship with her mother and with her therapist will give her the opportunity to tell; increased assertiveness and confidence will give her the ability.

Treatment should address all of the preconditions for child sexual abuse, and attempt to intervene on every level. Without discovery and comprehensive intervention the sexual abuse will not be adequately addressed. In cases in which there is no intervention, the powerlessness of the victim often continues even after the abuse itself has stopped, and long-term sequelae are common. The following excerpt was written by a college student about her sexual abuse experience. She was sexually molested from ages 7 to 14 by her stepfather. She was able to stop the abuse at age 14, but did not reveal it to anyone. Prior to college she had not received treatment. She entered treatment following a suicidal gesture her senior year. At the time she wrote the following, she had not revealed the abuse to her family and had never confronted her abuser. Socially isolated, she had never dated, and was repulsed by the thought of sexuality. Her own body disgusted her, and she literally refused to look down while taking a shower. She wrote the following about her interactions with her stepfather:

> I was hoping to get away from it all, but I can't, because it haunts me. It really does haunt me. Howard, his last words to me, they follow me everywhere. It's no different here, just because I'm at college.
>
> When he asked me about the letters I wrote this summer . . . "Why didn't you put a couple of X's and O's on your letters?"[1]
>
> Blood rushing to my face . . . feeling ashamed . . ."I dunno."
>
> "I saw the little X's and O's on the letters to the family."
>
> "Well . . . uh . . . they were to everyone and so . . . you know . . ." Mumbling so much. Thinking, this is your big chance . . . Tell him why. Tell him that he hurt you . . . Say it.
>
> "I think—" he talks now "—that the reason you didn't put the X's and O's on the letters to me is because you knew what they meant. Is that it?"
>
> "Well . . ." Guilt. Shame. Disgust for myself and this beast.
>
> "Is that it?"
>
> I smiled, gulped, chuckled nervously. "I guess so." THIS IS YOUR CHANCE, DAMMIT! Stop farting around and tell him what you think. The bastard.
>
> "I think it is. Well, you know I'll be waiting to hear from you, and I'll be looking for the X's and O's on your letters. Do you still remember what they mean?"
>
> No, you fucking bastard, I just forgot. It slipped my mind.
>
> "Yeah."
>
> "Will I see them on any letters?"
>
> I smiled. "Don't count on it."
>
> "Well, your feelings may change once you get to college. Think about it. Will you do that for me?"
>
> Why not? I've done everything else.
>
> "I guess so." Eyes always on the floor. Focus on the bread crumbs. On anything. Disgust. Feeling of nausea.
>
> "Well, I love you an awful lot. And I'm going to miss you."
>
> LIKE HELL YOU LOVE ME. Yeah, you'll miss me, but you won't miss ME, WHO I AM. You'll miss my physical presence, you disgusting pig.
>
> He continued: "I don't know what you think of your old stepfather—" If only you knew (so why don't you tell him, you asshole??!)"—But I hope you'll miss me a little bit, and write to me when you can."

How did it end? Oh, probably like all the other confrontations. I, head down, ashamed and blushed, mumble and shuffle out of the room. away . from . him. How many millions of times did I go through *that* routine? It was just a part in a play. All of the nightmare was just a little show that I was watching. I had watched it all my life. What did it matter that I was one of the actors?

And then later, when he came into my room and stood there watching me, smoking his damn cigarette, and the questions came again.

"I was just curious . . . I was wondering if you have any regrets about what we did?"

REGRETS!? This man ruined my life and he wants to know about REGRETS? FUCK YOU, HOWARD. If I answered truthfully, if I told you that you could be in prison now if I did something about it. REGRETS? IT WAS YOUR DAMN FAULT! NOT MINE. I WAS IN SECOND GRADE WHEN IT STARTED. Regrets? I regret Life. I regret ever seeing your face. I regret that YOU destroyed me inside so that I may never be whole again. Do I have any regrets?

"I don't know . . ." I was mumbling again. Staring at my hands. Hating myself.

"Are you glad we did it?"

To cry. To scream. No, I just sit passively and let the assault take place. I can't answer this one. My tongue tastes vile and my head spins with hatred and anger.

"Are you glad that we had all that fun?"

"No . . ." I smile. What the hell was I smiling for? Guilt? Shame?

"Did you like it?"

"No." My god, I said it. I answered. I told him I didn't like it.

"That's not what you used to think." OH YEAH?! You want to know what I used to think? My terror of the nights that Mom was out, my feeling of nausea every time you "just wanted to say goodnight." My total helplessness. My ruined childhood. You want to know what I "used to think"?!

"You used to tell me how much you loved it." He grins and his voice holds an edge of power, of sarcasm, of "I've got you, haven't I?"

I NEVER, NEVER, NEVER told you that! Stop putting words in my mouth! I NEVER, I swear by it, I NEVER told you any such thing! You lie just like my father.[2] You twist words, wait to spring upon innocent victims. You're a liar. A Fucking Liar!!

"Remember that?" His grin is bigger now. He's waiting for an answer. WHAT'S HIS PROBLEM!?

"Not really." I meant to be sarcastic, as if to say, "How am I supposed to remember what I never said?" But it didn't come out that way. Even if it had, he wouldn't have heard it . . .

"Well, I do." He says something else, who cares what, and leaves the room.

Why didn't I just tell him? Why didn't I just come right out and tell him everything I had felt?

I was afraid. I was afraid of his lies. Of his twisting words and cornering me and making me admit he's right. He's NOT right, but I was so afraid that he'd keep that silly, hungry grin and feed me more and more bullshit so that I got so confused I couldn't think. I was afraid that it would cause an argument that would be dragged out and awful.

Fear. Haven't I always felt it? Will I ever NOT feel it? And fear of Daddy, too. Even here. I'll never escape that. The anger and bitterness-that won't leave either. I can always leave, but all of it follows me, hunts me down, keeps on stabbing and stinging.

Well, so here I am. Back to base one I can tell that all the other players in the game are sneering. Pointing at me and laughing. So what the hell. Maybe someday I'll win.

This young woman subsequently told her family of the abuse, and confronted her offender. Her mother had been alienated from the stepfather for years, but had never left him, as the stepfather was wealthy and she had signed a prenuptial agreement that would have left her penniless in case of a divorce. She managed to persuade him that she would publicize the molestation if he did not provide for her financially. Unfortunately, the statute of limitations had run out in her state, and he could not be prosecuted. The mother had had a lover for some time, whom she introduced her daughter to following the separation from the stepfather. The lover, drunk at this first meeting, made a pass at her daughter in front of the mother. When the daughter objected, the mother told her not to be "so uptight. Loosen up." The young woman left the table, and took a bus to friends in another state, where she stayed for the remainder of her school vacation.

The picture of offender and victim that is revealed in the preceding vignette emerges frequently in child sexual abuse cases. All too often the victim is paralyzed by a sense of helplessness, immobilized by impotent rage. Standing on one foot and the other, shuffling back and forth, head down, afraid to confront the offender, too young to know her rights, too naive to understand that he not she, will be in trouble, too afraid of what will happen if she tells, she mumbles outside while she shouts inside.

Some victims go numb. "I don't feel anything anymore," said one young man to his mother when the sexual abuse by his employer over a period of years was finally exposed. "I could just go kill someone, and I wouldn't feel anything about it. I know I shouldn't do it and it's wrong. But I wouldn't feel anything." Other victims dissociate and watch themselves being molested by an offender while they hover somewhere in the top of the room. Much later, tragically, they find they cannot control the dissociation and that it comes, unbidden, when they want to be intimate with someone.

It is asking much of mental health clinicians, steeped in a tradition that combines absolute confidentiality, therapeutic neutrality, and empathy to treat sex offenders. The most cherished tenets of psychotherapy must be surrendered. Therapists must from the start place strict limits on confidentiality, must distrust much of what their clients say, must take a firm value stand often at odds with their clients, and must be hypervigilant for movement toward relapse. They cannot rely on the type of therapeutic relationship or on the kind of therapeutic techniques that have been effective for them with other clients.

Although the task is difficult, the community of mental health professionals must develop the skills and implement the programs necessary to treat child sexual abuse. With or without jail, most sex offenders will eventually return to the community. Without treatment, relapses will be frequent. There is nothing in the external controls of a prison that will teach internal controls. On the contrary, most offenders will spend their time in prison masturbating to deviant fantasies of children, far more often than they masturbated on the outside, and consequently return to the community with a more ingrained pattern of deviant arousal.

Gene Abel has said the following:

> We already have the treatment programs available. They have been available for quite some time. What is needed is for them to be implemented, and they are not being implemented. People are going to jail or prison and they rarely receive any treatment or specialized treatment there. Or, worse yet, they are on the street and no one does anything about it. And it is not really complicated. We have treatment programs and they must be brought to the offender. (Abel, as quoted in Knopp, 1984, p. 81)

The situation is actually a little worse than Abel describes. The models for the programs are there, but the programs themselves are not. Although sex offender treatment is still in its infancy, the techniques available today are vastly superior to earlier, nonspecialized treatment. Those techniques, developed and refined by a handful of treatment specialists in the country, have been utilized in only a few treatment programs. The need for many such programs is clear: Increased reporting by children has led to an influx of offenders into the system. More and more offenders are going to court; more and more courts would mandate treatment were it available. Treatment needs to be available everywhere.

NOTES

1. Her stepfather had previously told her that x's and o's on letters between them signified oral sex.
2. Her father physically abused her when she was a preschooler.

APPENDICES

APPENDIX A
Vermont Sexual Abuse/Assault Protocol
William M. Young

I. *Introduction and Definition*

  A. This protocol has been developed as a cooperative effort of all of the parties, representing concerned agencies and individuals in Bennington, Orange, Rutland, Windham and Windsor Counties. The purpose of the protocol is to help personnel from various disciplines recognize and respond appropriately to children and adolescents who have been sexually abused or assaulted, to their families, and to the perpetrator of the abuse/assault. The agencies and individuals involved are in agreement that the primary purpose of a sexual abuse program is to prevent victimization from occurring, or reoccurring, and to provide assistance to victims. This protocol is based on the philosophy that no attempt to prevent and treat sexual abuse is likely to be successful unless it involves a cooperative effort on the part of all involved agencies and individuals.

  B. For the purpose of this protocol sexual abuse of children and adolescents consists of any act or acts of any person involving sexual molestation or sexual exploitation of a child including, but *not limited to* incest as defined in 13 VSA 205, prostitution, sexual assault as defined in 13 VSA 3251 and 3252, or any lewd or lascivious conduct involving a child. It should be noted that present Vermont law protects anyone making a good faith report of possible child abuse to Social and Rehabilitative Services (SRS) from any civil liability for such a report.

II. *Guidelines for Reporting and Responding to Child/Adolescent Sexual Abuse Cases*

  The following is intended as a brief description of the reporting process and response to suspected or confirmed cases of child/adolescent abuse. More detailed protocols for each organization or agency may be developed by individual agencies for use by their own workers and, if so, are available upon request.

A. Reporting

SRS is the State agency mandated by law to deal with suspected or confirmed cases of child sexual abuse. In any case of child sexual abuse, SRS should be notified first. An oral report should be made as soon as there is reasonable cause to believe that abuse has occurred. A written report should follow as soon thereafter as possible.

Upon receipt of a report of child sexual abuse SRS will, in accordance with State law and Department policy, assign a social worker to investigate the report within 72 hours. In most situations an attempt will be made to investigate immediately. The Social Worker assigned to the case will be responsible for ensuring that the appropriate police agency (State, Local, or State's Attorney's Investigator)— is notified and will make arrangements to conduct a joint investigation. This will usually take the form of the initial face to face contact being made by the Social Worker and the police investigator together.

In emergencies where the police are involved prior to SRS action, the police will report the facts of their investigation to SRS, and if charges are brought, follow their usual procedure with the State's Attorney's office.

It is assumed that in cases of a violent, life threatening assault, or where an assault is in progress, the police will always be called, either by the original reporter, SRS, or the State's Attorney. The police agency in these situations is responsible for immediately ensuring that SRS also has the information. The SRS investigation and initial interview shall focus on the child victim and other non-offending family members, not on the alleged offender. If the SRS workers questions the alleged offender, any statements made may not be used in court. The alleged offender may, but need not, be informed by the SRS worker that any statements may be used against him or her. It is not until police have an alleged offender in their custody that the alleged offender *must* be informed of his or her Miranda rights. It is the responsibility of the assigned police investigator to interview the alleged offender and to carry out an investigation that may result in criminal charges being filed.

If in the initial SRS family interview, the alleged offender is present, it is appropriate for the SRS worker to notify him of the allegations, to explain the SRS role in the investigation, to inform him that SRS will report the situation to the police and State's Attorney and to inform him that there is the *possibility* of criminal charges. The SRS workers shall not give legal advice to the alleged offender nor shall they make statements about the police investigation other than the fact that there may be one. It is expected that in most situations the police investigator will be present and will address these issues with the alleged offender. During joint investigations and interviews, the police officer and the SRS worker should be working in a cooperative manner that complements each other's roles and in that capacity should be helpful to one another. This does not imply that their roles are the same. While the primary goal of both is to protect the child, the police officer remains concerned with the investigation of criminal activity; the SRS worker with such issues as family dynamics and treatment.

B. Responsibilities:

1. Social and Rehabilitation Services:

SRS has responsibility for the initial investigation and protection of the child. This will typically be done in conjunction with the police investigator. The Social Worker focuses on a determination regarding the facts of the abuse and establishing what environment will afford further protection for the child if the abuse is established. SRS may make recommendations to the State's Attorney regarding conditions of release for the offender when criminal charges are brought, and it is anticipated that SRS, the police, and the State's Attorney's office will cooperate with each other when there is doubt as to the appropriateness of criminal charges.

SRS prepares the juvenile court case, if any, and may make recommendations to the State's Attorney regarding sentencing disposition in the criminal cases, to include specific conditions of probation if deemed appropriate, (suggested conditions of release or bail and of probation or parole are attached).

SRS works with the family to establish concrete goals, monitor progress in specific terms and makes decisions regarding re-constitution of the family. The Mental Health professional involved with the case is consulted in all cases. In those areas with an established child sexual abuse treatment program the family members will be referred immediately to the program.

SRS has a primary responsibility for the protection of the victim. While contact with the family can and should be humanistic and therapeutic, SRS workers are not responsible for providing therapeutic services, but rather for assisting in arrangements for such services. The investigation role of SRS predominates, and in that role SRS makes its presence felt throughout the treatment process.

The SRS workers should always encourage/arrange for a medical evaluation for the child/adolescent, if this has not already been done. This is necessary not only to treat injuries, but also to assure the child that they have not been physically "damaged." While there may be situations where there are not obvious physical injuries, or where a medical exam would add more disturbance (e.g., parent is violently opposed) every effort should be made to have the child seen by a knowledgeable physician. If the child is in the custody of SRS and removed from the home, SRS will pay for evaluation/treatment if necessary.

In cases of child/adolescent sexual abuse within a family setting, the perpetrator will typically be asked (or ordered by the court) to leave the day abuse is substantiated in order to protect the child from further victimization and to facilitate treatment for all concerned (see police and State's Attorney protocols). Where the child cannot remain safely in the home—for example, where a spouse has participated in the abuse or is incapable of protecting the child—then SRS may seek custody and place the child as appropriate.

The above practices mean that some control of the case is given over to the police and the State's Attorney. Mental health clinicians gain the satisfaction of success obtained in providing therapy, but SRS gains a simplified role and a greater likelihood of long term success.

2. Police:

The role of law enforcement agencies regarding child/adolescent sexual abuse is to prevent continued victimization and to investigate and refer for criminal prosecution all cases of sexual abuse violating

Vermont law. While police officers should receive specialized training in appropriate methods of dealing with child sexual abuse, and should be familiar with this protocol, they are not expected to act as social workers any more than social workers should be expected to function as law enforcement officers. Both, however, must function in a coordinated manner if sexual abuse is to be dealt with adequately.

An allegation of child sexual abuse may be investigated by a local police department, the State Police, or the State's Attorney's investigator, or the Sheriff's Department. It may follow an initial SRS investigation or be a response to a direct report to the police, who will then notify SRS to coordinate the investigation.

The police investigator and the Social Worker are both responsible for arranging the investigation to include, for example, joint interviews with the victim, non-offending spouse and others as needed.

In cases being investigated by the State's Attorney's investigator, or the State Police, the investigating officer will inform the local police department of the investigation. This is not done just as a courtesy, but to gain the benefit of any information the local department may have, to assist the local department in the event of any future complaints regarding the same individual, and to aid in prevention efforts by making the police aware of potential problems in their area. All such information is confidential.

If the initial report is made to the police, the police response is dictated by the circumstances at the time. In cases where there is immediate danger or threat of violence the police agency will respond immediately and notify the SRS by telephone, SRS will respond within 72 hours, and immediately if necessary (particularly if there is a threat of violence). Continued investigation will be coordinated with the assigned caseworker.

In situations where the police receive the initial report and do not feel an emergency situation exists, they will contact the local SRS office and state that they are calling to notify the SRS of a report of child sexual abuse and to coordinate the investigation. The SRS supervisor/worker and the police officer may decide to 1) have SRS investigate alone, 2) do an initial interview with both SRS and the police, or 3) have the police make the initial contact alone. This and all subsequent aspects of the investigation should be closely coordinated between SRS and the police.

The role of the investigating officer is to determine the status of the victim, establish whether probable cause exists to believe that an offense has occurred, and deal with such issues as jurisdiction of the incident, continuing safety of the victim, evidence, and preparation of a report for the State's Attorney.

When first reported, medical attention shall be obtained immediately for the victim if needed. When in doubt, arrange for medical attention. A criminal investigation will start at this time. It will be the duty of the investigating officer and the SRS caseworker to determine if danger exists at this time for the victim and to take whatever action is needed to protect the victim such as, removing from the home to a safe location or to an SRS worker, by court order, if necessary. (See 33 VSA 639(3)). This should be done with the basic philosophy in mind that the offender should be the one to leave the house if at all possible, and that the offender and victim must be separated initially. Under Rule 3(c)(2)(C) of the Vermont Rules of Criminal Procedure, it is possible as one course of action for a law enforcement officer to tell a felony offender that, because of concern for possible continued victimization of the child, he will cite the offender in court if the offender will pack his clothes and find temporary lodging elsewhere, or he will arrest and lodge him if he refuses to do so. Another course, if probable cause exists, is to arrest the offender and seek appropriate conditions of release or bail.

In order to take any action, the officer must obviously establish probable cause that a criminal offense has occurred, and will pursue routine police procedures to do so. Cooperation with the agencies, the State's Attorney, SRS, mental health professionals, school nurses, and physicians may be necessary to continue the investigation and ensure the continued safety of the victim. Evidence will be collected and preserved in accordance with established police procedures. The report is the sum of all the facts that the State's Attorney must use in making a decision.

3. State's Attorney:

The State's Attorney office has two primary goals in dealing with child sexual abuse cases. The first is the primary goal of all agencies involved - to protect the child. The second is the normal prosecutorial function - to prosecute the perpetrator. The parties to the protocol adhere to the belief that, in a system where there is an inter-agency policy of cooperation, and where adequate treatment is available for the victim, the family, and the offender, the best interests of all concerned dictate prosecution of the offender, whenever it is possible to do so.

In the interests of reaching the best disposition of the case, however, the State's Attorney's office will seek the recommendation of the SRS caseworker and any involved mental health clinician prior to making a decision regarding prosecution or a recommendation to the court regarding sentencing. The recommendation of the probation officer is formalized in the form of a pre-sentence investigation. The PSI should include the opinion of the investigating police officer.

This type of cooperation is essential, particularly since it is anticipated that many offenders will be placed under probation supervision, and there will be a need to structure the supervision with appropriate conditions. Recommendations for release on bail by the State's Attorney will almost always include a condition that the offender remain out of the home, as well as other conditions designed to protect the victim. When it is necessary, a juvenile petition may be filed with the District Court. In an emergency situation a child may be taken into custody and placed temporarily in a foster home, or remain in their own home though in SRS custody.

If a child is found to be in need of care and supervision either by having a hearing to determine that fact or by a stipulation of the parties, the Court has three options. These are:

1. To allow the child to remain with his or her parents guardian, subject to such conditions and limitations as the court may prescribe, or
2. To place the child under protective supervision, or
3. To transfer legal custody or guardianship to the Commissioner of Social and Rehabilitation Services.

Ultimately the Court will make a determination as to which course of action is in the best interests of the child after receiving input from Social and Rehabilitation Services, the State's Attorney, the Attorney for the child, the parents, the Guardian Ad Litem for the child, and the parent's attorney. The prosecution of the perpetrator would be pursued through normal criminal procedures. The end result of such a prosecution could include the imposition by the Court of a suspended sentence with conditions of probation, a deferred sentence (only with the agreement of the State) with conditions, or incarceration. The Courts normally have input from the Defendant, State's Attorney and Department of Probation and Parole. Factors to be considered in the decision include the strength of the case, protection of the public, rehabilitation, public education, deterrence and punishment. It is important that the Office of the State's Attorney be involved as early as possible once a report is substantiated (unless the State's Attorney's investigator is acting as the police investigator and thus their office is already involved). It is only through the communication of the parties that the goal of victim protection may be achieved.

4. Medical Aspects of Sexual Abuse:

Each hospital in the area should be encouraged to have a protocol regarding treatment of child sexual abuse victims, and staff trained in providing treatment Agencies involved should attempt to use/recommend physicians who are knowledgeable in this special area. Further training should be pursued for medical staff in information sharing with other agencies, evidence collection, and treatment procedures. During the medical evaluation—preferably by a physician *aware* of the special needs of sexually abused child and also a physician *known* to the child—the physician attempts to establish evidence of abuse, diagnose and treat trauma and infections secondary to the abuse, and most of all begins to help the child deal with the psychological trauma caused by the abuse by examining the child in a non-threatening, gentle, caring manner. Even if there is no physical trauma, the examination can serve to reassure the child that they are not physically harmed or "damaged."

1. *All* children should have a medical evaluation. An examination should occur immediately upon discovery if the abuse is recent (within 72 hours) or if physical trauma is evident. The exam may be delayed up to a week if the abuse occurred in the past (more than 72 hours) and no physical trauma is present. The medical exam should include all appropriate tests, history and physical as outlined in *Guidelines for Physicians*.

2. The Social Worker must help parents understand the need for a physical exam in *all* cases of sexual abuse.
3. If a parent is violently opposed and the child has not been physically harmed, the SRS worker will have to decide whether the value of the exam outweighs the disruption of a forced exam. In cases where the Social Worker feels an exam must be done but cannot obtain parental permission, then a court order must be acquired prior to an exam.

5. School/Day Care Center/Pre-school:

All school and day care personnel are required by law to report suspected cases of child abuse to SRS. Schools and day care centers should develop their own internal procedures to ensure that this is done and that good communication exists with SRS. (SRS will provide information and assistance in this regard and will cooperate in establishing and maintaining good working relationships.)

School personnel should be aware that it is much easier to deal with such cases, particularly for the child, if SRS can be involved as early in the day as possible.

6. Mental Health:

Many areas in southern Vermont have a formal treatment program for child sexual abuse in place, with services available for child victims, mothers/spouses, and offenders, as well as for families in non-incest cases. Because each area program may differ somewhat regarding method of referral, etc., information about such services should be obtained from the local Social Services office (listings are in the front of this protocol).

7. Probation and Parole (Department of Corrections):

As the agency with primary responsibility for offender change, Probation and Parole is still concerned, as its first goal, with protection of the child, and any potential victims. Probation and Parole will coordinate its normal functions with the offender with the other involved agencies, particularly with SRS caseworker and the Mental Health clinician treating the offender. Maintaining confidentiality regarding the offender's issues is seen as a block to effective treatment and information will be shared freely with the involved caseworkers to facilitate treatment and protection of the child. A major function of the Probation Officer is seen as supervision, monitoring and surveillance of the offender.

There are a number of situations where the Probation Officer is involved:

1. If the perpetrator is under Probation or Parole supervision at the time of the offense the supervising officer could have him (a) removed from the home immediately via emergency arrest procedures; (b) have conditions added to his probation/parole conditions that would mandate counseling or other conditions deemed necessary to ensure the safety of the victim and treatment of the perpetrator; and (c) bring a violation of probation/parole and recommend (b) above, or incarceration.
2. Prior to sentencing, the probation officer will usually prepare the pre-sentence investigation report for the sentencing judge with

recommendations for disposition. In this situation, the probation officer would be relying heavily on the consensus among individuals involved in the case.

3. If the perpetrator is committed and placed on supervision as part of a deferred sentence or probation, the probation officer is responsible to see to it that the offender is following the court mandated treatment program and for coordinating activities with the SRS caseworker to ensure appropriate decisions affecting the child and family and with the mental health worker dealing with the offender. Under no circumstances will the probation officer allow the offender to return to the home without prior discussion and agreement with the SRS worker, the non-offending spouse, and the mental health worker(s) involved.

8. Adult Correctional Facilities (Dept. of Corrections):

In the event that an offender is incarcerated, the assigned institution counselor and probation and parole officer will always coordinate any release plans closely with the SRS worker involved with the family (if the offender is to return to live with his family). Special conditions of parole may be added that mandate continued involvement in a treatment program, level of contact with the offender's children, or other children, and any other special needs/precaution deemed appropriate by the case managers and approved by the Parole Board.

III. *Implementation and Modification*

This protocol shall take effect upon approval of the agencies and individuals involved. Any subsequent changes, additions, or deletions will be submitted to each of the parties to the protocol before being made.

The parties to the protocol recognize that no written document can cover all of the situations that may arise, but are committed to a cooperative effort in this area. Recognizing that problems will occur within and between agencies, the parties to this protocol are committed to a continual effort to improve methods of dealing with child sexual abuse, examining specific problems where they occur, and resolving them in a cooperative manner.

Child Sexual Abuse Treatment Program
Suggested Conditions of Release
and Conditions of Probation
for Child Sexual Offenders

The following suggested conditions are based on the belief that the primary goal of all agencies involved in child sexual abuse cases must be to prevent further victimization from occurring. They reflect the fact that, in order to lessen the disruption and trauma to the family in such cases, certain structured conditions should be considered for the accused or convicted offender.

1. Suggested conditions of release prior to conviction:
   a. For incest cases, unless otherwise recommended by the child protection services)
      You shall not reside with your children nor contact your children in any manner unless approved by the social worker assigned to the case. In addition, you shall not initiate, maintain or establish contact with any other minor child, nor attempt to do so, nor reside in the same residence with other minor children.
   b. (In cases of child molestation outside of a family setting)
      You shall not initiate, maintain, or establish contact with any minor child, nor attempt to do so, nor reside in the same residence with minor children.
   c. In cases where there is *no apparent* issue of alcohol abuse, a special condition of release should be added. You shall not use alcoholic beverages to the extent it interferes with your employment or the welfare of your family, yourself or others. If there is *any* question that alcohol abuse *may* be a problem, then a condition requiring total abstinence from alcohol should be imposed.
2. Suggested conditions of probation (or parole):
   a. In all cases of child molestation:
      1. You shall not initiate, maintain or establish contact with any minor child, nor attempt to do so, nor reside in the same residence with minor children, without permission of your probation officer.
      2. You shall participate in the Child Sexual Abuse Treatment Program and complete the same to the full satisfaction of your Probation Officer and the treatment staff of the program, fully complying with all program requirements. Program participation is defined as attendance at all meetings, prompt payment of fees, admission of responsibility for your offense and progress toward reasonable treatment goals.
      3. You shall contribute toward the cost of the Child Sexual Abuse Treatment program in the amount set by the program staff, but no less than $15 per week.
      4. Special conditions regarding alcohol abuse correspond with Section 1c above.
   b. For incest cases:
      1. All of the above, #'s 1-4.
      2. You shall not reside with your children, nor contact your children in any manner unless approved by your probation officer and the social worker assigned to the case.

APPENDIX C
Agreement of Nonconfidentiality

I/We _____ hereby agree to nonconfidentiality within the Child Sexual Abuse Treatment Program (CSATP). I understand that the CSATP includes representatives from the Child Protection Agency, Department of Corrections/Probation and Parole, the Prosecuting Attorney's office and mental health. I understand that information will be shared both verbally and in writing among team members. This communication shall include, but not be limited to, specific information concerning case management, participation in the treatment sessions and my/our progress in treatment. I/we also hereby authorize the Prosecuting Attorney's Office and the Department of Corrections/Probation & Parole to give the CSATP copies of existing and future court orders, victim statements, contact orders, or other stipulations related to my offense.

I understand that sexual assault is a criminal offense with serious consequences to the victim and the community. I understand that the CSATP is legally required and fully intends to report to the Prosecuting Attorney's Office, the State Police or local police and/or the Department of Corrections/Probation and Parole as appropriate any occurrence or potential occurrence of a sexual offense on my part, regardless of how the CSATP obtained the information. The purpose of my participation in the CSATP is to control my sexual assaultiveness in the community and I wish to be held fully accountable for such behavior.

Signed _____ Date _____

Northwest Treatment Associates, Seattle, Washington
Assignments

1. Sexual Autobiography
2. Index Cards
3. Incentives
4. Addiction List
5. Discovery Report
6. Victim Reminders
7. Empathy Paper
8. Reoffense Essay
9. Victim Agency
10. Forty Adults
11. Chronology
12. Offense Questionnaire
13. Bibliography
14. Impact Statement
15. Relationships
16. Questions Victims Ask
17. Controls
18. Group Therapy Examination

1. Sexual Autobiography

Purpose:

A. To Learn about the origin, development and maintenance of appropriate and inappropriate sexual behavior.

B. To Weaken denial, secrecy, alienation and over-confidence.

C. To Increase self-awareness and introspection.

D. To Inform others about oneself, thereby enhancing support and surveillance.

E. To Illuminate the ingrained pervasive and tenacious nature of sexual deviancy, thereby increasing motivation for treatment and change.

F. To Assist in prediction, extrapolation, and the selection of treatment rules and methodology.

Content:

Include names, ages and dates. Be detailed and follow chronological order.

1. Early sexual memories and experiences; how did you learn about sex? Include modeling, education, humor and myths. Explore the influence of family, peers, teachers and church community.

2. Self as victim, emotional, physical and sexual abuse.

3. Masturbation: Onset, frequency, antecedents, fantasy content, and relationship to outlet.

4. Homosexuality: Child-child, adult-child, adult-adult.

5. Pornography: When, why, feelings about and content.

APPENDIX D Continued

6. Dating-Courtship-Marriage: Begin with initial experiences, including kissing, petting, and intercourse. Compare frequency with peers. Examine selection of partner, self-confidence, and patterns. Any sexually transmitted diseases? If so, explore impact of these on feelings about self, partners, and sexuality. Comment on infidelity, sexual functioning-satisfaction, and fantasies employed during intimacy. Within the content of established relationships look at problem-solving, communication, anger management, and parenting.

Outlets:

Topless taverns
Massage parlors
Anonymous homosexual-heterosexual sex
Prostitution
Fetishism
Frottage
Beastiality
Sado-masochism
Obscene phone calls
Voyeurism
Exhibitionism
Child Molestation
Rape
Other

For each applicable outlet, discuss:

1. Origin and changes over time. What were the mechanisms by which change occurred, e.g., masturbatory conditioning, boldness, boredom with current form, etc.? What did you get out of the behavior and why did you continue? Was it in lieu of something else?
2. Disinhibitors (experiences that weaken inhibitions and controls).
3. Antecedents: Emotional, physical, cognitive (including rationalizations and fantasies) and environmental factors.
4. How did you set yourself up for offending? Consider rationalizations, substance abuse, creating conflicts within the primary relationship, pornography, and masturbation to deviant fantasy themes. Consider the stimulus-premeditation, relationship-predatory, and self-control-habit continuums.
5. Selection of victims.
6. How did you control victim before, during and after abuse, e.g., isolation, intimidation, favors, promises and threats?
7. Outlet in detail: Describe exactly what was said and done by you and victim. Frequency of each incident?
8. Resistance: Obvious and subtle, and your persistence.
9. Victim symptoms.

(continued)

10. Post-offense thoughts, feelings, and behaviors, e.g., fear of discovery, remorse and self-loathing. How did you bury-handle them?
11. Prior counseling: Secular, religious and specialized.
12. Attempts to control the problem: What methods were effective and which didn't work? What contributed to latency periods? How long did these last?
13. Who knows that you have this problem?
14. Impact of sexual deviancy on other significant aspects of your life, e.g., family, employment, friendships and health.
15. Discovery: Include all confrontations, accusations, and investigations. How did you respond to each of them?
16. Current legal status and restrictions.

2. Index Cards

Prepare 8 index cards. On each card write down the kind of excuse you have made in the past. For example, you might write, "It won't hurt just to go in and see how he's doing in the bath. After all, kids can get hurt in the bathtub."

Then on each card write down a challenge to your excuse. For example you might write, "Forget it. You're just trying to get in to take a look at him nude. You're thinking of offending again, and making your usual ridiculous excuses."

3. Incentives

Write down a list of 40 things you would lose by offending.

4. Addiction List

Make up a list of 20 reasons that prove you are addicted to child molesting.

5. Discovery Report

Write down the following:

1) what life was like prior to getting caught
2) how you got caught
3) what it was like being confronted by people important to you

6. Victim Reminders

When your daughter sees you and your spouse behaving appropriately together, after treatment is completed, write down what will remind her of your abuse. List 25 items.

7. Empathy Paper

Write down in the first person what it is like to be sexually abused. Describe the abuse in the present and include what the thoughts and feelings are of the victim.

APPENDIX D Continued

8. Reoffense Essay

Write about a reoffense as though it were happening today. Include the pressures you are under, the excuses and rationalizations you would use, how you would go about the offense, whom you would pick, how you would groom them, and how you would initiate the offense. Then write what is different now that would stop you from committing an offense. Include things that are different at home, at work, and in therapy.

9. Victim Agency

Contact an agency that treats victims of sexual assault. Make a donation, then talk to a counselor and ask her/him to tell you how a sexual assault affects victims.

10. Forty Adults

List 40 adults you know (e.g., employer, friend, etc.), what kind of relationship you have with them, whether that person knows about your problem or not and how they would react to reoffense.

11. Chronology

Prepare an outline listing significant events by age. Be brief and very clear in your description. Cover the following topics:

   a. Sexual behavior, appropriate and deviant. Include first names/ages of victims, list *all* forms of sexual deviancy. Include *all* forms of sexual conduct including masturbation, pornography, homosexuality, prostitution and affairs.
   b. You as victim of physical—sexual abuse and other crimes; include offender's first name, relationship and nature of abuse.
   c. Alcohol-drug use and abuse.
   d. You as physical abuser; include name and age of victim, and nature of abuse.
   e. List all crimes (sexual and otherwise). If caught, the consequences.
   f. Bracket the especially good and bad years. Indicate what made these years special or different for you.

12. Offense Questionnaire

1. When did you become a sex offender?
2. How have you arranged your life to make it easier to offend?
3. Which sex offender (character) traits do you employ before, during and after your offense?
4. How do you feel about yourself before, during and after offending?
5. What thoughts and feelings occur to you while thinking of outlet history?
6. How did you learn your outlet?
7. Write an essay about your victim prior to outlet abuse.

(continued)

8. How do you select your victim?

9. What factors (emotional, physical, mental, environmental) precede outlet behavior? These are your warning signs.

10. What cognitive and perceptual distortions (excuses and misrepresentations) have you employed to make offending easier to do?

11. How do you control your victim before, during and after offending?

12. What do you want from outlet and victim?

13. What do you get from outlet and victim; what keeps the behavior going?

14. How does victim show resistance (subtle and obvious, during and between incidents of abuse), how have you been persistent—forceful?

15. How has your sexual deviation changed over time?

    a. Variations and one outlet; fantasy, distance, frequency, severity, risk, target communication, ejaculation, compulsivity, etc.

    b. Multiple outlets: Discuss transition, direction and implications.

16. How is your fantasy of offense different from the actual behavior; e.g., in the fantasy the victim is older, sexually aggressive and unharmed.

17. How has sexual deviancy affected other areas of your life, historically, e.g., self-inmate, school-employment effectiveness, social life, family interactions, health, finances, sexual intimacy?

18. In what ways have you tried to terminate outlet? Discuss results.

19. What factors effect your motivation to terminate outlet?

20. How can outlet needs be met in nondestructive, nonaddictive ways?

21. What have you gotten out of being secretive and dishonest?

22. How do you show diminished selfishness?

23. What are your biggest fears and how are you dealing with them?

24. What is missing in your life now?

25. Discuss your relationship patterns with adults, e.g., lovers, care-givers and authority figures (male and female). Include relevant thoughts, feelings, criticisms and fears involving women. Do you seem to repeat unhealthy patterns?

26. What have you done to help/hurt your partner, and your treatment experience? To what extent have the men in your group seen the offender that the victim experienced?

27. Discuss your self-concept; is it realistic? What are your strengths and weaknesses?

28. What are the problem areas in your life now? the future? How might you handle them?

29. Discuss your short and long range plans and goals.

30. Provide a written and verbal summary of an article or book that relates to your problem.

APPENDIX D Continued

31. Recovering clients realize that they are important, they belong and contribute to the well being of others. Write briefly about recent volunteer experience, donations (money, food, blood, clothing, etc.) and participation in (social, political, religious, athletic) community organizations.
32. Briefly describe your nonsexual, nonaddictive outlets for excitement.
33. What are your new controls; objective and subjective? Discuss your use of these methods; be specific.

13. Bibliography

Allen, Charlotte Vale. *Daddy's Girl*
Armstrong, Louise. *Kiss Daddy Goodnight*
Barbach, Lonnie, Ph.D. *For Each Other* (Anchor Press, 1982)
Brady, Kathryn. *Father's Days*
Burns, David D., M.D. *Feeling Good* (William Morrow, 1980)
Carnes, Patrick, Ph.D. *Sexual Addiction* (CompCare Publications, 1983)
Halpern, Howard L. *How to Break Your Addiction to a Person* (McGraw-Hill, 1982)
Heiman, Julia; LoPiccolo, Leslie; LoPiccolo, Joseph. *Becoming Orgasmic: A Sexual Growth Program for Women* (Prentice-Hall, 1976)
Mackey, Gene; Swan, Helen. *Dear Elizabeth* (For adolescent victims)
NiCarthy, Ginny. *Getting Free* (Seal Press, 1982)
Wachter, Oralee. *No More Secrets for Me* (Little, Brown) (For adolescent victims)
Zilbergeld, Bernie, Ph.D. *Male Sexuality* (Bantam, 1978)
  Red Light, Green Light (School-age victims)
  My Very Own Book About Me (School-age victims)

14. Offending: Impact on
Other Areas in My Life

Prepare an essay on each topic and lead your group in a discussion of one of these. Add two topics of your own.

1. Primary Relationship
2. Employment
3. Self esteem
4. Friendship
5. Alcohol-drug usage
6. Sex
7. Finances
8. Health (including appetite, sleep, hygiene, psychosomatic disorders)
9. Recreation (including involvement in organizations)
10. Parenting and family life.
11. Mood.
12. Religion (include church attendance, prayer, role in controlling victim and as an aid in pushing guilt away and rationalizations, e.g., "I'm forgiven. I'm different now. God knows so nobody else needs to. I don't have to be accountable to man and his laws.")

(continued)

APPENDIX D Continued

15. Relationships

1. Examine motivation for dating.
2. Use good judgement regarding when to look for partners and where to go on dates.
3. No victim-aged children.
4. Age appropriate.
5. Has she been victimized—emotional impact
   counseling history
   dysfunctional patterns
6. Equal power—verbal, social and intellectual skills.
7. Don't rush things.
8. Share process of building relationship here—before sexual intimacy occurs.
9. Discuss birth control and pregnancy issues before becoming sexual.
10. Disclose regarding offender history, patterns, controls and treatment legal status when it appears relationship is becoming significant.

16. Questions Victims Ask

Prepare a brief, written response to each question. Add five questions-answers of your own.

1. Why did you do those things to me?
2. Will you ever do those things to me again?
3. Why me; what did I do?
4. Why did I have to keep secrets?
5. Was Mom in on this with you?
6. How do you feel about my telling, and being angry with you?
7. What if you weren't turned in—what would have happened?
8. Why do I feel badly about the offense, Mom's unhappiness and the breakup of our home?
9. Why did you seem the better parent rather than Mom?
10. What did you do to set me up and continue controlling me?
11. How will I know if you are about to hurt me again; should I trust you?
12. What can I do to protect myself; what if I feel you're about to do those things to me?
13. How will things be different at home; how will our relationship be different?
14. Will my friends be safe? Do they need to know? Who knows now?
15. Tell me about your counseling.

17. Controls

Add five items to each list.

External

1. Avoidance of high risk situations
2. Counseling

APPENDIX D Continued

3. Informed support system
4. Lock on children's door
5. No pornography
6. Minimize disinhibitors
   a. Alcohol
   b. Fatigue
   c. Drugs
   d. Unresolved conflicts
7. Alcohol-drugfree lifestyle
8. Alcoholics Anonymous/Narcotics Anonymous
9. Appropriate clothing
10. Healthy social activities
11. Healthy sexual activities
12. Name on bumper sticker
13. Photo of family on visor
14. Rubber band
15. Yell "Stop!"
16. Tapes—video
17. Assertiveness
18. Rewards for appropriate behavior

<u>Internal</u>

1. Covert scenes
2. Fear of incarceration
3. Knowledge of warning signs and controls
4. Empathy
5. Incentive lists
6. Responsibility
7. Knowledge of cycle and exits
8. Thought stopping
9. Excuses and challenges
10. Appropriate fantasy structure
11. Accept possibility of reoffense
12. Prosocial goals
13. Religion
14. Group as conscience
15. Self-acceptance
16. Avoid depression
17. Introspective attitude
18. Avoid procrastination

(continued)

APPENDIX D Continued

18. Group Therapy Examination

NAME: _____

GROUP TIME: _____

NUMBER OF GROUP SESSIONS: _____

SCORE (MAXIMUM 300 POINTS) _____

GROUP RANGE-AVERAGE _____

1. Name the four categories of warning signs and give five examples of each one. Why is this important?

>Score: 1 point for each sign (4)
>1 additional point for sub-category (3)
>1 point for each example (7 X 5 = 35)
>Maximum 3 points for importance (3)
>(Total maximum 45)

2. List eight ways in which sex offenders push away guilt.

>Score: 2 points each.

3. List 10 symptoms of sexual victimization.

>Score: 2 points each

4. What are the components of an appropriate masturbation fantasy?

>Score: 8 point maximum

5. Why not masturbate while dwelling on thoughts of sexual deviancy?

>Score: 2 points.

6. How did your victim(s) resist, and how were you forceful?

>Score: 4 points each, maximum 8

7. Might you reoffend?

>Score: 1 point for yes, no point for no!

>Why?   Score: 4 points for 4 reasons

8. Why is it important to believe that you might reoffend, in either similar or new expression of sexual deviancy?

>Score: 6 points maximum

9. Why is it important for significant others to know the nature of your sexual deviancy?

>Score: 3 points maximum.

10. a) Define the following terms: Outlet, grooming, lay-out, AB, plethysmograph, assertiveness, boredom tape, aversive tape.

>Score: 16 points maximum.

APPENDIX D Continued

11. Why chart deviant sexual impulses?

    Score: Maximum 4 points.

    Define the 1-10 impulse scale.

    Score: Maximum 10 points.

12. List 8 behavioral—"external" controls against reoffense.

    Score: Maximum 16 points.

13. List 8 group—"internal" controls against reoffense.

    Score: Maximum 16 points.

14. Challenge these reoffense justifications:

    Score: 2 points each—maximum 18.

    a. This will be the last time.
    b. Nobody will know.
    c. I'm just teaching about sex.
    d. She won't look if she doesn't want to see me.
    e. No intercourse, so it's really okay.
    f. Nobody will be hurt.
    g. I'm not getting love anywhere else.
    h. It's my daughter so it's OK.
    i. It's not my daughter so it's OK.
    j. & k. Write two additional justifications (1 point each)
        and a challenge for each (1 point each)

15. Connect offense behavior with masturbation to pornography/television.

    Score: Maximum 16 points.

16. What are the purposes of writing a sexual history?

    Score: Maximum 3 points.

17. List 8 sex offender character traits.

    Score: 8 points.

    Relate each to sexual deviancy.

    Score: 8 additional points.

18. What happens in group to lessen the likelihood of reoffense.

    Score: Maximum 16 points.

19. Why did you become a sexual offender?

    Score: 4 points.

20. How have you controlled your victim Before (2 ways = 2 points)
    During (2 ways = 2 points)
    and After (2 ways = 2 points
    your offense.

    Score: Maximum 6 points.

(continued)

21. Explain the cycle of reoffense and its purpose. (Score 2 points).
    Duplicate the cycle (2 points for each station—10 stations—maximum 20 points).
    Give an example for each station (Score 1 point each—maximum 10).
    Give an exit for each station (Score 1 point each—maximum 10).

SOURCE: Steven Silver and Northwest Treatment Associates, 315 W. Galer, Seattle, WA 98119; telephone (206) 283-8099. Reprinted by permission.

APPENDIX E

Northwest Treatment Associates Protocol for "Boredom Tapes"

Step 1 — Select a time and a place where you will not be disturbed for approximately one and a half hours.

Step 2 — a. Place your tape recorder where you intend to masturbate and load it with a blank C-90 cassette (45 minutes per side).

b. Press the button to record and say a few sentences in your normal voice from the position where you will be masturbating.

c. Rewind and press the play button and see if you can understand your recorded voice clearly without straining.

d. Repeat Steps 2b and 2c until you can understand yourself clearly without straining. Adjust recording volume and microphone position as needed.

Step 3 — Remove whatever clothing is required so you can masturbate.

Step 4 — Apply a generous amount of oil to your penis. This is not optional, it is required. You may use baby oil, massage oil, or any other sort of lubricant. One oil, particularly suggested, is sweet almond oil which may be obtained in a health food store.

Step 5 — Begin recording. State your initials, the date, the type of tape you are making, the name of your therapist, and say "appropriate side."

Step 6 — Begin to verbalize an appropriate fantasy while masturbating. Apply more oil if needed. Stop talking only after climax. Run the tape fast forward to the end. Your fantasy should outline an appropriate adult sexual interaction. It should not begin in bed. There should be some presexual behavior described—sharing, talking, enjoying each other's company. Watch the details of your fantasy. Try to get into as much detail as possible as far as your partner's feelings and responses. 10 to 15 minutes is a desirable length.

Step 7 — Turn tape over immediately and begin recording. State your initials, date and say "inappropriate fantasy side."

Step 8 — Begin to verbalize inappropriate fantasies without stopping until this side of the tape is completely filled. These fantasies should reflect all of your outlet behaviors. They can be things that have only happened in fantasies, but they should represent all of your excuses and outlet behaviors. Both excuses before outlet and excuses you used to block transitory guilt are to be included. Do not turn the tape off at any time. This must be done in one complete unit of approximately 45 minutes.

Note: For all fantasies, appropriate and inappropriate, please use the first person, present tense, i.e., say "I am" instead of "I was" or "I would." Record these fantasies as if they were actually happening now. You should attempt to visualize, to imagine the fantasies, and simply verbalize what it is that you are imagining. Some mild arousal during inappropriate fantasies is not uncommon during early stages of the utilization of this technique. When you note arousal, repeat the section over and over until arousal disappears. Keep your therapist informed of what things you are experiencing arousal to.

Add Note: Ejaculation to the appropriate fantasy is desirable but not a necessity. If the appropriate fantasy becomes work after 10 to 15 minutes—Stop!—note this verbally on the tape.

(continued)

BOREDOM TAPE REPORT

Client Name _____   Time of Day _____

Date of Tape _____   Week # _____

Therapist _____

Appropriate

    Length of fantasy _____ minutes

    Ejaculation Yes _____ No _____

    Brief summary of fantasy

_____

_____

_____

_____

_____

1. Arrousal today was:

1	2	3	4	5
Very difficult	Somewhat difficult	Neither difficult or easy	Somewhat easy	Very easy

2. Clearness of fantasy:

1	2	3	4	5
Very unclear	Somewhat unclear	Neither unclear or clear	Somewhat clear	Very clear

3. Today's fantasy:

1	2	3	4	5
Very enjoyable	Somewhat enjoyable	Neither enjoyable or unenjoyable	Somewhat unenjoyable	Very unenjoyable

Deviant

4. Today I was:

1	2	3	4	5
Not aroused	Minimally aroused	Aroused an average amount	Aroused an above average amount	Very aroused

    by my deviant fantasy.

Number of minutes aroused during deviant fantasy _____ (Max. 45 minutes).

5. Highest arousal level during deviant fantasy:

   1   2   3   4   5   6   7   8   9   10
   No arousal   Somewhat of   Ejaculation
                          an erection

What if anything did you learn about your outlet? _____

_____

Brief summary of deviant fantasies:

SOURCE: Steven Silver and Northwest Treatment Associates, 315 W. Galer, Seattle, WA 98119; telephone (206) 283-8099. Reprinted by permission.

APPENDIX F
Abel and Becker Cognitions Scale

DESCRIPTION

This is a 29-item scale that measures cognitive distortions regarding the sexual molestation of children.

SCORING

Respondents mark each item on a scale from 1 ("strongly agree") to 5 ("strongly disagree"). The items are noted clinically rather than scored quantitatively. Each item represents statements that have been made by sex offenders to justify their behavior.

INTERPRETATION

Agreement with any of the items represents an example of distorted cognitions to be addressed in therapy.

REFERENCE

Abel, G., Becker, J., Cunningham-Rathner, J., Rouleau, J., Kaplan, M., & Reich, J. (1984). *The treatment of child molesters* (Available from SBC-TM, 722 West 168th Street, Box 17, NY, NY 10032).

ABEL and BECKER COGNITIONS SCALE

Read each of the statements below carefully, and then circle the number that indicates your agreement with it.

1. Strongly Agree
2. Agree
3. Neutral
4. Disagree
5. Strongly Disagree

	Strongly Agree				Strongly Disagree
1. If a young child stares at my genitals it means the child likes what she (he) sees and is enjoying watching my genitals.	1	2	3	4	5
2. A man (or woman) is justified in having sex with his (her) children or stepchildren, if his wife (husband) doesn't like sex.	1	2	3	4	5
3. A child 13 or younger can make her (his) own decision as to whether she (he) wants to have sex with an adult or not.	1	2	3	4	5

APPENDIX F Continued

	Strongly Agree				Strongly Disagree
4. A child who doesn't physically resist an adult's sexual advances really wants to have sex with the adult.	1	2	3	4	5
5. If a 13-year-old (or younger) child flirts with an adult, it means he (she) wants to have sex with the adult.	1	2	3	4	5
6. Sex between a 13-year-old (or younger) child and an adult causes the child no emotional problems.	1	2	3	4	5
7. Having sex with a child is a good way for an adult to teach the child about sex.	1	2	3	4	5
8. If I tell my young child (stepchild or close relative) what to do sexually and they do it, that means they will always do it because they really want to.	1	2	3	4	5
9. When a young child has sex with an adult, it helps the child learn how to relate to adults in the future.	1	2	3	4	5
10. Most children 13 (or younger) would enjoy having sex with an adult and it wouldn't harm the child in the future.	1	2	3	4	5
11. Children don't tell others about having sex with a parent (or other adult) because they really like it and want to continue.	1	2	3	4	5
12. Sometime in the future, our society will realize that sex between a child and an adult is all right.	1	2	3	4	5
13. An adult can tell if having sex with a young child will emotionally damage the child in the future.	1	2	3	4	5
14. An adult, just feeling a child's body all over without touching her (his) genitals, is not really being sexual with the child.	1	2	3	4	5
15. I show my love and affection to a child by having sex with her (him).	1	2	3	4	5
16. It's better to have sex with your child (or someone else's child) than to have an affair.	1	2	3	4	5

(continued)

APPENDIX F Continued

	Strongly Agree				Strongly Disagree
17. An adult fondling a young child or having the child fondle the adult will not cause the child any harm.	1	2	3	4	5
18. A child will never have sex with an adult unless the child really wants to.	1	2	3	4	5
19. My daughter (son) or other young child knows that I will still love her (him) even if she (he) refuses to be sexual with me.	1	2	3	4	5
20. When a young child asks an adult about sex, it means that she (he) wants to see the adult's sex organs or have sex with the adult.	1	2	3	4	5
21. If an adult has sex with a young child, it prevents the child from having sexual hang-ups in the future.	1	2	3	4	5
22. When a young child walks in front of me with no or only a few clothes on, she (he) is trying to arouse me.	1	2	3	4	5
23. My relationship with my daughter (son) or other child is strengthened by the fact that we have sex together.	1	2	3	4	5
24. If a child has sex with an adult, the child will look back at the experience as an adult and see it as a positive experience.	1	2	3	4	5
25. The only way I could do harm to a child when having sex with her (him) would be to use physical force to get her (him) to have sex with me.	1	2	3	4	5
26. When children watch an adult masturbate, it helps the child learn about sex.	1	2	3	4	5
27. An adult can know just how much sex between him (her) and a child will hurt the child later on.	1	2	3	4	5
28. If a person is attracted to sex with children, he (she) should solve that problem themselves and not talk to professionals.	1	2	3	4	5
29. There's no effective treatment for child molestation.	1	2	3	4	5

Please reread each question and this time place an "X" over the number which corresponds with the way you would have answered it before others (family, friends, the police) became aware of your deviant behavior.

SOURCE: For Abel and Becker Cognitions Scale, Abel and Becker (1984). Copyright © 1984 by Abel and Becker. Reprinted by permission.

Attitudes Toward Women Scale

DESCRIPTION

The Attitudes Toward Women (ATW) scale is a 15-item version of the original 55-item scale. The scale focuses on the rights and roles of women, and asks subjects to respond to each statement on a four point scale from "agree strongly" to "disagree strongly."

SCORING

Items are scored from 0 to 3. Three indicates a more egalitarian attitude toward women. The following items are therefore scored with A ("agree strongly") scoring 0 and D ("disagree strongly") scoring 3: 1, 5, 7, 8, 9, 12, 13, 15. The remaining items are scored in reverse, with A scoring 3 and D scoring 0. Scores range from 0 to 45.

INTERPRETATION

Salters, Kairys, and Teague, in previously unpublished research, found a sample of 59 male factory workers to score an average of 29.3 on the ATW with a standard deviation of 7.5. These scores were obtained from a working-class sample; it is to be expected that scores will differ by social class. While limited research is currently available on the ATW by social class, it is not necessary or possible solely to score the ATW quantitatively. The face validity of the items is such that a clinician can derive information regarding the degree of sex role stereotyping in which an offender engages by analysis of the individual items.

REFERENCES

Spence, J. T., & Helmreich, R. L. (1978). *Masculinity and femininity: Their psychological dimensions, correlates and antecedents*. Austin: University of Texas Press.

Spence, J. T., & Helmreich, R. L. (1972). The attitudes toward women scale: An objective instrument to measure attitudes toward the rights and roles of women in contemporary society. *Psychological Documents, 2*, 153.

ATTITUDES TOWARD WOMEN

The statements listed below describe attitudes toward the roles of women in society which different people have. There are no right or wrong answers, only opinions. You are asked to express your feeling about each statement by indicating whether you (A) agree strongly, (B) agree mildly, (C) disagree mildly, or (D) disagree strongly.

	agree strongly			disagree strongly
1. Swearing and obscenity are more repulsive in the speech of a woman than a man.	A	B	C	D

(continued)

APPENDIX G Continued

	agree strongly			disagree strongly
2. Under modern economic conditions with women being active outside the home, men should share in household tasks such as washing dishes and doing the laundry.	A	B	C	D
3. It is insulting to women to have the "obey" clause remain in the marriage service.	A	B	C	D
4. A woman should be as free as a man to propose marriage.	A	B	C	D
5. Women should worry less about their rights and more about becoming good wives and mothers.	A	B	C	D
6. Women should assume their rightful place in business and all the professions along with men.	A	B	C	D
7. A woman should not expect to go to exactly the same places or to have quite the same freedom of action as a man.	A	B	C	D
8. It is ridiculous for a woman to run a locomotive and for a man to darn socks.	A	B	C	D
9. The intellectual leadership of a community should be largely in the hands of men.	A	B	C	D
10. Women should be given equal opportunity with men for apprenticeship in the various trades.	A	B	C	D
11. Women earnings as much as their dates should bear equally the expense when they go out together.	A	B	C	D
12. Sons in a family should be given more encouragement to go to college than daughters.	A	B	C	D
13. In general, the father should have greater authority than the mother in the bringing up of children.	A	B	C	D
14. Economic and social freedom is worth far more to women than acceptance of the ideal of femininity which has been set up by men.	A	B	C	D
15. There are many jobs in which men should be given preference over women in being hired or promoted.	A	B	C	D

SOURCE: For Attitudes Toward Women questionnaire, Spence, J. T., & Helmreich, R. L. (1978). *Masculinity and Femininity: Their Psychological Dimensions, Correlates and Antecedents.* Copyright © 1978, University of Texas Press. Reprinted by permission.

Burt Rape Myth Acceptance Scale

DESCRIPTION

This is a 19-item scale measuring the acceptance or rejection of myths about rape. This scale is the equivalent of Abel and Becker's Cognitions Scale; the difference is that the Cognitions Scale measures cognitive distortions around child molestation, while the Burt measures cognitive distortions around rape.

SCORING

Items 1-11 are scored on a 7-point scale from "strongly disagree" to "strongly agree." Numbers 12 and 13 are scored on a 7-point scale ranging from "almost none" to "almost all." Items 14 through 19 are scored on a 7-point scale from "never" to "always." The scoring is reversed on item 2 and on items 14-19.

INTERPRETATION

Salters, Kairys, and Teague, in previously unpublished research found that 57 male factory workers had a mean score of 53.4 on the Burt Scale, with a standard deviation of 18. Scores ranged from 19 to 96. (The total range on the Burt is from 19 to 103.) A mean score of 53.4 suggests that many subjects adhered to a number of rape myths. This was reflected not only by the quantitative scoring, but by informal comments made by subjects. One man, for example, who had a score of 53 wrote on his questionnaire, "99.9% of the time my wife enjoys being forced, & thanks me after. Have found this true before married also." It remains to be seen whether rapists score higher than working class men on rape myths. However, the issue may not be the absolute score but adherence to rape myths *in combination with* other factors—for example, the motivation to rape and the belief that one could do so without being caught. It is, therefore, not recommended that clinicians be unconcerned by the presence of rape myths reflected in scores that are not in excess of working class samples. Rather, the existence of rape myths in a sexual offender should be taken seriously, regardless of the absolute score; attitudes that may not be dangerous in an individual with no history of sexual acting out may be dangerous in someone with such a history. For these purposes, the Burt may be used clinically rather than scored formally. Those distortions that the offender holds should be dealt with therapeutically in the same manner that distortions that support child molestation are.

REFERENCES

Burt, M. R. (1980). Cultural myths and supports for rape. *Journal of Personality and Social Psychology, 38*(2), 217-230.
Burt, M. R. (1983). Justifying personal violence: A comparison of rapists and the general public. *Victimology: An International Journal, 8*(3-4), 131-150.
Burt, M. R., & Albin, R. S. (1981). Rape myths, rape definitions, and probability of conviction. *Journal of Applied Social Psychology, 11*(3), 212-230.

(continued)

RAPE MYTH ACCEPTANCE SCALE

For the statements which follow, please circle the number that best indicates your opinion—what you believe. If you strongly disagree you would answer "1"; if you strongly agree you would answer "7"; if you feel neutral you would answer "4"; and so on.

	disagree strongly	disagree some-what	disagree slightly	neutral	agree slightly	agree some-what	agree strongly
1. A woman who goes to the home or apartment of a man on their first date implies that she is willing to have sex.	1	2	3	4	5	6	7
2. Any female can get raped.	1	2	3	4	5	6	7
3. One reason that women falsely report a rape is that they frequently have a need to call attention to themselves.	1	2	3	4	5	6	7
4. Any healthy woman can successfully resist a rapist if she really wants to.	1	2	3	4	5	6	7
5. When women go around braless or wearing short skirts or tight tops, they are just asking for trouble.	1	2	3	4	5	6	7
6. Women who get raped while hitchhiking get what they deserve.	1	2	3	4	5	6	7
7. A woman who is stuck-up and thinks she is too good to talk to guys on the street deserves to be taught a lesson.	1	2	3	4	5	6	7
8. Many women have an *unconscious* wish to be raped, and may then *unconsciously* set up a situation in which they are likely to be attacked.	1	2	3	4	5	6	7

APPENDIX H Continued

	disagree strongly	disagree some-what	disagree slightly	neutral	agree slightly	agree some-what	agree strongly
9. If a woman gets drunk at a party and has intercourse with a man she's just met there, she should be considered "fair game" to other males at the party who want to have sex with her too, whether she wants to or not.	1	2	3	4	5	6	7
10. In the majority of rapes, the victim is promiscuous or has a bad reputation.	1	2	3 .	4	5	6	7
11. If a girl engages in necking or petting and she lets things get out of hand, it is her own fault if her partner forces sex on her.	1	2	3	4	5	6	7

Please use the following key to answer the next two questions.

	Almost None	A Few	Some	About Half	Many	A Lot	Almost All

Circle the number that shows what fraction you believe to be true.

12. What percentage of women who report a rape would you say are lying because they are angry and want to get back at the man they accuse?	1	2	3	4	5	6	7
13. What percentage of reported rapes would you guess were merely invented by women who discovered they were pregnant and wanted to protect their own reputation?	1	2	3	4	5	6	7

(continued)

APPENDIX H Continued

Please use the following key to answer the next question.

	Never	Rarely	Some-times	Half the Time	Often	Usually	Always
14. A person comes to you and claims they were raped. How likely would you to be to believe their statement if the person were: Your best friend?	1	2	3	4	5	6	7
15. An Indian woman?	1	2	3	4	5	6	7
16. A neighborhood woman?	1	2	3	4	5	6	7
17. A young boy?	1	2	3	4	5	6	7
18. A black woman?	1	2	3	4	5	6	7
19. A white woman?	1	2	3	4	5	6	7

SOURCE: For Rape Myth Acceptance Scale, Burt, M. R. (1980). Cultural Myths and Supports for Rape. *Journal of Personality and Social Psychology, 38*(2), 217-230. Copyright © 1980, American Psychological Association. Reprinted by permission.

Buss-Durkee Hostility Inventory

DESCRIPTION

This is a 66-item true/false questionnaire that includes seven subscales: negativism, resentment, indirect hostility, assault, suspicion, irritability, and verbal hostility.

SCORING

One point is assigned for every answer that matches the following scoring key:

NE	RE	IN	AS	SU	IR	VE
1. T	2. T	3. T	4. T	5. T	6. T	7. T
8. T	9. T	10. F	11. F	12. T	13. F	14. T
15. T	16. T	17. T	18. T	19. T	20. T	21. T
22. T	23. T	24. F	25. T	26. T	27. T	28. T
29. T	30. T	31. T	32. T	33. T	34. F	35. F
	36. F	37. T	38. F	39. T	40. T	41. T
	42. T	43. F	44. T	45. T	46. T	47. T
	48. T	49. T	50. T	51. T	52. T	53. T
		54. T	55. T	56. F	57. T	58. F
			59. T	60. F	61. F	62. T
					63. T	64. T
						65. F
						66. F

A total score is obtained by summing scores on all items.

INTERPRETATION

In the original 1957 study of college students, Buss obtained the following means and standard deviations:

Abbr.	Scale Name	Mean	SD
NE	Negativism	2.19	1.34
RE	Resentment	2.26	1.89
IN	Indirect Hostility	4.47	2.23
AS	Assault	5.07	2.48
SU	Suspicion	3.33	2.07
VE	Verbal Hostility	7.61	2.74
IR	Irritability	5.94	2.65
	Total	30.87	10.24

The particular scores used as cutoffs for "high" and "average" scores are to some degree arbitrary. Utilizing one standard deviation above the mean would be conservative, as this represents the top 16% of the sample. That can be obtained by simply adding the means and standard deviations. The top 25% of the sample can be determined by the use of z-scores.

(continued)

APPENDIX I Continued

Abbr.	High Score Top 25%
NE	3
RE	4
IN	6
AS	7
SU	5
VE	9
IR	8

REFERENCE

Buss, A. H., & Durkee, A. (1957). An inventory for assessing different kinds of hostility. *Journal of Consulting Psychology, 21*(4), 343-349.

BUSS-DURKEE HOSTILITY INVENTORY

Please read each of the following statements carefully and decide if it is true (T) or false (F) for you. If it is true for you, circle T. If it is false for you, circle F. Be sure to put your name and the date on your answer sheet. Thank you.

T F 1. Unless somebody asks me in a nice way, I won't do what they want.

T F 2. I don't seem to get what's coming to me.

T F 3. I sometimes spread gossip about people I don't like.

T F 4. Once in a while I cannot control my urge to harm others.

T F 5. I know that people tend to talk about me behind my back.

T F 6. I lose my temper easily but get over it quickly.

T F 7. When I disapprove of my friend's behavior, I let them know it.

T F 8. When someone makes a rule I don't like, I am tempted to break it.

T F 9. Other people always seem to get the breaks.

T F 10. I never get mad enough to throw things.

T F 11. I can think of no good reason for ever hitting anyone.

T F 12. I tend to be on my guard with people who are somewhat more friendly than I expected.

T F 13. I am always patient with others.

T F 14. I often find myself disagreeing with people.

T F 15. When someone is bossy, I do the opposite of what he asks.

T F 16. When I look back on what's happened to me, I can't help feeling mildly resentful.

T F 17. When I am mad, I sometimes slam doors.

T F 18. If somebody hits me first, I let him have it.

T F 19. There are a number of people who seem to dislike me very much.

APPENDIX I Continued

T	F	20.	I am irritated a great deal more than people are aware of.
T	F	21.	I can't help getting into arguments with people when they disagree with me.
T	F	22.	When people are bossy, I take my time just to show them.
T	F	23.	Almost every week I see someone I dislike.
T	F	24.	I never play practical jokes.
T	F	25.	Whoever insults me or my family is asking for a fight.
T	F	26.	There are a number of people who seem to be jealous of me.
T	F	27.	It makes my blood boil to have somebody make fun of me.
T	F	28.	I demand that people respect my rights.
T	F	29.	Occasionally when I am mad at someone I will give him the "silent treatment."
T	F	30.	Although I don't show it, I am sometimes eaten up with jealousy.
T	F	31.	When I am angry, I sometimes sulk.
T	F	32.	People who continually pester you are asking for a punch in the nose.
T	F	33.	I sometimes have the feeling that others are laughing at me.
T	F	34.	If someone doesn't treat me right, I don't let it annoy me.
T	F	35.	Even when my anger is aroused, I don't use "strong language."
T	F	36.	I don't know any people that I downright hate.
T	F	37.	I sometimes pout when I don't get my way.
T	F	38.	I seldom strike back, even if someone hits me first.
T	F	39.	My motto is "Never trust strangers."
T	F	40.	Sometimes people bother me by just being around.
T	F	41.	If somebody annoys me, I am apt to tell him what I think of him.
T	F	42.	If I let people see the way I feel, I'd be considered a hard person to get along with.
T	F	43.	Since the age of ten, I have never had a temper tantrum.
T	F	44.	When I really lose my temper, I am capable of slapping someone.
T	F	45.	I commonly wonder what hidden reason another person may have for doing something nice for me.
T	F	46.	I often feel like a powder keg ready to explode.
T	F	47.	When people yell at me, I yell back.
T	F	48.	At times I feel I get a raw deal out of life.
T	F	49.	I can remember being so angry that I picked up the nearest thing and broke it.
T	F	50.	I get into fights about as often as the next person.
T	F	51.	I used to think that most people told the truth but now I know otherwise.
T	F	52.	I sometimes carry a chip on my shoulder.
T	F	53.	When I get mad, I say nasty things.
T	F	54.	I sometimes show my anger by banging on the table.
T	F	55.	If I have to resort to physical violence to defend my rights, I will.
T	F	56.	I have no enemies who really wish to harm me.
T	F	57.	I can't help being a little rude to people I don't like.
T	F	58.	I could not put someone in his place, even if he needed it.
T	F	59.	I have known people who pushed me so far that we came to blows.

(continued)

APPENDIX I Continued

T F 60. I seldom feel that people are trying to anger or insult me.
T F 61. I don't let a lot of unimportant things irritate me.
T F 62. I often make threats I don't really mean to carry out.
T F 63. Lately, I have been kind of grouchy.
T F 64. When arguing, I tend to raise my voice.
T F 65. I generally cover up my poor opinion of others.
T F 66. I would rather concede a point than get into an argument about it.

SOURCE: For Buss-Durkee Hostility Inventory, Buss and Durkee (1957). Copyright © 1957, American Psychological Association. Reprinted by permission.

Interpersonal Reactivity Index

DESCRIPTION

This is a 28-item index that measures four components of empathy. They are "Perspective Taking" (PT), a cognitive measure of the ability to appreciate other people's point of view; "Empathic Concern" (EC), an affective measure of the ability to feel compassion and concern for others having negative experiences; "Fantasy" (FS), a measure of the ability to identify with fictitious characters, and "Personal Distress" (PD), a measure of the extent to which an individual shares the negative emotions of others. While this latter is said merely to denote identification with the feelings of others, in fact it appears to measure the inability to cope with negative feelings. For example, items include "I tend to lose control during emergencies" and I sometimes feel helpless when I am in the middle of a very emotional situation."

SCORING

Items are scored on a 5-point scale from 0 ("does not describe me well") to 4 ("describes me very well"). The scales with their associated items are as follows:

PT	EC	FS	PD
3(−)	2	1	6
8	4(−)	5	10
11	9	7(−)	13(−)
15(−)	14(−)	12(−)	17
21	18(−)	16	19(−)
25	20	23	24
28	22	26	27

Minus signs note items to be scored in reverse.

INTERPRETATION

In a sample of 500 male college students and 582 female students, Davis (1980) obtained the following mean scores:

	PT	EC	FS	PD
f.	17.96	21.67	18.75	12.28
m.	16.78	19.04	15.73	9.46

Standard deviations were not reported. A previously unpublished study of 138 male factory workers by Salter, Kairys, and Teague, found the following mean scores and standard deviations:

	PT	EC	FS	PD
Means	18.35	20.19	13.4	11.09
SD	4.4	4.25	6.3	5.73

(continued)

APPENDIX J Continued

REFERENCES

Davis, M. H. (1980). A multidimensional approach to individual differences in empathy. *JSAS Catalog of Selected Documents in Psychology, 10,* 85.
Davis, M. H. (1983). The effects of dispositional empathy on emotional reactions and helping: A multidimensional approach. *Journal of Personality, 51*(2), 67-184.

INTERPERSONAL REACTIVITY INDEX

The following statements inquire about your thoughts and feelings in a variety of situations. For each item, indicate how well it describes you by choosing the appropriate letter on the scale at the top of the page: A, B, C, D or E. When you have decided on your answer, fill in the letter in the answer space following the item. READ EACH ITEM CAREFULLY BEFORE RESPONDING. Answer as honestly and as accurately as you can. Thank you.

ANSWER SCALE

A	B	C	D	E
Does Not Describe Me Well				Describes Me Very Well

ITEM

1. I daydream and fantasize, with some regularity, about things that might happen to me. _____

2. I often have tender, concerned feelings for people less fortunate than me. _____

3. I sometimes find it difficult to see things from the "other guy's" point of view. _____

4. Sometimes I don't feel very sorry for other people when they are having problems. _____

5. I really get involved with the feelings of the characters in a novel. _____

6. In emergency situations, I feel apprehensive and ill-at-ease. _____

7. I am usually objective when I watch a movie or play and I don't often get completely caught up in it. _____

8. I try to look at everybody's side of a disagreement before I make a decision. _____

9. When I see someone being taken advantage of, I feel kind of protective towards them. _____

10. I sometimes feel helpless when I am in the middle of a very emotional situation. _____

11. I sometimes try to understand my friends better by imagining how things look from their perspective. _____

APPENDIX J Continued

12. Becoming extremely involved in a good book or movie is somewhat rare for me. _____

13. When I see someone get hurt, I tend to remain calm. _____

14. Other people's misfortunes do not usually disturb me a great deal. _____

15. If I'm sure I'm right about something, I don't waste much time listening to other people's arguments. _____

16. After seeing a play or movie, I have felt as though I were one of the characters. _____

17. Being in a tense emotional situation scares me. _____

18. When I see someone being treated unfairly, I sometimes don't feel very much pity for them. _____

19. I am usually pretty effective in dealing with emergencies. _____

20. I am often quite touched by things that I see happen. _____

21. I believe that there are two sides to every question and try to look at them both. _____

22. I would describe myself as a pretty soft-hearted person. _____

23. When I watch a good movie, I can very easily put myself in the place of a leading character. _____

24. I tend to lose control during emergencies. _____

25. When I'm upset at someone, I usually try to "put myself in his shoes" for a while. _____

26. When I am reading an interesting story or novel, I imagine how I would feel if the events in the story were happening to me. _____

27. When I see someone who badly needs help in an emergency, I go to pieces. _____

28. Before criticizing somebody, I try to imagine how I would feel if I were in their place. _____

SOURCE: For Interpersonal Reactivity Index, Davis (1980). Copyright © 1980, American Psychological Association. Reprinted by permission.

MAST: Michigan Alcoholism Screening Test

DESCRIPTION

The MAST is 24-item yes/no questionnaire designed to detect alcoholism. Included here is the revised 1980 version.

SCORING

Items are weighted differentially. See the MAST itself for the scoring (to the left of the questions). Positive answers are alcoholic responses except where indicated otherwise.

INTERPRETATION

        3 or less points—nonalcoholic
        4 points—suggests alcoholism
        5 or more points—indicates alcoholism

Programs using the above scoring system find it very sensitive at the five-point level, and it tends to find more people alcoholic than anticipated. However, it is a screening test, and should be sensitive at its lower levels.

REFERENCES

Selzer, M. L. (1971). The Michigan Alcoholism Screening Test: the quest for a new diagnostic instrument. *American Journal of Psychiatry, 127*(12), 1653-1658.
Skinner, H. A., & Sheu, W. (1982). Reliability of alcohol use indices. The lifetime drinking history and the MAST. *Journal of Studies on Alcohol, 43*(11), 1157-1170.

MAST: MICHIGAN ALCOHOLISM SCREENING TEST

Points

      0. Do you enjoy a drink now and then?

(2) *1. Do you feel you are a normal drinker? (By normal we mean you drink less than or as much as most other people.)

(2) 2. Have you ever awakened the morning after some drinking the night before and found that you could not remember a part of the evening?

(1) 3. Does your wife, husband, a parent, or other near relative ever worry or complain about your drinking?

(2) *4. Can you stop drinking without a struggle after one or two drinks?

(1) 5. Do you ever feel guilty about your drinking?

(2) *6. Do friends or relatives think you are a normal drinker?

(2) *7. Are you always able to stop drinking when you want to?

(5) 8. Have you ever attended a meeting of Alcoholics Anonymous (AA)?

(1) 9. Have you gotten into physical fights while drinking?

APPENDIX K Continued

(2) 10. Has drinking ever created problems between you and your wife, husband, a parent, or other relative?

(2) 11. Has your wife, husband (or other family member) ever gone to anyone for help about your drinking?

(2) 12. Have you ever lost friends because of drinking?

(2) 13. Have you ever gotten into trouble at work because of drinking?

(2) 14. Have you ever lost a job because of drinking?

(2) 15. Have you ever neglected your obligations, your family, or your work for two or more days in a row because you were drinking?

(1) 16. Do you ever drink before noon fairly often?

(2) 17. Have you ever been told you have liver trouble? Cirrhosis?

**(2) 18. After heavy drinking have you ever had delirium tremens (DTs), severe shaking, or heard voices or seen things that weren't there?

(5) 19. Have you ever gone to anyone for help about your drinking?

(5) 20. Have you ever been in a hospital because of drinking?

(2) 21. Have you ever been a patient in a psychiatric hospital or a psychiatric ward of a general hospital where drinking was part of the problem that resulted in hospitalization?

(2) 22. Have you ever been seen at a psychiatric or mental health clinic, or gone to a doctor, social worker, or clergyman for help with an emotional problem in which drinking had played a part?

***(2) 23. Have you ever been arrested for drunk driving, driving while intoxicated, or driving under the influence of alcoholic beverages?
(If YES, How many times? _____)

***(2) 24. Have you ever been arrested, or taken into custody even for a few hours, because of other drunk behavior?
(If YES, How many times? _____)

*Negative responses are alcoholic responses.
**5 points for Delirium Tremens.
***2 points for each arrest.

SOURCE: For Michigan Alcoholism Screening Test, Seltzer, M. L. (1971). The Michigan Alcoholism Screening Test: The quest for a new diagnostic instrument. *American Journal of Psychiatry, 127,* 1653-1658. Copyright © 1971, the American Psychiatric Association. Reprinted by permission.

APPENDIX L
Social Avoidance and Distress Scale

DESCRIPTION

This is a 28-item true/false scale that measures distress in social situations and the avoidance of social interactions.

SCORING

Assign one point for each answer that matches the following scoring key:

1. F	15. F
2. T	16. T
3. F	17. F
4. F	18. T
5. T	19. F
6. F	20. T
7. F	21. T
8. T	22. F
9. F	23. T
10. T	24. T
11. T	25. F
12. F	26. T
13. T	27. F
14. T	28. F

INTERPRETATION

Watson and Friend (1969) studied 205 college students (145 females and 60 males). The distribution of scores was skewed, with high scores being rare; the modal score was 0. Mean scores differed by sex: males had a mean of 11.2 and females had a mean score of 8.24. The overall mean was 9.11, the median was 7 and the standard deviation 8.01. Watson and Friend divided their sample into high, average and low scorers as follows:

Low Scorers	0 or 1
Average Scorers	2 to 11
High Scorers	12 and up

REFERENCE

Watson, D. & Friend, R. (1969). Measurement of social-evaluative anxiety, *Journal of Consulting and Clinical Psychology*, 33(4), 448-457.

SOCIAL AVOIDANCE AND DISTRESS SCALE

This questionnaire consists of a number of statements. We want you to decide for each one if it is TRUE or FALSE, as applied to you. If the statement is TRUE or MOSTLY TRUE as applied to you, mark T in the space to the left of the item number. If the statement is FALSE or MOSTLY FALSE as applied to you, mark F in the space to the left of the item number.

APPENDIX L Continued

Remember to give your own opinion of yourself. Try not to leave any statements unanswered. Put your name and the date on your answer sheet.

_____ 1. I feel relaxed even in unfamiliar social situations.

_____ 2. I try to avoid situations which force me to be very sociable.

_____ 3. It is easy for me to relax when I am with strangers.

_____ 4. I have no particular desire to avoid people.

_____ 5. I often find social occasions upsetting.

_____ 6. I usually feel calm and comfortable at social occasions.

_____ 7. I am usually at ease when talking to someone of the opposite sex.

_____ 8. I try to avoid talking to people unless I know them well.

_____ 9. If the chance comes to meet new people, I often take it.

_____ 10. I often feel nervous or tense in casual get-togethers in which both sexes are present.

_____ 11. I am usually nervous with people unless I know them well.

_____ 12. I usually feel relaxed when I am with a group of people.

_____ 13. I often want to get away from people.

_____ 14. I usually feel uncomfortable when I am in a group of people I don't know.

_____ 15. I usually feel relaxed when I meet someone for the first time.

_____ 16. Being introduced to people makes me tense and nervous.

_____ 17. Even though a room is full of strangers, I may enter it anyway.

_____ 18. I would avoid walking up and joining a large group of people.

_____ 19. When my superiors want to talk with me, I talk willingly.

_____ 20. I often feel on edge when I am with a group of people.

_____ 21. I tend to withdraw from people.

_____ 22. I don't mind talking to people at parties or social gatherings.

_____ 23. I am seldom at ease in a large group of people.

_____ 24. I often think up excuses in order to avoid social engagements.

_____ 25. I sometimes take the responsibility for introducing people to each other.

_____ 26. I try to avoid formal social occasions.

_____ 27. I usually go to whatever social engagements I have.

_____ 28. I find it easy to relax with other people.

SOURCE: For Social Avoidance and Distress Scale, Watson, David & Friend, Ronald (1969). Measurement of Social-Evaluative Anxiety. *Journal of Consulting and Clinical Psychology, 33*(4), 448-457. Copyright © 1969, American Psychological Association. Reprinted by permission of the publisher and the authors.

Wilson Sexual Fantasy Questionnaire

DESCRIPTION

This is a 40-item questionnaire that lists sexual fantasies and asks the respondent to indicate how frequently each fantasy occurs to him/her. The 40 items have been empirically grouped into four themes as follows: (1) intimate themes, such as kissing and coitus with a loved one; (2) exploratory themes, such as engaging in an orgy or exchanging mates; (3) impersonal themes, such as having intercourse with a stranger, using vibrators or pornography; and (4) sadomasochistic themes involving the use of force or humiliation.

SCORING

Each item is scored on a 6 point scale from "never" (scored 0) to "regularly" (scored 5). The four fantasy factors consist of the following items:

Exploratory	5, 6, 9, 22, 26, 29, 32, 33, 34, 36
Intimate	1, 2, 3, 10, 11, 16, 17, 18, 38, 40
Impersonal	4, 12, 13, 19, 23, 30, 31, 35, 37, 39
Sado-masochistic	7, 8, 14, 15, 20, 21, 24, 25, 27, 28

Scores for each of these themes are added up separately. Since scores range from 0 to 5 for each item, the total of the scores for the 10 items in each category ranges from 0 to 50.

INTERPRETATION

Sexual fantasies can be used clinically to determine suitable material for covert sensitization and boredom tapes without reference to formal scoring. For those who wish to know how far from the norm a particular offender's fantasies may be, see the studies by Wilson and Gosselin cited below for research regarding sexual fantasies of "normal" people as well as particular subgroups, such as fetishists, tranvestites, and sadomasochists. In the Gosselin and Wilson study, means for the control group for the four categories of sexual fantasy were as follows:

Intimate	16.9
Exploratory	8.1
Impersonal	7.6
Sado-masochistic	2.3
Total	34.9 (Ch. 4, p. 81)

REFERENCES

Wilson, Glenn (1978). *The secrets of sexual fantasy*. London: J. M. Dent & Sons.

Gosselin, Chris & Wilson, Glenn (1980). *Sexual variations: fetishism, sado-masochism, and transvestism*. New York: Simon & Schuster.

APPENDIX M Continued

WILSON SEX FANTASY QUESTIONNAIRE

Indicate how often you fantasize about the following themes using the scale;
0 — Never, 1 — Seldom, 2 — Occasionally, 3 — Sometimes, 4 — Often, 5 — Regularly.

1. Making love out of doors in a romantic setting,
   e.g., field of flowers, beach at night   0 1 2 3 4 5
2. Having intercourse with a loved partner   0 1 2 3 4 5
3. Intercourse with someone you know but have
   not had sex with   0 1 2 3 4 5
4. Intercourse with an anonymous stranger   0 1 2 3 4 5
5. Sex with two other people   0 1 2 3 4 5
6. Participating in an orgy   0 1 2 3 4 5
7. Being forced to do something   0 1 2 3 4 5
8. Forcing someone to do something   0 1 2 3 4 5
9. Homosexual activity   0 1 2 3 4 5
10. Receiving oral sex   0 1 2 3 4 5
11. Giving oral sex   0 1 2 3 4 5
12. Watching others have sex   0 1 2 3 4 5
13. Sex with an animal   0 1 2 3 4 5
14. Whipping or spanking someone   0 1 2 3 4 5
15. Being whipped or spanked   0 1 2 3 4 5
16. Taking someone's clothes off   0 1 2 3 4 5
17. Having your clothes taken off   0 1 2 3 4 5
18. Making love elsewhere than bedroom
    (e.g., kitchen or bathroom)   0 1 2 3 4 5
19. Being excited by material or clothing
    (e.g., rubber, leather, underwear)   0 1 2 3 4 5
20. Hurting a partner   0 1 2 3 4 5
21. Being hurt by a partner   0 1 2 3 4 5
22. Mate-swapping   0 1 2 3 4 5
23. Being aroused by watching someone
    urinate   0 1 2 3 4 5
24. Being tied up   0 1 2 3 4 5
25. Tying someone up   0 1 2 3 4 5
26. Having incestuous sexual relations   0 1 2 3 4 5
27. Exposing yourself provocatively   0 1 2 3 4 5
28. Transvestism (wearing clothes of the
    opposite sex)   0 1 2 3 4 5
29. Being promiscuous   0 1 2 3 4 5
30. Having sex with someone mucn younger
    than yourself   0 1 2 3 4 5
31. Having sex with someone much older
    than yourself   0 1 2 3 4 5

(continued)

APPENDIX M Continued

32. Being much sought after by the opposite sex	0	1	2	3	4	5
33. Being seduced as an "innocent"	0	1	2	3	4	5
34. Seducing an "innocent"	0	1	2	3	4	5
35. Being embarrassed by failure of sexual performance	0	1	2	3	4	5
36. Having sex with someone of a different race	0	1	2	3	4	5
37. Using objects for stimulation (e.g., vibrators, candles)	0	1	2	3	4	5
38. Being masturbated to orgasm by a partner	0	1	2	3	4	5
39. Looking at obscene pictures or film	0	1	2	3	4	5
40. Kissing passionately	0	1	2	3	4	5

SOURCE: For Wilson Sex Fantasy Questionnaire, Wilson, Glenn (1978). *The Secrets of Sexual Fantasy*. Copyright © 1978, J. M. Dent & Sons, London. Reprinted by permission.

Abel and Becker Sexual Interest Card Sort
(Optional)

DESCRIPTION:

The original 260-item card sort has been revised to 75 items. There are 5 questions each in 15 categories. The categories, along with the individual items which belong to them, are as follows:

adult homosexual	1, 23, 26, 53, 55
adult heterosexual	5, 39, 41, 62, 72
voyeurism	2, 4, 37, 69, 70
exhibitionism	13, 14, 54, 57, 71
frottage	9, 16, 17, 50, 74
female pedophilia	3, 8, 27, 61, 65
male pedophilia	24, 49, 58, 60, 75
female incest	11, 18, 21, 33, 38
male incest	7, 20, 40, 42, 59
rape	19, 22, 31, 45, 67
sadism	6, 12, 15, 30, 66
masochism	10, 43, 46, 51, 52
sexual identity female	25, 32, 36, 47, 63
sexual identity male	29, 34, 48, 64, 73
transvestism	28, 35, 44, 56, 68

At this length the measure may be used as a questionnaire or as a card sort. Card sorts tend to be easier for the subject to use. If used as a card sort, each item should be typed on a separate index card with the statement on the front and an abbreviation for the category (e.g., HO for adult homosexual) plus a number from 1-5 on the back to facilitate scoring.

The top card should contain the following instructions:

There are 7 blue cards. Read them, and place them separately on the table. These 7 cards go from HIGHLY AROUSING (exciting) to HIGHLY REPULSIVE (gross).

Read the white cards AS IF YOU WERE ACTUALLY IN THAT SITUATION. Place each white card on one of the blue cards. If you were in the situation described on the white card, would you find it sexually highly arousing, neutral, moderately repulsive, or extremely repulsive.

When finished, place each blue card on top of each stack of white cards and leave them on the table.

A set of 7 blue index cards would accompany the white item cards. Each would have one of the following typed on it: "highly repulsive," "moderately repulsive," "slightly repulsive," "neutral (neither repulsive nor arousing)," "slightly arousing," "moderately arousing," "highly arousing."

(continued)

SCORING

After the subject has completed the task, the cards are turned over and scored by placing a number from −3 ("highly repulsive") to +3 ("highly arousing") in the appropriate box on the scoring form. (See attached scoring form.) Each category score is then averaged presenting the offender's report of his sexual arousal pattern. (See attached scoring summary.)

INTERPRETATION

At present there are no adequate norms for the card sort. While, however, this makes it impossible to use the card sort to distinguish groups; e.g., sex offenders from nonoffenders or pedophiles from rapists, nonetheless it can be used clinically to measure the relative strength of different forms of deviant arousal. This is obviously most true in offenders who are honest about the extent of their sexual deviancy, i.e., a minority of offenders. However, while denying offenders may flatly deny the particular type of deviant arousal involved in the crime for which they have been charged, nonetheless this author has been impressed with the extent that offenders will rate those items to which they are attracted as *less* repulsive than others, or as neutral. Thus the relative differences in scores may be useful clinically.

Name _____
Date _____

CARDS

CATEGORIES		1	2	3	4	5	$\overline{X}$
Adult Homosexual	(Ho)						
Adult Heterosexual	(He)						
Voyeurism	(V)						
Exhibitionism	(E)						
Frottage	(F)						
Homosexual Incest	(HoI)						
Heterosexual Incest	(HeI)						
Homosexual Pedophilia	(HoP)						
Heterosexual Pedophilia	(HeP)						
Transvestism	(T)						
Sadism	(S)						
Masochism	(M)						
Rape	(R)						
Male Sexual Identity	(MSI)						
Female Sexual Identity	(FSI)						

Figure N.1   Card Sort Raw Data Scoring Form

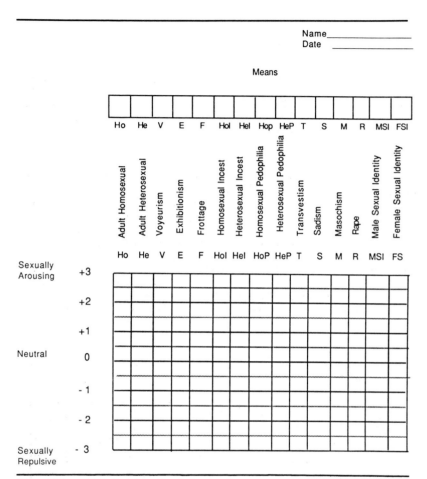

Figure N.2   ABEL Card Sort Graph Scoring Summary

ABEL AND BECKER SEXUAL INTEREST CARD SORT

Instructions: Please *circle the number beside each statement* which best describes how you feel about that statement at the present.

> −3 = extremely sexually repulsive
> −2 = moderately sexually repulsive
> −1 = slightly sexually repulsive
> 0 = neutral (neither sexually arousing nor sexually repulsive)
> +1 = slightly sexually arousing
> +2 = moderately sexually arousing
> +3 = extremely sexually arousing

1. A 25 year old man and I are lying side by side naked touching each other all over.
   −3 −2 −1   0 +1 +2 +3

2. I'm peering through a girl's window. She's an attractive brunette with a great figure; she's taking a shower.
   −3 −2 −1   0 +1 +2 +3

3. I have an erection. My penis is between an 8 year old girl's legs.
   −3 −2 −1   0 +1 +2 +3

4. I'm looking through the partially drawn window shades. I'm watching a woman sleeping. The covers have fallen off her nude body.
   −3 −2 −1   0 +1 +2 +3

5. A beautiful woman is stroking my dick and balls as she lays beside me. We are both getting excited.
   −3 −2 −1   0 +1 +2 +3

6. I'm standing over a woman I've just beaten up. She's bruised and bleeding. She can't move any more.
   −3 −2 −1   0 +1 +2 +3

7. I'm lying on top of my son. I feel his hot body beneath mine as I kiss his back and feel his skin.
   −3 −2 −1   0 +1 +2 +3

8. A 10 year old girl and I are lying on the couch. I'm rubbing her soft skin, all over her body. I'm feeling her breasts.
   −3 −2 −1   0 +1 +2 +3

9. The subway train is extremely packed. I've really got a stiff hard-on. I'm face to face with a young woman, pushing my dick right up against her. She's trying to move away but she can't.
   −3 −2 −1   0 +1 +2 +3

10. I'm pleading with a tall woman to stop hitting me with her belt. The pain is tremendous.
    −3 −2 −1   0 +1 +2 +3

APPENDIX N Continued

---

11. I'm lying back naked on the bed with   −3   −2   −1   0   +1   +2   +3
my daughter sitting on top of me. I'm
stroking her naked body with my hands
and pushing my fingers into her cunt.

12. I'm pinching a 25 year old woman's   −3   −2   −1   0   +1   +2   +3
breasts with pliers. She's beginning
to bleed. She's crying.

13. I see two good looking 22 year old   −3   −2   −1   0   +1   +2   +3
girls walking down the street. I drive
slowly by with no clothes on, rubbing
my penis. I get excited as they look
at me with disbelief.

14. I followed a 20 year old blonde girl   −3   −2   −1   0   +1   +2   +3
into the parking lot at the public
library. I take my dick out and begin
to beat it as she sees me and looks
tense.

15. I'm holding a burning cigarette butt   −3   −2   −1   0   +1   +2   +3
against the big tits of a 30 year old
brunette. She's screaming for me
to stop.

16. It's packed in the train and I've pinned   −3   −2   −1   0   +1   +2   +3
a woman up against the people in front
of her. I'm rubbing her ass with my
hands. She tells me to stop. She can't
get away from me. I just keep rubbing
her.

17. It's very crowded in the subway train.   −3   −2   −3   0   +1   +2   +3
I'm facing a beautiful girl. I'm rubbing
her tits and her crotch. She has a blank
expression on her face.

18. I'm unbuttoning my daughter's blouse.   −3   −2   −1   0   +1   +2   +3
I'm feeling her small tits. She likes it.

19. I've pulled an attractive woman to the   −3   −2   −3   0   +1   +2   +3
ground. I've pulled her panties off.
I'm forcing my penis in her. She is
screaming.

20. I'm kneeling beside my son, holding   −3   −2   −1   0   +1   +2   +3
him close to me. I'm kissing his fore-
head and getting an erection.

21. I'm pulling down my little daughter's   −3   −2   −3   0   +1   +2   +3
shorts and underwear. I'm going to
fingerfuck her.

(continued)

APPENDIX N Continued

22.	I've forced my way into an apartment. I've forced a brunette to take off her clothes. I'm raping her.	−3	−2	−1	0	+1	+2	+3
23.	I'm lying on a deserted beach with a real handsome guy. He has wrapped his arms and legs around me. He really enjoys making love with me.	−3	−2	−1	0	+1	+2	+3
24.	I have a hard on. My dick is between the legs of a young boy.	−3	−2	−1	0	+1	+2	+3
25.	I would like to be a wife.	−3	−2	−1	0	+1	+2	+3
26.	We're in the 69 position with me on top. I'm sucking a young guy's dick as he sucks mine. I'm starting to come.	−3	−2	−1	0	+1	+2	+3
27.	A 12 year old girl is sucking my cock. I'm about to come.	−3	−2	−1	0	+1	+2	+3
28.	I'm thinking about putting on some sheer nylon tights with no crotch. I'm feeling them in my hands.	−3	−2	−1	0	+1	+2	+3
29.	I would like to have a good physique.	−3	−2	−1	0	+1	+2	+3
30.	I have a woman spread eagled on the floor. I'm torturing her, burning her fingertips.	−3	−2	−1	0	+1	+2	+3
31.	An attractive woman looks surprised as I tell her I'm going to rape her. I make her undress and put my dick between her legs as I hold her down.	−3	−2	−1	0	+1	+2	+3
32.	I would like to be a mother.	−3	−2	−1	0	+1	+2	+3
33.	I can feel myself getting turned on as my daughter hugs me. I want to screw her.	−3	−2	−1	0	+1	+2	+3
34.	I would like to be a husband.	−3	−2	−1	0	+1	+2	+3
35.	I've broken into a house. No one is home. I've found some women's underclothes and I'm pulling on some cotton panties.	−3	−2	−1	0	+1	+2	+3
36.	I would like to wear beautiful, feminine clothes.	−3	−2	−1	0	+1	+2	+3
37.	I go by the girl's gym at college and look through the dressing room window. I can see several girls there, all partly undressed.	−3	−2	−1	0	+1	+2	+3
38.	I have a hard-on. My dick is between my daughter's legs as I'm ejaculating.	−3	−2	−1	0	+1	+2	+3

39. I feel my partner on top of me, with her knees holding my hips. She is moving up and down on my dick. −3 −2 −1 0 +1 +2 +3

40. My son is curled up beside me in bed. I'm gently rubbing his small penis; he is getting an erection. −3 −2 −1 0 +1 +2 +3

41. I've fucked a 25 year old woman. She has come again and again. She is thinking that I'm really great in bed. −3 −2 −1 0 +1 +2 +3

42. I've gotten my son to rub my cock. I'm getting hard. −1 −2 −3 0 +1 +2 +3

43. A beautiful woman is pinching my skin with pliers. I'm afraid she's going to pinch my balls with it, too. −3 −2 −1 0 +1 +2 +3

44. I'm in my sister's bedroom alone. I'm pulling on a pair of beige nylon panties. −3 −2 −1 0 +1 +2 +3

45. I'm forcing a well-stacked girl to hold still as I push my dick into her. She cries out as I rape her. −3 −2 −1 0 +1 +2 +3

46. My hands and legs are tied up. The ropes are biting into my skin. A woman in high heeled black boots is coming towards me, snapping a whip in her hand. −3 −2 −1 0 +1 +2 +3

47. I would like to be a woman. −3 −2 −1 0 +1 +2 +3

48. I would like to have male genitals. −3 −2 −1 0 +1 +2 +3

49. A 12 year old boy is sucking my cock. I'm about to come. −3 −2 −1 0 +1 +2 +3

50. I'm following a woman off the subway train. I move in right behind her as she waits for the next train. The crowd moves forward onto the next train. I start to rub her ass from behind. −3 −2 −1 0 +1 +2 +3

51. I'm chained to a wall. A woman in tall, black boots is holding a burning cigarette butt close to my nipples. She smiles as she brings the cigarette closer. −3 −2 −1 0 +1 +2 +3

52. I'm lying face down on the ground. An attractive woman is sitting on my ass, slashing my back with a razor blade. I'm pleading with her to stop. The blood is gushing out. −3 −2 −1 0 +1 +2 +3

(continued)

53. A good-looking man is pressing   −3 −2 −1   0 +1 +2 +3
against me as we kiss very tenderly.
We hold each other close.

54. I am following a nicely built blond,   −3 −2 −1   0 +1 +2 +3
18 year old girl down the stairs at
school. I take my dick out, holding
my books in front of it and begin
to beat it. As I follow her, I feel it
get hard.

55. A handsome man is lying on top of   −3 −2 −1   0 +1 +2 +3
me in bed. He has his tongue in my
ear and his hand on my dick. I'm
really excited.

56. I'm wearing a matching bra, panties   −3 −2 −1   0 +1 +2 +3
and slip, all lacy. I'm touching and
feeling the underclothes against my
body.

57. I'm standing naked beside the car.   −3 −2 −1   0 +1 +2 +2
A 20 year old girl in a bikini is coming
from the swimming pool. I feel my
hard penis in my hand as she sees
me and looks shocked.

58. I've gotten a young boy to rub my   −3 −2 −1   0 +1 +2 +3
cock. I feel it getting hard.

59. I'm sucking my son's small dick. He   −3 −2 −1   0 +1 +2 +3
seems to like it.

60. A lovely little boy is curled up beside   −3 −2 −1   0 +1 +2 +3
me in bed. I'm gently rubbing his
small penis.

61. I've lured a 9 year old girl into the   −3 −2 −1   0 +1 +2 +3
house. She's really good looking. I'm
pulling her shorts and underwear down.

62. I'm lying on top of my partner. She is   −3 −2 −1   0 +1 +2 +3
digging her hands into my back, lifting
her ass up. She is really excited.

63. I would like to have female genitals.   −3 −2 −1   0 +1 +2 +3

64. I would like to wear masculine clothes.   −3 −2 −1   0 +1 +2 +3

65. A 10 year old girl with long blond hair   −3 −2 −1   0 +1 +2 +3
is holding my dick. She seems to be
fascinated by it.

66. I've got a young woman tied down in   −3 −2 −1   0 +1 +2 +3
the woods. I'm sticking needles into her
vagina. She is screaming with terror.

APPENDIX N Continued

67.	A girl in the women's bathroom has taken her clothes off. I've pinned her down. I'm starting to rape her.	−3	−2	−1	0	+1	+2	+3
68.	I'm lying on a couch, wearing only my feminine underclothes, bright red panties, large-cupped bra, sheer hose, and a see-through slip.	−3	−2	−1	0	+1	+2	+3
69.	At an apartment complex a 25 year old girl is just dressed in her panties. I'm looking at her through the window.	−3	−2	−1	0	+1	+2	+3
70.	I'm looking from my upstairs window down into the apartment across the way. I can see a woman with big tits reading with a see-through negligee on.	−3	−2	−1	0	+1	+2	+3
71.	I've walked out of the field house shower so a young girl can see me. The 13 year old girl is surprised as she looks at my penis.	−3	−2	−1	0	+1	+2	+3
72.	My partner and I are in the bath tub. She is sitting between my legs, leaning back against me. I'm playing with her tits.	−3	−2	−1	0	+1	+2	+3
73.	I would like to be a man.	−3	−2	−1	0	+1	+2	+2
74.	There are very few people on the suburban train. I sit down next to an attractive woman and let my hand fall down into her crotch. I start to rub her.	−3	−2	−1	0	+1	+2	+3
75.	A 10 year old boy with soft dark hair is holding my dick. He seems to be fascinated by it.	−3	−2	−1	0	+1	+2	+3

APPENDIX O
Nowicki-Strickland Internal/External Scale
(Optional)

DESCRIPTION

This is a 40-item yes/no questionnaire that measures the extent to which individuals feels that events are contingent on *their* behavior and the extent to which they feel events are controlled externally.

SCORING

Scoring is done by assigning one point for every answer that matches the following answer key:

1. Y	21. Y
2. N	22. N
3. Y	23. Y
4. N	24. Y
5. Y	25. N
6. N	26. N
7. Y	27. Y
8. Y	28. N
9. N	29. Y
10. Y	30. N
11. Y	31. Y
12. Y	32. N
13. N	33. Y
14. Y	34. N
15. N	35. Y
16. Y	36. Y
17. Y	37. Y
18. Y	38. N
19. Y	39. Y
20. N	40. N

INTERPRETATION

The Nowicki has been far more studied with college adults than noncollege adults. A complete bibliography is available from Nowicki (see reference below). Studies of college adults consistently find a mean of approximately 8, with standard deviations of approximately 3.5 (based on 15 studies cited in the Adult Nowicki-Strickland manual). Two studies of noncollege adults (Nowicki & Duke, 1973 and Nowicki, 1975) found means of 10.96 (sd = 5.61) and 10.61 (sd = 4.81). Since items are scored in the external direction, low scores indicate more of a reliance on and belief in the individual's power over his/her life, and high scores represent a belief that external factors control events.

APPENDIX O Continued

REFERENCES

Nowicki, S., & Strickland, B. (1973). A locus of control scale for children. *Journal of Consulting and Clinical Psychology, 40*(1), 148-154.

Nowicki, S., & Duke, M. P. (1974). A locus of control scale for college as well as non-college adults. *Journal of Personality Assessment, 38*, 136-137.

Nowicki, S. (1975). The effect of locus of control on peer relationships across age groups, *Journal of Genetic Psychology, 43*, 275-280.

Nowicki, S. (1976). The factor structure of locus of control at three different ages. *Journal of Genetic Psychology, 129*, 13-17.

Nowicki, S. *Adult Nowicki-Strickland Internal-External Locus of Control.* (test manual). Available from S. Nowicki, Department of Psychology, Emory University, Atlanta, Georgia 30322.

NOWICKI-STRICKLAND INTERNAL/EXTERNAL SCALE

We are trying to find out what men and women your age think about certain things. We want you to answer the following questions the way *you* feel. There are no right or wrong answers. Don't take too much time answering any one question, but do try to answer them all.

One of your concerns during the test may be, "What should I do if I can answer both yes and no to a question?" It's not unusual for that to happen. If it does, think about whether your answer is just a little more one way than the other. For example, if you'd assign a weighting of 51 percent to "yes" and assign 49 percent to "no," mark the answer "yes." Try to pick one or the other response for all questions and not leave any blanks.

Circle yes or no next to each item. Be sure to put your name and the date on your answer sheet.

Thank you.

1. Do you believe that most problems will solve themselves if you just don't fool with them?   YES   NO

2. Do you believe that you can stop yourself from catching a cold?   YES   NO

3. Are some people just born lucky?   YES   NO

4. Most of the time do you feel that getting good grades meant a great deal to you?   YES   NO

5. Are you often blamed for things that just aren't your fault?   YES   NO

6. Do you believe that if somebody studies hard enough he or she can pass any subject?   YES   NO

7. Do you feel that most of the time it doesn't pay to try hard because things never turn out right anyway?   YES   NO

(continued)

APPENDIX O Continued

---

8. Do you feel that if things start out well in the morning it is going to be a good day no matter what you do? YES NO

9. Do you feel that most of the time parents listen to what their children have to say? YES NO

10. Do you believe that wishing can make good things happen? YES NO

11. When you get punished does it usually seem it's for no good reason at all? YES NO

12. Most of the time do you find it hard to change a friend's (mind) opinion? YES NO

13 Do you think that cheering more than luck helps a team to win? YES NO

14. Did you feel that it was nearly impossible to change your parent's mind about anything? YES NO

15. Do you believe that parents should allow children to make most of their own decisions? YES NO

16. Do you feel that when you do something wrong there's very little you can do to make it right? YES NO

17. Do you believe that most people are just born good at sports? YES NO

18. Are most of the other people your age stronger than you are? YES NO

19. Do you feel that one of the best ways to handle most problems is just not to think about them? YES NO

20. Do you feel that you have a lot of choice in deciding whom your friends are? YES NO

21. If you find a four-leaf clover, do you believe that it might bring you good luck? YES NO

22. Did you often feel that whether you did your homework has much to do with what kind of grades you got? YES NO

23. Do you feel that when a person your age decides to hit you there's little you can do to stop him or her? YES NO

24. Have you ever had a good-luck charm? YES NO

25. Do you believe that whether or not people like you depends on how you act? YES NO

26. Did your parents usually help if you ask them to? YES NO

27. Have you felt that when people were angry to you it was usually for no reason at all? YES NO

28. Most of the time, do you feel that you can change what might happen tomorrow by what you do today? YES NO

29. Do you believe that when bad things are going to happen they just are going to happen no matter what you try to do to stop them? YES NO

APPENDIX O Continued

30. Do you think that people can get their own way if they just keep trying?	YES	NO
31. Most of the time do you find it useless to try to get your own way at home?	YES	NO
32. Do you feel that when good things happen they happen because of hard work?	YES	NO
33. Do you feel that when somebody your age wants to be your enemy there's little you can do to change matters?	YES	NO
34. Do you feel that it's easy to get friends to do what you want them to?	YES	NO
35. Do you usually feel that you have little to say about what you get to eat at home?	YES	NO
36. Do you feel that when someone doesn't like you there's little you can do about it?	YES	NO
37. Did you usually feel that it was almost useless to try in school because most other children were just plain smarter than you were?	YES	NO
38. Are you the kind of person who believes that planning ahead makes things turn our better?	YES	NO
39. Most of the time, do you feel that you have little to say about what your family decides to do?	YES	NO
40. Do you think it's better to be smart than to be lucky?	YES	NO

SOURCE: For Nowicki-Strickland Internal/External Scale, Nowicki, Stephen, Jr., & Strickland, Bonnie (1973). A Locus of Control Scale for Children. *Journal of Consulting and Clinical Psychology, 40*(1), 148-154. Copyright © 1973, American Psychological Association. Reprinted by permission.

APPENDIX P
Fear of Negative Evaluation Scale
(Optional)

DESCRIPTION

This is a 30-item true/false test that measures sensitivity to negative evaluations by others, expectations, and avoidance of criticism.

SCORING

One point is given for each answer that matches the scoring key. The scoring key is as follows:

1. F	16. F
2. T	17. T
3. T	18. F
4. F	19. T
5. T	20. T
6. F	21. F
7. T	22. T
8. F	23. F
9. T	24. T
10. F	25. T
11. T	26. F
12. F	27. F
13. T	28. T
14. T	29. T
15. F	30. T

INTERPRETATION

Low Scores (0-8) 25% of college-based sample
Average Scores (9-18) 50%
High Scores (19-30) 25%

High scorers are sensitive to possible criticism. They expect the worst and read into situations evaluations where none may be intended. They become nervous when being evaluated, and avoid such situations when possible. They also seek approval in addition to avoiding disapproval. They tend to be more defensive, less autonomous, less dominant and more self-effacing than their low-scoring counterparts.

REFERENCE

Watson, David, & Friend, Ronald (1969). Measurement of social-evaluative anxiety. *Journal of Consulting and Clinical Psychology, 33*(4), 448-457.

APPENDIX P Continued

FEAR OF NEGATIVE EVALUATION SCALE

Carefully read each of the 30 statements listed below. Decide whether each statement is true (T) or false (F) as it pertains to you personally. If you are unsure which is the better answer, decide which one is slightly more applicable to how you are feeling at the moment and answer accordingly. Try to answer based on your first reaction to the statement. Don't spend too long on any one item. Mark your answer on the answer sheet.

1. I rarely worry about seeming foolish to others.
2. I worry about what people will think of me even when I know it doesn't make any difference.
3. I become tense and jittery if I know someone is sizing me up.
4. I am unconcerned even if I know people are forming an unfavorable impression of me.
5. I feel very upset when I commit some social error.
6. The opinions that important people have of me cause me little concern.
7. I am often afraid that I may look ridiculous or make a fool of myself.
8. I react very little when other people disapprove of me.
9. I am frequently afraid of other people noticing my shortcomings.
10. The disapproval of others would have little effect on me.
11. If someone is evaluating me, I tend to expect the worst.
12. I rarely worry about what kind of impression I am making on someone.
13. I am afraid that others will not approve of me.
14. I am afraid that people will find fault with me.
15. Other people's opinions of me do not bother me.
16. I am not necessarily upset if I do not please someone.
17. When I am talking to someone, I worry about what they may be thinking of me.
18. I feel that you can't help making social errors sometimes, so why worry about it.
19. I am usually worried about what kind of impression I make.
20. I worry a lot about what my superiors think of me.
21. If I know someone is judging me, it has little effect on me.
22. I worry that others will think I am not worthwhile.
23. I worry very little about what others may think of me.
24. Sometimes I think I am too concerned with what other people think of me.
25. I often worry that I will say or do the wrong things.
26. I am often indifferent to the opinions others have of me.
27. I am usually confident that others will have a favorable impression of me.
28. I often worry that people who are important to me won't think very much of me.
29. I brood about the opinions my friends have about me.
30. I become tense and jittery if I know I am being judged by my superiors.

SOURCE: For Fear of Negative Evaluation Scale, Watson, David & Friend, Ronald (1969). Measurement of social evaluative-anxiety. *Journal of Consulting and Clinical Psychology, 33*(4), 448-457. Copyright © 1969, American Psychological Association. Reprinted by permission of the publisher and the author.

Northwest Treatment Associates Partner Alert List

These lists are intended to lessen the likelihood of offense by serving as a vehicle for communication and by assisting the partner in surveillance of client's offense-linked behavior. He will add three items related to his own pattern. Endorsement of some items could be insignificant. However, multiple items suggest the need for communication and intervention, especially when dealing with known offender or victim. Trust your judgment. If you feel that something is not quite right, initiate discussion with partner and counselor. Consider posting the list.

A. The Client: Change in Pattern

1. Minimizing previous offenses and stated over-confidence regarding the possibility of reoffense.
2. Abuse of alcohol and other drugs.
3. Discrediting treatment program; not attending sessions or completing assigned work.
4. Loss of control over nonsexual behaviors, e.g., gambling, eating, battering.
5. Any invasion of child's privacy, e.g., entering their bedroom or bathroom unchaperoned without being asked to do so.
6. Rapid religious conversion.
7. Job stress: fired, laid off, change in job description.
8. Change in sexual functioning: frequency, dysfunction, abuse, infidelity.
9. Unresolved marital conflicts: refusal to discuss problems.
10. Client retreats to childhood: clothing, language, cultivation of younger friends, involvement in youth programs.
11. Isolating the child: with client, or away from others including mother, friends, counselor and physician.
12. Critical interest in victim's social-sexual behavior; unduly concerned regarding child's clothing and cosmetics.
13. Involvement in child's hygiene: bathing, massage, apparel, grooming.
14. Initiating-prolonging physical contact with target.
15. Sexual preoccupation: pornography, staring, offensive, offensive humor, aggressivity.
16. Difficulty accounting for time; unstructured or unmonitored time.
17. Cruise in car with no destination, unexplained mileage.
18. Discipline: favoritism, harsh, erratic.
19. Sleep disturbance: fitful, last to bed, up at night, first to rise.
20. Inappropriate apparel: broken zipper, poor hygiene, robe only, no underwear.
21. Leaving bedroom-bathroom door open.
22. Difficulty accounting for money spent: alcohol, drugs, gifts, pornography, gasoline for cruising, prostitution, topless taverns, and massage parlors.
23. Repeated "accidental" contacts with victim.
24. Attempting to establish authority over potential victims.
25. Offender traits, e.g., self-centeredness, dishonesty, deviousness, withdrawal, aggressivity and procrastination.
26. Challenging wife's authority over children; making excuses for child.

APPENDIX Q Continued

27. Attempting to intimidate child: bullying, staring, isolating and ultimatums.
28. Contact with victim's body: massage, inspection, wrestling, and "medicinal."
29. Medical deterioration: ulcer, elevated blood pressure, indigestion, sexually transmitted disease, hypochrondical complaints.
30. Seeking to establish contacts with friends who have children.
31. Experiencing assaults to self-esteem and competency including interpersonal, sexual, medical and vocational disappointments.
32. Disinhibitors including drug abuse, unresolved conflicts, pornography and depression.
33. Secretive readings of self-help books.
34. Attempts to establish peer-like relationships with children.
35. Sexual conversation in presence of child, e.g., regarding clothing, body, humor and "sex education."
36. Insisting on going places alone (exhibitionist, voyeur, predatory pedophile).
37. Rationalizing the breaking of rules and laws.
38. Victim stance: self-piteous, blaming, regressed and brittle.
39. Discrediting child: unjustified criticisms, name-calling, disproportionate intensity.
40. Prolonged sexual abstinence; sexually transmitted disease although partner is asymptomatic (prostitution, anonymous gay sex, promiscuity, etc.).
41. Reluctance to discuss offense-related matters.
42. Avoidance of peers who are knowledgeable regarding offense and warning signs.
43. "Penance behaviors" vis-à-vis victim, e.g., favoritism, rescuing, deference and gift-giving.
44. _____
45. _____
46. _____

B. The Victim: Change in Pattern

1. Sleep disturbance: nightmares, bedwetting, sleeping in clothing.
2. Avoidance of offender: clinging to partner, loss of eye contact with offender, addressing father-offender by first name, refusal to talk with or discuss offender, ignoring Father's Day and his birthday, sleeping with siblings, refusal to attend family vacations and discussions, hiding in bedroom, frequently home late, distancing from other men and running away.
3. Appetite-weight change.
4. Unexplained fears and anxieties.
5. Victim questions mother about marital status-separation.
6. Bedroom door shut-locked.
7. Change in peer relationships: stops bringing friends home, protective of siblings.
8. Rebellious in home.
9. Legal problems: theft, alcohol, drugs, vandalism.

(continued)

APPENDIX Q Continued

10. Flight into adulthood (because childhood is painful).
11. School difficulty: discipline, truancy, homework not done, declining grades.
12. Escapes: suicide attempts, alcohol and drug abuse, running away, pregnancy, early marriage, home late, sleeping elsewhere.
13. Acute physical discomfort: infection, rash, abrasions, bloodstained clothing, complaints regarding frequent sore throats (forced sodomy) and sexually transmitted disease.
14. Medical complaints with no apparent basis in fact.
15. Pseudo-sophisticated or atypical sexual knowledge and behavior.
16. Compulsive cleanliness rituals, e.g., excessive washing of body and clothing.
17. Victim symptoms: including suicide attempts, severe depression, insecurity, promiscuity, poor hygiene, interpersonal problems, delinquency, withdrawal, and regressive behaviors; e.g., bedwetting, frequent crying, the creating of a fantasy world and thumb sucking.
18. Attempting to make self unattractive: obesity, unkempt appearance, poor hygiene, and self-mutilation.
19. Child reports victimation (believe her-him).
20. Child becomes physically-sexually abusive of siblings or others.
21. Collection of gifts, money, candy or privileges that child is reluctant to discuss.
22. _____
_____
23. _____
_____
24. _____
_____

SOURCE: Steven Silver and Northwest Treatment Associates, 315 W. Galer, Seattle, WA 98119; telephone (206) 283-8099. Reprinted by permission.

REFERENCES

Abel, G. G., Barlow, D. H., Blanchard, E. B., & Guild, D. (1977). The components of rapists' sexual arousal. *Archives of General Psychiatry, 34,* 895-903.

Abel, G. G., Becker, J. V., Cunningham-Rathner, J., Rouleau, J., Kaplan, M., & Reich, J. (1984). *The treatment of child molesters.* (Available from SBC-TM, 722 West 168th Street, Box 17, New York, NY 10032.)

Abel, G. G., Becker, J. V., Murphy, W. D., & Flanagan, B. (1981). Identifying dangerous child molesters. In R. B. Stuart (Ed.), *Violent behavior.* New York: Brunner/Mazel.

Abel, G. G., Blanchard, E. B., Barlow, D. H., & Mavissakalian, M. (1975). Identifying specific erotic cues in sexual deviation by audiotaped descriptions. *Journal of Applied Behavior Analysis, 8,* 247-260.

Abel, G. G., Blanchard, E. B., & Becker, J. V. (1978). An integrated treatment program for rapists. In R. Rada (Ed.), *Clinical aspects of the rapist.* New York: Grune & Stratton.

Abel, G. G., Blanchard, E. B., Becker, J. V., & Djenderedjian, A. (1978). Differentiating sexual aggressives with penile measures. *Criminal Justice and Behavior, 5,* 315-332.

Abel, G. G., Mittelman, M. S., & Becker, J. V. (1985). Sexual offenders: Results of assessment and recommendations for treatment. In M. H. Ben-Aron, S. J. Huckle, & C. D. Webster (Eds.), *Clinical criminology: The assessment and treatment of criminal behavior* (pp. 191-205). Toronto: M & M Graphic.

Abraham, K. (1927). The experiencing of sexual traumas as a form of sexual activity. In K. Abraham, *Selected papers* (pp. 47-62). London: Hogarth.

Achenbach, T. M. (1966). The classification of children's psychiatric symptoms: A factor-analytic study. *Psychological Monographs, 80*(7) 615, 1-37.

Achenbach, T. M., & Edelbrock, C. S. (1978). The classification of child psychopathology: A review and analysis of empirical efforts. *Psychological Bulletin, 85,* 1275-1301.

Achenbach, T. M., & Edelbrock, C. S. (1983). *Manual for the child behavior checklist and revised child behavior profile.* Burlington: University of Vermont, Department of Psychiatry.

Achenbach, T. M., & Edelbrock, C. S. (1984). Psychopathology of childhood. *Annual Review of Psychology, 35,* 227-256.

Alberti, R. E., & Emmons, M. L. (1982). *Your perfect right: A guide to assertive living.* San Luis Obispo, CA: Impact.

Alexander, P. C. (1985). A systems theory conceptualization of incest. *Family Process, 24,* 79-87.

Alter-Reid, K., Gibbs, M. S., Lachenmeyer, J. R., Sigal, J., & Massoth, N. A. (1986). Sexual abuse of children: A review of the empirical findings. *Clinical Psychology Review, 6,* 249-266.

American Psychiatric Association. (1968). *Diagnostic and statistical manual for mental disorders* (2nd ed.). Washington, DC: Author.

American Psychiatric Association. (1980). *Diagnostic and statistical manual of mental disorders* (3rd ed.). Washington, DC: Author.

Amir, M. (1971). *Patterns in forcible rape.* Chicago: University of Chicago Press.

Anderson, S. C., Bach, C. M., & Griffith, S. (1981, April). *Psychosocial sequelae in intrafamilial victims of sexual assault and abuse.* Paper presented at the Third International Congress on Child Abuse and Neglect, Amsterdam.

Annon, J. S. (1973). The composite fear inventory. In A. L. Comrey, T. E. Becker, & E. M. Glaser (Eds.), *A sourcebook for mental health measures.* Los Angeles: Human Interaction Research Institute.

Annon, J. S. (1974, 1975). *The behavioral treatment of sexual problems* (2 vols.). Honolulu: Enabling Systems.

Armentrout, J. A., & Hauer, A. L. (1978). MMPIs of rapists of adults, rapists of children, and non-rapist sex offenders. *Journal of Clinical Psychology, 34*(2), 330-332.

Badgley, R. (1984). *Sexual offenses against children: Report of the Committee on Sexual Offenses Against Children and Youths.* Ottawa: Government of Canada.

Bagley, C. (1985). Child sexual abuse: A child welfare perspective. In K. Levitt & B. Wharf (Eds.), *The challenge of child welfare* (pp. 66-92). Vancouver: University of British Columbia Press.

Bagley, C., & McDonald, M. (1984). Adult mental health sequels of child sexual abuse, physical abuse and neglect in maternally separated children. *Canadian Journal of Community Mental Health, 3,* 15-26.

Bandura, A. (1977). Self-efficacy: Toward a unifying theory of behavior change. *Psychological Review, 84,* 191-215.

Barbaree, H. E., Marshall, W. L., & Lanthier, R. D. (1979). Deviant sexual arousal in rapists. *Behavioral Research and Therapy, 17,* 215-222.

Barr, R. G., & Feuerstein, M. (1983). Recurrent abdominal pain syndrome: How appropriate are our basic clinical assumptions? In P. G. McGrath &

P. Firestone (Eds.), *Pediatric and adolescent behavioral medicine: Issues in treatment* (pp. 13-27). New York: Springer.

Bauer, D. H. (1977). An exploratory study of developmental changes in children's fears. In S. Chess & A. Thomas (Eds.), *Annual progress in child psychiatry and child development* (pp. 141-148). New York: Brunner/Mazel.

Becker, J. V., & Coleman, E. M. (in press). Incest. In V. B. Hasselt, R. L. Morrison, A. S. Bellack, & M. Hersen (Eds.), *Handbook of family violence.* New York: Plenum.

Becker, J. V., Skinner, L. J., Abel, G. G., & Cichon, J. (1986). Level of postassault sexual functioning in rape and incest victims. *Archives of Sexual Behavior, 15*(1), 37-49.

Bell, A. P., & Hall, C. S. (1971). *The personality of a child molester.* New York: Aldine.

Bender, L., & Blau, A. (1937, October). The reaction of children to sexual relations with adults. *American Journal of Orthopsychiatry,* pp. 500-518.

Benward, J. B., & Densen-Gerber, J. (1975). Incest as a causative factor in antisocial behavior: An exploratory study. *Contemporary Drug Problems, 4*, 323-340.

Berliner, L., & Ernst, E. (1984). Group work with preadolescent sexual assault victims. In I. R. Stuart & J. G. Greer (Eds.), *Victims of sexual aggression: Treatment of children, women and men* (pp. 105-124). New York: Van Nostrand Reinhold.

Black, C. (1981). *It will never happen to me.* Denver: M.A.C.

Blick, L. C., & Porter, F. S. (1982). Group therapy with female adolescent incest victims. In S. M. Sgroi, *Handbook of clinical intervention in child sexual abuse* (pp. 147-175). Lexington, MA: Lexington Books.

Blythe, M. J., & Orr, D. P. (1985, January). Childhood sexual abuse: Guidelines for evaluation. *Indiana Medicine,* pp. 11-18.

Brecher, E. M. (1978). *Treatment programs for sex offenders.* Washington, DC: Government Printing Office.

Briere, J. (1984, April). *The effects of childhood sexual abuse on later psychological functioning: Defining a post-sexual-abuse syndrome.* Paper presented at the Third National Conference on Sexual Victimization of Children, Washington, DC.

Briere, J., & Runtz, M. (1985, August). *Symptomatology associated with prior sexual abuse in a nonclinical sample.* Paper presented at the annual meeting of the American Psychological Association, Los Angeles.

Browne, A., & Finkelhor, D. (1986). Impact of child sexual abuse: A review of the research. *Psychological Bulletin, 99*(1), 66-77.

Browning, D., & Boatman, B. (1977). Incest: Children at risk. *American Journal of Psychiatry, 134*(1), 69-72.

Burt, M. R. (1980). Cultural myths and supports for rape. *Journal of Personality and Social Psychology, 38*(2), 217-230.

Burt, M. R. (1983). Justifying personal violence: A comparison of rapists and the general public. *Victimology: An International Journal, 8*(3-4), 131-150.

Burt, M. R., & Albin, R. S. (1981). Rape myths, rape definitions, and probability of conviction. *Journal of Applied Social Psychology, 11*(3), 212-230.

Buss, A. H., & Durkee, A. (1957). An inventory for assessing different kinds of hostility. *Journal of Consulting Psychology, 21*(4), 343-349.

Chaney, E. F., O'Leary, M. R., & Marlatt, G. A. (1978). Skill training with alcoholics. *Journal of Consulting and Clinical Psychology, 46,* 1092-1104.

Check, J. B., & Malamuth, N. (1985). An empirical assessment of some feminist hypotheses about rape. *International Journal of Women's Studies, 8,* 414-423.

Clark, C. A., O'Neil, J. A., & Laws, D. R. (1981). A comparison of intrafamilial sexual and physical sexual abuse. In M. Cook & K. Howells (Eds.), *Adult sexual interest in children* (pp. 3-39). New York: Academic Press.

Condiotte, M. M., & Lichtenstein, E. (1981). Self-efficacy and relapse in smoking cessation programs. *Journal of Consulting and Clinical Psychology, 49,* 648-658.

Cormier, B. M., Kennedy, M., & Sangowicz, J. (1962). Psychodynamics of father-daughter incest. *Canadian Psychiatric Association Journal, 7*(5), 203-217.

Crawford, D. A. (1981). Treatment approaches with pedophiles. In M. Cook & K. Howells (Eds.), *Adult sexual interest in children* (pp. 181-217). New York: Academic Press.

Crisci, G. A. (1983). *Personal safety curriculum: Prevention of child sexual abuse.* (Available from Personal Safety Program, P.O. Box 763, Hadley, MA 01035.)

Crooks, R., & Baur, K. (1987). *Our sexuality.* Menlo Park, CA: Benjamin.

Crystal, J. C., & Bolles, R. N. (1974). *Where do I go from here with my life?* Berkeley, CA: Ten Speed.

Cummings, C., Gordon, J., & Marlatt, G. A. (1980). Strategies of prevention and prediction. In W. R. Miller (Ed.), *The addictive behaviors: Treatment of alcoholism, drug abuse, smoking, and obesity.* New York: Pergamon.

Curran, J. P., & Monti, P. M. (1982). *Social skills training: A practical handbook for assessment and treatment.* New York: Guilford.

Davis, M. H. (1980). A multidimensional approach to individual differences in empathy. *JSAS catalog of selected documents in psychology, 10,* 85.

Davis, M. H. (1983a). The effects of dispositional empathy on emotional reactions and helping: A multidimensional approach. *Journal of Personality, 51*(2), 167-184.

Davis, M. H. (1983b). Empathic concern and the muscular dystrophy telethon: Empathy as a multidimensional construct. *Personality and Social Psychology Bulletin, 9*(2), 223-229.

Davis, M. H. (1983c). Measuring individual differences in empathy:

Evidence for a multidimensional approach. *Journal of Personality and Social Psychology, 44,* 113-126.

DeYoung, M. (1982). *The sexual victimization of children.* Jefferson, NC: McFarland.

Donaldson, M. A. (1983, November). *Incest victims years after: Methods and techniques for treatment.* Paper presented at the National Association of Social Workers Professional Symposium, Washington, DC.

Eisenhower, M. S. (1969). *To establish justice, to insure domestic tranquility.* Final Report of the National Commission on Causes and Prevention of Violence. Washington, DC: Government Printing Office.

Eist, H. I., & Mandel, A. U. (1968). Family treatment of ongoing incest behavior. *Family Process, 7,* 216-232.

Elkind, D. (1984). *All grown up and no place to go: Teenagers in crisis.* Reading, MA: Addison-Wesley.

Eysenck, H. J. (1953). *The structure of human personality.* New York: John Wiley.

Fattah, E. A. (1967). Towards a criminological classification of victims. *International Review of Criminal Police, 209,* 162-169.

Fay, J. J., & Flerchinger, B. J. (1982). *Top secret* (Available from King County Rape Relief, 305 South 43rd, Renton, Washington 98055.)

Field, L. H., & Williams, M. (1970). The hormonal treatment of sexual offenders. *Medicine, Science and the Law, 10,* 27-34.

Finkelhor, D. (1979). *Sexually victimized children.* New York: Free Press.

Finkelhor, D. (1984). *Child sexual abuse: New theory and research.* New York: Free Press.

Forward, S., & Buck, C. (1978). *Betrayal of innocence: Incest and its devastation.* New York: J. P. Tarcher.

Freeman-Longo, R. E., & Wall, R. V. (1986, March). Changing a lifetime of sexual crime. *Psychology Today,* pp. 58-64.

Freud, A. (1981). A psychoanalyst's view of sexual abuse by parents. In P. B. Mrazek & C. H. Kempe, *Sexually abused children and their families* (pp. 33-34). New York: Pergamon.

Freund, K., McKnight, C. K., Langevin, R., & Cibiri, S. (1972). The female child as a surrogate object. *Archives of Sexual Behavior, 2*(2), 119-133.

Friedlander, K. (1947). *The psycho-analytical approach to juvenile delinquency.* London: Kegan Paul, Trench, Trubner.

Friedrich, W. N., Urquiza, A. J., & Beilke, R. L. (1986). Behavior problems in sexually abused young children. *Journal of Pediatric Psychology, 11*(1), 47-57.

Frisbie, L. (1969). *Another look at sex offenders in California* (Research Monograph No. 12). Sacramento: California Department of Mental Hygiene.

Fritz, G. S., Stoll, K., & Wagner, N. (1981). A comparison of males and females who were sexually molested as children. *Journal of Sex and Marital Therapy, 7*(1), 54-59.

Fromuth, M. F. (1983). *The long term psychological impact of childhood sexual abuse.* Unpublished doctoral dissertation, Auburn University, Alabama.

Gagnon, J. H. (1965). Female child victims of sex offense. *Social Problems, 13*(2), 176-192.

Gebhard, P. H., Gagnon, J. H., Pomeroy, W. B., & Christenson, C. V. (1965). *Sex offenders: An analysis of types.* New York: Harper & Row.

Giarretto, Henry (1982). *Integrated treatment of child sexual abuse.* Palo Alto, CA: Science & Behavior.

Glasser, W. (1976). *Positive addiction.* New York: Harper & Row.

Golla, F. L., & Hodge, R. S. (1949). Hormone treatment of the sexual offender. *Lancet, 1,* 1006-1007.

Goodwin, J., McCarthy, T., DiVasto, P. (1981). Prior incest in mothers of abused children. *Child Abuse and Neglect, 5,* 87-96.

Goodwin, J., McCarty, T., DiVasto, P. (1982). Physical and sexual abuse of the children of adult incest victims. In J. Goodwin (Ed.), *Sexual abuse: Incest victims and their families* (pp. 139-154). Littleton, MA: PSG.

Gordon, L. (1955). Incest as revenge against the pre-Oedipal mother. *Psychoanalytic Review, 42,* 284-292.

Gosselin, C., & Wilson, G. (1980). *Sexual variations: Fetishism, sado-masochism, and transvestism.* New York: Simon & Schuster.

Groth, A. N. (1982). The incest offender. In S. Sgroi, *Handbook of clinical intervention in child sexual abuse* (pp. 215-239). Lexington, MA: Lexington Books.

Groth, A. N. (1983). Treatment of the sexual offender in a correctional institution. In J. G. Greer & I. R. Stuart (Eds.), *The sexual aggressor: Current perspectives on treatment.* New York: Van Nostrand Reinhold.

Groth, Nicholas (1979). *Men who rape: The psychology of the offender.* New York: Plenum.

Group for the Advancement of Psychiatry (1977). *Psychiatry and sex psychopath legislation: The 30's to the 80's.* New York: Group for the Advancement of Psychiatry.

Gruber, K. J., & Jones, R. J. (1983). Identifying determinants of risk of sexual victimization of youth: A multivariate approach. *Child Abuse and Neglect, 7,* 17-24.

Gutheil, T. G., & Avery, N. C. (1977). Multiple overt incest as family defense against loss. *Family Process, 16*(1), 105-116.

Hall, G. C., Maiuro, R. D., Vitaliano, P. P., & Proctor, W. C. (1986). The utility of the MMPI with men who have sexually assaulted children. *Journal of Consulting and Clinical Psychology, 54*(4), 493-496.

Hamilton, G. V. (1929). *A research in marriage.* New York: Albert & Charles Boni.

Harrison, P. A., & Lumry, A. E. (1984, August). *Female sexual abuse victims: Perspectives on family dysfunction, substance use and psychiatric disorders.* Paper presented at the Second National Conference for Family Violence Researchers, University of New Hampshire, Durham.

Hayman, C. R., Stewart, W. F., Lewis, F. R., & Grant, M. (1968). Sexual assault on women and children in the District of Columbia. *Public Health Reports, 83*(12), 1021-1028.

Heims, L. W., & Kaufman, I. (1963). Variations on a theme of incest. *American Journal of Orthopsychiatry, 33*(2), 311-312.

Henderson, D. J. (1975). Incest. In A. M. Freedman, H. I. Kaplan, & B. J. Sadock (Eds.), *Comprehensive textbook of psychiatry* (2nd ed., pp. 1530-1539). Baltimore: Williams & Wilkins.

Henderson, J. (1983). Is incest harmful? *Canadian Journal of Psychiatry, 28,* 34-40.

Herman, J., & Hirschman, L. (1977). Father-daughter incest. *Signs: Journal of Women in Culture and Society, 2*(4), 735-756.

Herman, J., & Hirschman, L. (1981). Families at risk for father-daughter incest. *American Journal of Psychiatry, 138*(7), 967-970.

Herman, Judith (1981). *Father-daughter incest.* Cambridge, MA: Harvard University Press.

Hindman, J. (1985). *A very touching book.* (Available from McClure-Hindman Associates, P.O. Box 208, Durkee, OR.)

Howells, K. (1981). Adult sexual interest in children: Considerations relevant to theories of aetiology. In M. Cook & K. Howells (Eds.), *Adult sexual interest in children* (pp. 55-94). New York: Academic Press.

Hunt, W. A., Barnett, L. W., & Branch, L. G. (1971). Relapse rates in addiction programs. *Journal of Clinical Psychology, 27,* 455-456.

Hursch, C. J. (1977). *The trouble with rape.* Chicago: Nelson-Hall.

James, B., & Nasjleti, M. (1983). *Treating sexually abused children and their families.* Palo Alto, CA: Consulting Psychologists.

James, J., & Meyerding, J. (1977). Early sexual experiences and prostitution. *American Journal of Psychiatry, 134,* 1381-1385.

Janus, M., Scanlon, B., & Price, V. (1984). Youth prostitution. In A. W. Burgess (Ed.), *Child pornography and sex rings* (pp. 127-146). Lexington, MA: Lexington Books.

Jones, D. P., & McGraw, J. M. (1987). Reliable and fictitious accounts of sexual abuse to children. *Journal of Interpersonal Violence, 2*(1), 27-45.

Justice, B., & Justice, R. (1979). *The broken taboo.* New York: Human Services.

Kaplan, H. S. (1974). *The new sex therapy: Active treatment of sexual dysfunctions.* New York: Brunner/Mazel.

Katz, S., & Mazur, M. A. (1979). *Understanding the rape victim: A synthesis of research findings.* New York: John Wiley.

Kaufman, I., Peck, A. L., Tagiuri, C. K. (1954). The family constellation and overt incestuous relationships between father and daughter. *American Journal of Orthopsychiatry, 24,* 266-279.

Kent, C. A. (1982) *No easy answers: A sexual abuse prevention curriculum for junior and senior high students.* (Available from Illusion Theater, 304 N. Washington, Minneapolis, MN 55401.)

Kercher, G. A. (1980). *Responding to child sexual abuse: A report to the 67th Session of the Texas Legislature*. Huntsville, TX: Sam Houston State University, Criminal Justice Center.

Kerns, D. L. (1981). Medical assessment of child sexual abuse. In P. B. Mrazek & C. H. Kempe, *Sexually abused children and their families* (pp. 129-141). New York: Pergamon.

Kilpatrick, A. C. (1986). Some correlates of women's childhood sexual experiences: A retrospective study. *Journal of Sex Research, 22*(2), pp. 221-242.

Kinsey, A. C., Pomeroy, W. B., Martin, C. E., & Gebhard, P. H. (1948). *Sexual behavior in the human male*. Philadelphia: Saunders.

Kinsey, A. C., Pomeroy, W. B., Martin, C. E., & Gebhard, P. H. (1953). *Sexual behavior in the human female*. Philadelphia: Saunders.

Knight, R. A., Rosenberg, R., & Schneider, B. A. (1985). Classification of sexual offenders: Perspectives, methods, and validation. In A. W. Burgess (Ed.), *Rape and sexual assault: A research handbook* (pp. 222-293). New York: Garland.

Knittle, B. J., & Tuana, S. J. (1980). Group therapy as primary treatment for adolescent victims in intrafamilial sexual abuse. *Clinical Social Work Journal, 8*(4), 236-242.

Knopp, F. H. (1982). *Remedial intervention in adolescent sex offenses: Nine program descriptions*. Orwell, VT: Safer Society.

Knopp, F. H. (1984). *Retraining adult sex offenders: Methods and models*. Orwell, VT: Safer Society.

Koss, M. P. (1985). *Hidden rape: Survey of psychopathological consequences* (final report of NIMH Grant RO1MH31618).

Koss, M. P., Leonard, K. E., Beezley, D. A., & Oros, C. J. (1981, August). *Personality and attitudinal characteristics of sexually aggressive men.* Paper presented at the annual meeting of the American Psychological Association, Los Angeles.

Koss, M. P., Leonard, K. E., Beezley, D. A., & Oros, C. J. (1985). Nonstranger sexual aggression: A discriminant analysis of the psychological characteristics of undetected offenders. *Sex Roles, 12*(9/10), 981-991.

Krasner, W., Meyer, L. C., & Carroll, N. E. (1976). *Victims of rape*. Washington, DC: Government Printing Office.

Krieger, M. J., Rosenfeld, A. A., Gordon, A., & Bennett, M. (1980). Problems in the psychotherapy of children with histories of incest. *American Journal of Psychotherapy, 34*(1), 81-88.

Kubo, S. (1959). Researches and studies on incest in Japan. *Hiroshima Journal of Medical Sciences, 8*(1), 99-159.

Landis, C. (1940). *Sex in development*. New York: Hoeber.

Landis, J. T. (1956). Experiences of 500 children with adult sexual deviation. *Psychiatric Quarterly Supplement, 30* (Part 1), 91-109.

Langevin, R. (1983). *Sexual strands: Understanding and treating sex anomalies in men*. Hillsdale, NJ: Lawrence Erlbaum.

Langevin, R., Paitich, D., Freeman, R., Mann, K., & Handy, L. (1978). Personality characteristics and sexual anomalies in males. *Canadian Journal of Behavioral Science, 10*(3), 222-238.

Lanyon, R. I. (1986). Theory and treatment in child molestation. *Journal of Consulting and Clinical Psychology, 54*(2), 176-182.

Laws, D. R., & Osborn, C. A. (1983). How to build and operate a laboratory to evaluate and treat sexual deviance. In J. G. Greer & I. R. Stuart (Eds.), *The sexual aggressor: Current perspectives on treatment.* New York: Van Nostrand Reinhold.

Liberman, R. P., King, L. W., DeRisi, W. J., & McCann, M. J. (1976). *Personal effectiveness training: Guiding people to assert their feelings and improve their social skills.* Champaign, IL: Research.

Lubell, D., & Soong, W. (1982). Group therapy with sexually abused adolescents. *Canadian Journal of Psychiatry, 27,* 311-315.

Lukianowicz, N. (1972). Incest I: Paternal incest. *British Journal of Psychiatry, 120,* 301-313.

Lustig, N., Dresser, J. W., Spellman, S. W., & Murray, T. B. (1966). Incest: A family group survival pattern. *Archives of General Psychiatry, 14,* 31-40.

Lutz, S. E., & Medway, J. P. (1984). Contextual family therapy with the victims of incest. *Journal of Adolescence, 7,* 319-327.

MacDonald, J. M. (1971). *Rape offenders and their victims.* Springfield, IL: Charles C Thomas.

Machotka, P., Pittman, F. S., & Flomenhaft, K. (1967). Incest as a family affair. *Family Process, 6,* 98-116.

MacVicar, K. (1979). Psychotherapeutic issues in the treatment of sexually abused girls. *Journal of the American Academy of Child Psychiatry, 18,* 342-353.

Mahoney, M. J. (1979). *Self-change: Strategies for solving personal problems.* New York: Norton.

Maisch, H. (1972). *Incest.* New York: Stein & Day.

Marlatt, G. A. (1982). Relapse prevention: A self-control program for the treatment of addictive behaviors. In R. B. Stuart (Ed.), *Adherence, compliance, and generalization in behavioral medicine.* New York: Brunner/Mazel.

Marlatt, G. A., & Gordon, J. (1980). Determinants of relapse: Implications for maintenance of change. In P. O. Davidson & S. M. Davidson (Eds.), *Behavioral medicine: Changing health lifestyles.* New York: Brunner/Mazel.

Marlatt, G. A., & Gordon, J. R. (1985). *Relapse prevention.* New York: Guilford.

Masson, J. M. (1984). *The assault on truth.* New York: Farrar, Straus & Giroux.

Mayer, A. (1983). *Incest: A treatment manual for therapy with victims, spouses and offenders.* Holmes Beach, FL: Learning.

McCown, D. E. (1981, July/August). Father/daughter incest: A family problem. *Pediatric Nursing,* pp. 25-28.

Meichenbaum, D. (1977). *Cognitive-behavior modification*. New York: Plenum.

Meiselman, K. (1978). *Incest*. San Francisco: Jossey-Bass.

Meyer, A. (1983). Origins and prevention of emotional disturbances among learning disabled children. *Topics in Learning Disabilities, 3*(2), 59-70.

Mian, M., Wehrspann, W., Klajner-Diamond, H., LeBaron, D., & Winder, C. (1986). Review of 125 children 6 years of age and under who were sexually abused. *Child Abuse and Neglect, 10*, 223-229.

Miller, W. R. (1980). The addictive behaviors. In W. R. Miller (Ed.), *The addictive behaviors: Treatment of alcoholism, drug abuse, smoking, and obesity*. New York: Pergamon.

Mohr, J. W. (1981). Age structures in pedophilia. In M. Cook & K. Howells *Adult sexual interest in children* (pp. 41-53). New York: Academic.

Mohr, J. W., Turner, R. E., & Jerry, M. B. (1964). *Pedophilia and exhibition-ism*. Toronto: University of Toronto Press.

Molnar, G., & Cameron, P. (1975). Incest syndromes: Observations in a general psychiatric unit. *Canadian Psychiatric Association Journal, 20*(5), 373-377.

Mrazek, P. J., & Bentovim, A. (1981). Incest and the dysfunctional family system. In P. B. Mrazek & C. H. Kempe, *Sexually abused children and their families* (pp. 167-177). New York: Pergamon.

Mrazek, P. J., Lynch, M. A., & Bentovim, A. (1983). Sexual abuse of children in the United Kingdom. *Child Abuse and Neglect, 7*, 147-153.

Mulvihill, D., Tumin, M., & Curtis, L. (1969). *Crimes of violence: A staff report submitted to the National Commission on the Causes and Prevention of Violence* (Vol 2). Washington, DC: Government Printing Office.

Murphy, W. D., Haynes, M. R., Stalgaitis, S. J., & Flanagan, B. (1986). Differential sexual responding among four groups of sexual offenders against children. *Journal of Psychopathology and Behavioral Assessment, 8*(4), 339-353.

Nichols, H. R., & Molinder, I. (1984). *Multiphasic sex inventory manual*. (Available from Nichols & Molinder, 437 Bowes Drive, Tacoma, WA 98466.)

Novaco, R. W. (1977). Stress inoculation: A cognitive therapy for anger and its application to a case of depression. *Journal of Consulting and Clinical Psychology, 45*, 600-608.

Nowicki, S. (1975). The effect of locus of control on peer relationships across age groups. *Journal of Genetic Psychology, 43*, 275-280.

Nowicki, S. (1976). The factor structure of locus of control at three different ages. *Journal of Genetic Psychology, 129*, 13-17.

Nowicki, S. (n.d.). *Adult Nowicki-Strickland Internal-External Locus of Control Scale*. (Test manual available from S. Nowicki, Jr., Department of Psychology, Emory University, Atlanta, GA 30322.)

Nowicki, S., & Duke, M. P. (1974). A locus of control scale for college as well as non-college adults. *Journal of Personality Assessment, 38*, 136-137.

Olson, D. H., Portner, J., & Lavee, Y. (1985). *FACES III*. (Available from Family Social Science, University of Minnesota, 290 McNeal Hall, St. Paul, MN 55108.)

Overholser, J. C., & Beck, S. (1986). Multimethod assessment of rapists, child molesters, and three control groups on behavioral and psychological measures. *Journal of Consulting and Clinical Psychology, 54*(5), 682-687.

Pacht, A. R., Halleck, S. L., & Ehrmann, J. C. (1962). Diagnosis and treatment of the sexual offender: A nine-year study. *American Journal of Psychiatry, 118,* 802-808.

Paitich, D., Langevin, R., Freeman, R., Mann, K., & Handy, L. (1977). The Clark Sexual History Questionnaire: A clinical sex history questionnaire for males. *Archives of Sexual Behavior, 6*(5), 421-435.

Panton, J. H. (1978). Personality differences appearing between rapists of adults, rapists of children and non-violent sexual molesters of female children. *Research Communications in Psychology, Psychiatry and Behavior, 3*(4), 385-393.

Panton, J. H. (1979). MMPI profile configurations associated with incestuous and non-incestuous child molesting. *Psychological Reports, 45,* 335-338.

Peters, J. J. (1976). Children who are victims of sexual assault and the psychology of offenders. *American Journal of Psychotherapy, 30,* 398-421.

Peterson, D. R. (1961). Behavior problems of middle childhood. *Journal of Consulting Psychology, 25,* 205-209.

Pithers, W. D., Buell, M. M., Kashima, K. M., Cumming, G. F., & Beal, L. S. (1987). Precursors to sexual offenses. *Proceedings of the First Annual Meeting of the Association for the Behavioral Treatment of Sexual Aggressors.* Newport, OR.

Pithers, W. D., Marques, J. K., Gibat, C. C., & Marlatt, G. A. (1983). Relapse prevention with sexual aggressives: A self-control model of treatment and maintenance of change. In J. G. Greer & I. R. Stuart (Eds.), *The sexual aggressor: Current perspectives on treatment.* New York: Van Nostrand Reinhold.

Plummer, K. (1981). Pedophilia: Constructing a sociological baseline. In M. Cook & K. Howells (Eds.), *Adult sexual interest in children* (pp. 221-250). New York: Academic Press.

Poznanski, E., & Blos, P. (1975, October). Incest. *Medical Aspects of Human Sexuality,* pp. 46-76.

Quinsey, V. L. (1977). The assessment and treatment of child molesters: A review. *Canadian Psychological Review, 18*(3), 204-220.

Quinsey, V. L., Arnold, L. S., & Pruesse, M. G. (1980). MMPI profiles of men referred for a pretrial assessment as a function of offense type. *Journal of Clinical Psychology, 36*(2), 410-417.

Quinsey, V. L., Bergersen, S. G., & Steinman, C. M. (1976). Changes in physiological and verbal responses of child molesters during aversion therapy. *Canadian Journal of Behavioral Science, 8*(2), 202-212.

Quinsey, V. L., Chaplin, T. C., & Carrigan, W. F. (1979). Sexual preferences among incestuous and nonincestuous child molesters. *Behavior Therapy, 10,* 562-565.

Quinsey, V. L., Chaplin, T. C., & Carrigan, W. F. (1980). Biofeedback and signaled punishment in the modification of inappropriate sexual age preferences. *Behavior Therapy, 11,* 567-576.

Quinsey, V. L., & Marshall, W. L. (1983). Procedures for reducing inappropriate sexual arousal: An evaluation review. In J. G. Greer & I. R. Stuart (Eds.), *The sexual aggressor: Current perspectives in treatment.* New York: Van Nostrand Reinhold.

Rada, R. T. (1976). Alcoholism and the child molester. *Annals of the New York Academy of Science, 273,* 492-496.

Rascovsky, M. W., & Rascovsky, A. (1950). On consummated incest. *International Journal of Psychoanalysis, 31,* 42-47.

Reich, J. W., & Gutierres, S. E. (1979). Escape/aggression incidence in sexually abused juvenile delinquents. *Criminal Justice and Behavior, 6,* 239-243.

Revitch, E., & Weiss, R. G. (1962). The pedophiliac offender. *Diseases of the Nervous System, 23,* 73-78.

Riemer, S. (1940). A research note on incest. *American Journal of Sociology, 7,* 566-575.

Rosen, R. C., & Fracher, J. C. (1983). Tension-reduction training in the treatment of compulsive sex offenders. In J. G. Greer & I. R. Stuart (Eds.), *The sexual aggressor: Current perspectives in treatment.* New York: Van Nostrand Reinhold.

Rush, F. (1980). *The best kept secret: Sexual abuse of children.* New York: McGraw-Hill.

Russell, D. (1975). *The politics of rape: The victim's perspective.* New York: Stein & Day.

Russell, D. (1984). *Sexual exploitation: Rape, child sexual abuse, and workplace harassment.* Beverly Hills, CA: Sage.

Sarles, R. M. (1975). Incest. *Pediatric Clinics of North America, 22*(3), 633-642.

Schiff, A. F. (1969). Statistical features of rape. *Journal of Forensic Sciences, 14*(1), 102-110.

Sedney, M. A., & Brooks, B. (1984). Factors associated with a history of childhood sexual experiences in a nonclinical female population. *Journal of the American Academy of Child Psychiatry, 23*(2), 215-218.

Seghorn, T., Boucher, R., & Cohen, M. (1983, May 22-27). Paper presented at the Sixth World Congress for Sexology, Washington, DC.

Seidner, A. L., Calhoun, K. S., & Kilpatrick, D. G. (1985, August). *Childhood and/or adolescent sexual experiences: Predicting variability in subsequent adjustment.* Paper presented at the 93rd Annual Convention of the American Psychological Association, Los Angeles.

Selzer, M. L. (1971). The Michigan Alcoholism Screening Test: The quest for a new diagnostic instrument. *American Journal of Psychiatry, 127,* 1653-1658.

Sgroi, S. (1982). *Handbook of clinical intervention in child sexual abuse.* Lexington, MA: Lexington Books.

Sgroi, S. M., Porter, F. S., & Blick, L. C. (1982). Validation of child sexual abuse. In S. M. Sgroi, *Handbook of clinical intervention in child sexual abuse* (pp. 39-79). Lexington, MA: Lexington Books.

Silbert, M. H. (1984). Treatment of prostitute victims of sexual assault. In I. R. Stuart & J. G. Greer (Eds.), *Victims of sexual aggression: Treatment of children, women, and men* (pp. 251-269). New York: Van Nostrand Reinhold.

Silbert, M. H., & Pines, A. M. (1981). Sexual child abuse as an antecedent to prostitution. *Child Abuse and Neglect, 5,* 407-411.

Silver, L. B. (1984). *The misunderstood child.* New York: McGraw-Hill.

Silver, R. L., Boon, C., & Stones, M. H. (1983). Searching for meaning in misfortune: Making sense of incest. *Journal of Social Issues, 39*(2), 81-102.

Skinner, H. A., & Sheu, W. (1982). Reliability of alcohol use indices: The lifetime drinking history and the MAST. *Journal of Studies on Alcohol, 43*(11), 1157-1170.

Slovenko, R. (1971). Statutory rape. *Medical Aspects of Human Sexuality, 5,* 155-167.

Solomon, R. L. (1980). The opponent process theory of acquired motivation: The costs of pleasure and the benefits of pain. *American Psychologist, 35,* 691-712.

Sorrenti-Little, L., Bagley, C., & Robertson, S. (1984). An operational definition of the long-term harmfulness of sexual relations with peers and adults by young children. *Canadian Children: Journal of the Canadian Association for Young Children, 9*(1).

Spence, J. T., & Helmreich, R. L. (1972). The Attitudes Toward Women Scale: An objective instrument to measure attitudes towards the rights and roles of women in contemporary society. *Psychological Documents, 2*(153).

Spence, J. T., & Helmreich, R. L. (1978). *Masculinity and femininity: Their psychological dimensions, correlates and antecedents.* Austin: University of Texas Press.

Strong, B., Wilson, S., Robbins, M., & Johns, T. (1981). *Human sexuality: Essentials* (2nd ed.). St. Paul, MN: West.

Sturgeon, H., Taylor, J., Goldman, R., Hunter, M., & Webster, D. (1979). *Report on mentally disordered sex offenders released from Atascadero State Hospital.* Atascadero, CA: Atascadero State Hospital.

Sturkie, K. (1983). Structured group treatment for sexually abused children. *Health and Social Work, 8,* 299-308.

Sturup, G. K. (1972). Castration: The total treatment. In H.L.P. Resnick & M. E. Wolfgang (Eds.), *Sexual behaviors: Social, clinical, and legal aspects.* Boston: Little, Brown.

Summit, R., & Kryso, J. (1978). Sexual abuse of children: A clinical spectrum. *American Journal of Orthopsychiatry, 48*(2), 237-251.

Svalastoga, K. (1962). Rape and social structures. *Pacific Sociological Review, 5*, 48-53.

Swanson, D. W. (1968). Adult sexual abuse of children. *Diseases of the Nervous System, 29*(10), 677-683.

Sweet, P. E. (1981). *Something happened to me.* Racine, WI: Mother Courage.

Taylor, E. A. (1986). Childhood hyperactivity. *British Journal of Psychiatry, 149*, 562-573.

Taylor, R. L. (1984). Marital therapy in the treatment of incest. *Social Casework: The Journal of Contemporary Social Work, 65*(4), 195-202.

Teague, G. B. (1979). *Alienation, systems, and praxis: Toward a concept of public practice.* Unpublished doctoral dissertation, Harvard University.

Terman, L. (1951). Correlates of orgasm adequacy in a group of 556 wives. *Journal of Psychology, 32*, 115-172.

Terman, L. M. (1938). *Psychological factors in marital happiness.* New York: McGraw-Hill.

Thoinot, L., & Weysse, A. W. (1911). *Medicolegal aspects of moral offenses.* Philadelphia: F. A. Davis.

Tongue, E., & Blair, B. (1975). Appendix 1. *Proceedings of the 31st International Conference on Alcoholism and Drug Dependence.*

Toobert, S., Bartelme, K., & Jones, E. S. (1959). Some factors related to pedophilia. *International Journal of Social Psychiatry, 4*, 272-279.

Tormes, Y. (1968). *Child victims of incest.* Denver: American Humane Association, Children's Division.

Virkkunen, M. (1974). Incest offenses and alcoholism. *Medicine, Science, & the Law, 14*, 124-128.

Virkkunen, M. (1975). Victim-precipitated pedophilia offenses. *British Journal of Criminology, 15*(2), 175-180.

Virkkunen, M. (1981). The child as participating victim. In M. Cook & K. Howells (Eds.), *Adult sexual interest in children* (pp. 121-134). New York: Academic Press.

Wallerstein, J. S., & Kelly, J. B. (1980). *Surviving the breakup: How children and parents cope with divorce.* New York: Basic Books.

Wasserman, J., & Kappel, S. (1985). *Adolescent sex offenders in Vermont.* (unpublished)

Watson, D., & Friend, R. (1969). Measurement of social-evaluative anxiety. *Journal of Consulting and Clinical Psychology, 33*(4), 448-457.

Weinberg, S. K. (1955, 1976). *Incest behavior.* New York: Citadel.

Weiner, I. B. (1962). Father-daughter incest: A clinical report. *Psychiatric Quarterly, 36*(1), 607-632.

Weiss, J., Rogers, E., Darwin, M. R., & Dutton, C. E. (1955). A study of girl sex victims. *Psychiatry Quarterly, 29*, 1-27.

Wender, P. H. (1987). *The hyperactive child, adolescent and adult.* New York: Oxford University Press.

West, D. J. (1981). Adult sexual interest in children: Implications for social control. In M. Cook & K. Howells (Eds.), *Adult sexual interest in children* (pp. 251-270). New York: Academic.

Wilson, Glenn (1978). *The secrets of sexual fantasy.* London: J. M. Dent.

Wright, R. (1980). Rape and physical violence. In D. J. West (Ed.), *Sex offenders in the criminal justice system.* Cambridge: Institute of Criminology.

Yochelson, S., & Samenow, S. (1976). *The criminal personality: Vol 1. A profile for change.* New York: Jason Aronson.

Young, W., & Waite, C. (1982). *Final report: Sex offender planning grant, Vermont Department of Corrections.* (unpublished)

Zilbergeid, B. (1978). *Male sexuality: A guide to sexual fulfillment.* New York: Brown.

INDEX

Note: f *after page number indicates figure;* t *indicates table.*

therapy, 126-128; maintaining therapeutic gains, 140-170; misconceptions about therapy, 138-140, 146; nonconfrontational techniques, 147; precursors to, 134-138, 136t, 137t; recidivism rates, 139; and the relapse process, 141-146, 142f; research studies, 134, 135, 157-158, 136t, 137t; stages of treatment, 140; successful coping, 141; tenets of a modified model, 141; treatment procedures, 153-169, 154f; unsuccessful coping, 141-142

Research studies: Abel et al. (1975), 197; (1977), 197; (1978), 197; (1981), 190-191, 197; (1985), 46, 103, 122, 184, 186-187, 190-191, 193, 201; Achenback (1966), 228; Achenbach and Edelbrock (1978), 229; (1984), 229; on adolescents as victims and offenders, 16-17, 19-21, 46, 70, 18t, 21t; on age of offenders, 16, 20, 47, 70; on age of victims, 16, 19-21, 46, 70, 18t, 21t; on alcoholism and sexual aggression, 193, 202f; Amir (1971), 20; Armentrout and Hauer (1978), 194; on assertiveness, 122; on attitudes toward women, 189, 280; Badgley (1984), 19-20, 21, 18t; Bagley (1985), 20, 18t; Barbaree et al. (1979), 197; Becker and Coleman (forthcoming), 41-42, 49; on behavioral indicators, 228-229; Benward and Densen-Gerber (1975), 234; Briere and Runtz (1985), 18t; Burt (1980), 189; (1983), 190; Burt and Albin (1981), 190; Buss and Durkee (1957), 286; Chaney et al. (1978), 157-158; Check and Malamuth (1985), 190; of clinical interviews, 186-187; of clinical populations, 16; on college populations, 17; Cummings et al. (1980), 135; and data analysis by age, 19; Davis (1983c), 192, 290; on defining sexual abuse, 17, 21; on delinquent behavior of victims, 234-235; Donaldson (1983), 223; on empathy, 192, 290, 202f; on external/internal control of behavior, 309; on false reporting of sexual abuse, 236-237; on family adaptability and cohesion, 192, 202f; Finkelhor (1979), 17, 18t; (1984), 223; Freeman-Longo and

Wall (1986), 46; Freidrich et al. (1986), 229; Fritz et al. (1981), 16, 17, 18t; Fromuth (1983), 18t; Gagnon (1965), 22, 28-29, 21t; Gebhard et al. (1965), 31-32, 47; Gosselin and Wilson (1980), 297; Groth (1979), 47; Hall et al. (1986), 194; Hamilton (1921), 21; (1929), 21, 21t; Herman and Hirschman (1981), 234; Himmelweit (in Eysenck, 1953), 228; of homosexual incest, 23; Horowitz et al. (in Jones and McGraw, 1987), 237; on hostility, 190-191, 286; Howells (1981), 198, 201; Hunt et al. (1971), 134-135; on internalizing and externalizing symptoms, 229; Jones and McGraw (1987), 236-237; Jones and Seig (in Jones and McGraw, 1987), 241; Katz and Mazur (1979), 20, 237; Kercher (1980), 18t; Kilpatrick (1986), 19, 18t; Kinsey et al. (1948), 24; (1953), 21-24, 21t; Knopp (1984), 48; Koss (1985), 100; Koss et al. (1981), 189; (1985), 189; Landis (1940), 21, 22; (1956), 22, 21t, Langevin (1983), 47-48; Langevin et al. (1978), 194; on marital status of offenders, 47, 49; Meiselman (1978), 234; Mian et al. (1986), 54, 241; Mohr et al. (1964), 46, 47; Mulvihill et al. (1969), 20; methodologies of, 16-24; on multiple deviant behavior, 103; of myths about rape, 189-190, 282; on negative evaluation, 201, 202f; of nonclinical populations, 16; of noncollege populations, 17; Nowicki (1975), 309; Nowicki and Duke (1973), 309; on offender denial, 100; on offenders as sexually abused children, 47-48; older, 21t; Olson et al. (1985), 192; on overall reporting of sexual abuse, 223-224; Overholser and Beck (1986), 201; Panton (1978), 194; of pedophiles, 46-49; of personality profiles, 194; of personality types of offenders, 184; Peters (1976), 20, 55, 190, 193, 237; Pithers et al. (1987), 135, 136t, 137t; of precursors to sexual aggression, 135, 136t, 137t; Quinsey et al. (1976), 197; (1980), 194, 197; Rada (1976), 47, 193; of rape myth beliefs, 189-190, 282; recent, 18t;

ABOUT THE CONTRIBUTORS

Anna C. Salter, Ph.D., is Assistant Professor of Clinical Psychiatry and Maternal and Child Health at Dartmouth Medical School. This joint appointment in Psychiatry and Pediatrics (Maternal and Child Health) involves her in teaching psychological interns, psychiatric residents, and pediatric residents. As Director of Psychosocial Education for the Pediatric Residency Program, she is responsible for behavioral pediatric training within the Department of Maternal and Child Health. She is also the Codirector of the Parenting Clinic at the Hitchcock Medical Center.

Dr. Salter received her Ph.D. in clinical psychology and public practice from Harvard University and a master's degree in child study from Tufts University. She was a teaching fellow at both universities. She has worked in the field of sexual deviancy for approximately eight years. She currently treats sex offenders and their families, coleads a group for adolescent offenders, supervises adult offender therapists and child victim therapists, and is a consultant to the National Institute of Corrections.

As the Assistant Director of the Children at Risk Program at Dartmouth Hitchcock Medical Center, Dr. Salter is currently conducting a research project titled "Correlates of Sexual Offending: The Role of Psychopathology, Empathy, and Life Stress." She is also the head of the Child Abuse Treatment Program, a new program that is developing and piloting specialized treatment for parents who physically abuse their children. She lectures widely on child physical and sexual abuse.

Linda S. Beal, M.A., is a Probation and Parole Officer, and is a member of the treatment team for the Vermont Treatment Program for Sexual Aggressors. She has been centrally involved in creating the relapse prevention approach to the supervision of sexual aggressors. She has conducted training for probation and parole officers and mental health clinicians in many states, and is the coauthor of several papers on the relapse prevention approach. She is currently serving as a consultant for the National Institute of Corrections in the area of sexual transgressors.

Georgia F. Cumming, B.A., is Program Coordinator for the Vermont Treatment Program for Sexual Aggressors. Previous to this position, she was a probation and parole officer for twelve years. She has been instrumental in adapting the relapse prevention model to the supervision of sexual offenders on probation and parole. She has conducted training for probation and parole officers and mental health clinicians in many states, and is the coauthor of several papers on the relapse prevention approach. She is currently serving as a consultant for the National Institute of Corrections in the area of sexual transgressors.

Kennon M. Kashima, M.A., is a member of the core faculty in psychology at Goddard College. He was formerly Clinical Instructor in the Department of Psychology at the University of Vermont and Assistant Director of the Vermont Treatment Program for Sexual Aggressors.

William D. Pithers, Ph.D., is a clinical psychologist who has conducted treatment and research with sexual aggressors for ten years. He currently serves as Clinical Director of the Vermont Treatment Program for Sexual Aggressors, which provides therapy for offenders at three inpatient and twenty outpatient sites. He has written more than forty papers on the topic of sexual abuse. He is best known for originating the adaptation of relapse prevention for sexual aggressors and for identification of precursors to sexual abuse. He also has functioned as a consultant to the National Institute of Corrections, the Center for Studies of Antisocial and Violent Behavior at the National Institute of Mental Health, and numerous treatment programs and probation departments.

William M. Young, B.A., is currently the Commissioner of Social and Rehabilitation Services in Vermont, dealing with programs serving children and people with disabilities. A former member of the Governor's Commission on Women, he headed the 1981 project that resulted in Vermont's first program for the treatment of incarcerated sexual offenders, and subsequently developed Vermont's statewide network of child sexual abuse treatment programs. He has overseen major improvements in the state's foster parent system, renewed emphasis on innovative programs for people with disabilities, and advocated for the massive increases in state support for abused and neglected children that took place in 1987 in Vermont.